PHILOSOPHICAL ESSAYS & LECTURES, VOL. 4

TYRANNY & WISDOM

PLATO'S *GREATER ALCIBIADES* & *GORGIAS*

by

GREG JOHNSON

Counter-Currents Publishing Ltd.
San Francisco
2025

Copyright © 2025 by Greg Johnson
All rights reserved

Cover image:
Marcello Bacciarelli, *Alcibiades Being Taught by Socrates*, 1776–77

Published in the United States by
COUNTER-CURRENTS PUBLISHING LTD.
http://www.counter-currents.com/

Hardcover ISBN: 978-1-64264-059-5
Paperback ISBN: 978-1-64264-060-1
E-book ISBN: 978-1-64264-061-8

Contents

Preface ❖ iii

1. Introduction: Tyranny & Wisdom ❖ 1

PART I: PLATO'S *GREATER ALCIBIADES*

2. The Greatest Pick-Up Line of All Time ❖ 15
3. The Question of Justice ❖ 30
4. Justice & Expediency ❖ 37
5. Raising the Stakes ❖ 44
6. Expertise vs. Common Knowledge ❖ 52
7. Knowing the Self ❖ 58
8. The Mirror of the Soul ❖ 66
9. Virtue vs. Tyranny ❖ 76

PART II: PLATO'S *GORGIAS*

10. "War & Battle" ❖ 85
11. Philosophy vs. Rhetoric ❖ 106
12. A Knack for Pandering ❖ 122
13. Crime & Punishment ❖ 141
14. Might & Right ❖ 163
15. Two Ways of Life ❖ 174
16. The Best Should Rule ❖ 183
17. Pleasure & Goodness ❖ 192
18. The True Statesman ❖ 215
19. Socrates the Dog ❖ 228

APPENDIX

20. A Note on Plato's *Lesser Alcibiades* ❖ 239

Bibliography ❖ 243
Index ❖ 249
About the Author ❖ 266

Preface

Originally this book was a series of lectures that accompanied the reading of Plato's *Greater Alcibiades* and *Gorgias*. It is not a substitute for reading Plato's originals. It is a companion to be read alongside them, or an introduction to be read immediately before them.

The original course was entitled *What Socrates Knew*. It was presented to about a dozen students in The Invisible College, my adult education organization, in Atlanta. The class was held on Tuesday evenings, beginning August 24, 1999, and ending on October 12. This is the outline of the class:

Lecture 1: Introduction: Thirty Socratic Theses
Lecture 2: Socratic Ignorance, Eros, & the *Daimonion*
Lecture 3: The *Greater Alcibiades*
Lecture 4: The *Gorgias* I, Socrates' Discussion with Gorgias
Lecture 5: The *Gorgias* II, Socrates' Discussion with Polus
Lecture 6: The *Gorgias* III, Socrates' Discussion with Callicles, I
Lecture 7: The *Gorgias* IV, Socrates' Discussion with Callicles, II
Lecture 8: The *Gorgias* V, Socrates' Discussion with Callicles, III

This book is primarily based upon my original lecture notes, supplemented by transcripts of the recorded lectures. I also draw a bit upon the notes and transcripts for another class on the *Gorgias* that I taught online in 2023.

The first two lectures have been set aside for a short book to be called *What Socrates Knew*. Thus the present volume deals entirely with the *Greater Alcibiades* (also called the *Alcibiades I*) and the *Gorgias*. Splitting the original lecture course was necessary because the topic turned out to be too big for a single lecture course or book. My original notes were quite voluminous, and many points had to be left out when I delivered the actual lectures. Because the original introductory lecture has been set aside, I have written a new Introduction to this volume. I also added a brief appendix on the *Lesser Alcibiades* (or *Alcibiades II*) showing the dialogue's tight connections with both the *Greater Alcibiades* and the *Gorgias*.

My decision to teach the *Greater Alcibiades* followed by the *Gorgias* was influenced by the Neoplatonic curriculum of Iamblichus.[1] I wanted to see if it had any merit. I also wanted to test the hermeneutic approach of the Neoplatonists, who held that the dialogues are organic wholes written to communicate a single message, although they have exoteric and esoteric levels. The dialogues are also to be read as dramas, not just collections of arguments. I did not, however, have access to Olympiodorus' commentary on the *Gorgias*.[2] But I did read the tantalizing fragment of Proclus' commentary on the *Greater Alcibiades*, as well as Olympiodorus' complete but much briefer commentary.[3] As a rule, these readings are very "top-down" and "metaphysical," harmonizing the dialogues with Plotinus' synthesis of Plato and Aristotle. They are quite different from my interpretations.

My approach to reading both dialogues was also influenced

---

[1] The Neoplatonic canon for studying Plato was created by Iamblichus (c. 245–c. 325 CE). The first ten dialogues were: *Greater Alcibiades, Gorgias, Phaedo, Cratylus, Theaetetus, Sophist, Statesman, Phaedrus, Symposium, Philebus*. These were followed by two more advanced dialogues, the *Timaeus* and *Parmenides*. Iamblichus gave the *Greater Alcibiades* first place because he believed that in the dialogue, the "entire subsequent development" was "anticipated as it were in seminal form." See Fragment 1 in Iamblichi Chalcidensis, *In Platonis Dialogos Commentariorum Fragmenta*, ed. and trans. John M. Dillon (Lydney, UK: The Prometheus Trust, 2009).

[2] Olympiodorus, *Commentary on Plato's Gorgias*, trans. Robin Jackson, Kimon Lycos, and Harold Tarrant (Leiden: E.J. Brill, 1998).

[3] Proclus, *Alcibiades I: A Translation and Commentary*, trans. William O'Neill, 2nd ed. (Dordrect: Springer, 1971). Olympiodorus, *Commentary on the First Alcibiades of Plato*, trans. L.G. Westerink, 2nd ed. (Amsterdam: Hakkert, 1982). Cf. Olympiodorus, *Life of Plato and On Plato First Alcibiades 1–9*, trans. Michael Griffin (London: Bloomsbury, 2015); and Olympiodorus, *On Plato First Alcibiades 10–28*, trans. Michael Griffin (London: Bloomsbury, 2016).

by Leo Strauss, whose hermeneutic principles were similar to the Neoplatonists but whose readings were very different. Strauss did not, however, write about the *Greater Alcibiades*, and his extensive comments on the *Gorgias* in two lecture courses on the dialogue, as well as at the beginning of his course on the *Protagoras*, were not available at the time.[4] I was surprised at how different Strauss's readings are from mine.

The most important resource for my reading of the *Gorgias* is E.R. Dodds' magisterial 1959 edition of and commentary on the Greek text.[5]

With the *Greater Alcibiades*, I was pretty much on my own, for the dialogue had long been regarded as spurious and had attracted very little useful commentary.[6] In the last quarter century, however, most reservations about its authenticity have disappeared, and a great deal of useful literature has appeared. I particularly wish I'd had access to Nicholas Denyer's magnificent edition of and commentary on the original Greek text,[7] as well as François Renaud and Harold Tarrant's *The Platonic Alcibiades I: The Dialogue and its Ancient Reception*.[8]

For translations, I have primarily relied upon Carnes Lord for the *Greater Alcibiades*[9] and Donald Zeyl, Tom Griffith, and

---

[4] Leo Strauss, *On Plato's Protagoras*, ed. Robert C. Bartlett (Chicago: University of Chicago Press, 2022); Plato's *Gorgias* (1957) Transcript, ed. Devin Stauffer (Leo Strauss Center, Audio and Transcripts); Plato's *Gorgias* (1963) Transcript, ed. Devin Stauffer (Leo Strauss Center, Audio and Transcripts).

[5] Plato, *Gorgias: A Revised Text with Introduction and Commentary* by E. R. Dodds (Oxford: Clarendon Press, 1959.

[6] Jakub Jirsa, "Authenticity of the *Alcibiades* I: Some Reflections," *Listy filologické*, vol. 132 (2009): 225–44.

[7] Plato, *Alcibiades*, ed. Nicholas Denyer (Cambridge: Cambridge University Press, 2001).

[8] François Renaud and Harold Tarrant, *The Platonic* Alcibiades I: *The Dialogue and its Ancient Reception* (Cambridge: Cambridge University Press, 2015).

[9] In Plato, *The Roots of Political Philosophy: Ten Forgotten Socratic Dialogues*, ed. Thomas L. Pangle (Ithaca, N.Y.: Cornell University Press, 1987).

R.E. Allen for the *Gorgias*[10] — although I did consult other translations.[11] I did, however, alter the translations in two ways. First and foremost, I made the translations of important concepts like justice (*dike*), righteousness (*dikaiosyne*), prudence (*phronesis*), wisdom (*sophia*), and moderation (*sophrosyne*) consistent. Second, I edited them for style.

When I quote Plato, I use double quotation marks. When I paraphrase Plato, I use single quotation marks.

I wish to thank everyone connected to The Invisible College, especially the students who took these lectures. I also wish to thank those who studied the *Gorgias* with me in 2023 for many challenging questions. I want to thank Michael Polignano for digitizing the original recordings, V.S. for transcribing the 1999 lectures, and J.H. for transcribing the 2023 set. I also wish to thank Collin Cleary and David Zsutty for their careful editing, James O'Meara for the index, G.J. for the cover design, Collin Cleary and F. Roger Devlin for their kind words of praise, and the Counter-Currents Brain Trust for their thoughts about Marcello Bacciarelli's cover painting, in which Socrates shows Alcibiades a horse's bridle as a symbol of the virtue of moderation.

This book is dedicated to tyrannicides of all nations.

Newport Beach
27 October 2025

---

[10] See Plato, *Complete Works*, ed. John M. Cooper (Indianapolis: Hackett, 1997) for the Zeyl translation. Plato, *Gorgias, Menexenus, Protagoras*, ed. Malcolm Schofield, trans. Tom Griffith (Cambridge: Cambridge University Press, 2010). Plato, *The Dialogues of Plato*, vol. 1, trans. R. E. Allen (New Haven: Yale University Press, 1984).

[11] I consulted the *Greater Alcibiades* translations of W.R.M. Lamb (Loeb Classical Library, Plato, vol. XII [Cambridge, Mass.: Harvard University Press, 1927]); D.S. Hutchinson (Plato, *Complete Works*, ed. Cooper); and David M. Johnson (Plato and Aeschines of Spettus, *Socrates and Alcibiades*, ed. David M. Johnson [Newburyport, Mass.: Focus Philosophical Library, 2003]) and the *Gorgias* translations of W.R.M. Lamb (Loeb Classical Library, Plato, vol. III [Cambridge, Mass.: Harvard University Press, 1925]) and Benjamin Jowett (Plato, *The Dialogues of Plato*, 2 vols., trans. Benjamin Jowett [New York: Random House, 1937]).

INTRODUCTION

Socrates and Plato were enemies of tyranny. Indeed, in books VIII and IX of Plato's *Republic*, Socrates sets forth one of history's oldest and most influential denunciations of tyrants and tyranny. Yet some of their best friends and students were tyrants.

Socrates was a friend and teacher of Alcibiades, a would-be tyrant, and of Critias and Charmides, who were actual members of the Thirty Tyrants who ruled Athens in 404–403 BCE.

Plato had even closer connections with the Thirty. He was a cousin of Critias and a nephew of Charmides. Plato initially supported the Thirty.[1] His older brother Glaucon may have supported them as well.[2]

Plato also knew four tyrants of Syracuse: Dionysius I; his son and successor, Dionysius II; Dion, who was the son-in-law of Dionysius I and the brother-in-law of Dionysius II; and Calippus.[3] Plato sought the favor of Dionysius I because he wished to advise him. But they quickly became enemies when Plato hectored him about the evils of tyranny. Plato, however, became close friends with Dion. When Dionysius II came to power, Plato sought to make him a better ruler but found him ineducable.

Dionysius II exiled Dion, who spent most of this time in Athens in the company of Plato and his school. With the help of Plato's nephew, Speusippus, Dion deposed Dionysius II and became tyrant in his place. Although Dion sought to rule lawfully, in accordance with Platonic principles, he found that impossible and was later assassinated by Calippus, another student of Plato. Calippus then ruled Syracuse for a year as tyrant before fleeing to become a mercenary captain.

---

[1] Plato, *Seventh Letter*, 324b–c.

[2] This is central to Jacob Howland's *Glaucon's Fate: History, Myth, and Character in Plato's Republic* (Philadelphia: Paul Dry Books, 2018). See also Mark Munn, *The School of History: Athens in the Age of Socrates* (Berkeley: University of California Press, 2000), p. 239.

[3] James Romm, *Plato and the Tyrant: The Fall of Greece's Greatest Dynasty and the Making of a Philosophic Masterpiece* (New York: Norton, 2025).

Tyrants were dangerous men to know. Indeed, Socrates' associations with Alcibiades, Charmides, and Critias were the chief cause of his trial and execution on the charges of impiety and corrupting the youth. Plato, moreover, was imprisoned and sold into slavery by Dionysius I. (Luckily, he was quickly ransomed by his friends.) Plato also could have lost his life in the conflict between Dionysius II and Dion.

Why, then, did wise men like Socrates and Plato associate with tyrants?

Ancient Greek city states were both small and rife with tyrants and would-be tyrants. So any freeborn Greek could be only a few degrees of separation from tyrants without even trying. This was certainly the case with Plato, who was born into the family of Critias and Charmides.

But Socrates and Plato actively courted tyrants. As we will see in Plato's *Greater Alcibiades*, Socrates intentionally befriended Alcibiades and offered to help realize his dreams of universal tyranny. Plato, moreover, intentionally cultivated relationships with the tyrants of Syracuse. Socrates and Plato were not fools, so they must have thought such relationships were worth the risk.

To explain this, we must first define tyranny. Tyranny is a form of one-man rule. But so is monarchy. What is the difference? The word "tyrant" originally had the sense of "usurper," as opposed to a legitimate king. But some tyrants established dynasties, and their successors were styled tyrants as well, not kings. For instance, in the sixth century BCE, Peisistratus became tyrant of Athens, and his sons Hippias and Hipparchus followed him. This pattern was followed in Plato's time by Dionysius I and II in Syracuse. Thus some Greeks—like Aeschylus and Sophocles—used "king" and "tyrant" interchangeably.

Plato understood that, at first glance, tyrants and kings might be indistinguishable. They both share the pomps and prerogatives of one-man rule. For Plato, however, tyrants and kings can be distinguished quite cleanly in terms of the inner character of the ruler, the aim of the regime, and the effects they have on society. A monarch is a virtuous man who rules for the common good, whereas a tyrant is a vicious man who rules for his own interests. Thus, a tyranny and a monarchy may look the same at the beginning. But, since character is destiny, with the passage of time, the consequences diverge ever more radically. Monarchical regimes will be happy, harmonious, and stable. Tyrannical regimes will be unhappy, fractious, and fleeting.

In the *Republic*, Plato develops a systematic analogy between the human soul and the city. The human soul has three parts: reason, which loves truth; spiritedness (*thumos*), which loves honor; and desire, which loves the gratification of physical appetites. The different parts of the soul can come into conflict. For instance, desires can be unreasonable or dishonorable. Honor can be unreasonable or undesirable. Ideas can be dishonorable or undesirable. There are three basic kinds of men, depending on which part of the soul wins out in such conflicts: rational men, in whom reason triumphs over spiritedness and desire; spirited men, in whom honor trumps reason and desire; and appetitive men, in whom desire rules over both reason and spiritedness.

The political regime corresponding to the rational man is the rule of philosopher-kings. The political regime corresponding to the spirited man is a warrior aristocracy. (Historically speaking, monarchies also correspond to the rule of the spirited element.) There are three regimes based on the rule of desire: oligarchy (where the rich rule), democracy (where the many rule), and tyranny, in which we return to one-man rule, but this time desire is in control, not reason or spirit.

Desire, in principle, is infinite, i.e., open-ended. You can always want more. Order, however, is a matter of limits. The sovereignty of desire, therefore, subverts order. The passage from oligarchy to democracy is accompanied by increasing spiritual and social disorder, which leads to tyranny. Tyranny is a form of disorder, but it also feeds upon a desire to reassert order by concentrating power into the hands of a single man. Unfortunately, a leader cannot impose order if he lacks it in himself, and the tyrannical man is even more desire-driven than ordinary democrats, for he has the means to gratify even the most extravagant and depraved fantasies.

If both the tyrannical and the democratic types are ruled by desire, what is the difference? What allows a tyrannical man to rise to power in a democracy? For Plato, tyrants are rare because superior gifts are required to seize control of a society. Thus, as Roger Boesche puts it, Plato had "a certain disconsolate admiration for the tyrant" because he saw tyrants as men with great potential who had gone bad.[4] As Socrates says in the *Republic*:

> Won't we say for souls . . . that . . . those with the best natures become exceptionally bad when they get bad instruction? Or do you suppose an ordinary nature is the source of great injustices and unmixed villainy? Don't you suppose, rather, that it's a vigorous one corrupted by its rearing, while a weak nature will never be the cause of great things either good or bad?[5]

What makes tyrants genuinely tragic is that their superior gifts are harnessed by their desires and the desire-driven society they must rule over, leading to the ruin of everyone involved. The greater the gifts, the greater the ruin.

Thus far, we have an explanation for why Socrates and Plato regarded tyrants as philosophically and psychologically interesting figures fit for tragic drama. But all these traits can be safely appreciated at a distance. So why get closer? Why would they personally associate with such people? What could overcome their inevitable feelings of fear and revulsion?

Socrates and Plato were not just interested in tyranny but in one-man rule in general. They were idealists who wanted to radically reform a corrupt and fallen society in which self-interest had completely eclipsed the common good, so nothing good could emerge by leaving individuals at liberty. They believed that the only way to save such a society is to concentrate all power in the hands of one man.

But one-man rule cannot regenerate society unless the ruler is wise and good. This is the origin of the idea of the "philosopher-

---

[4] Roger Boesche, *Theories of Tyranny from Plato to Arendt* (University Park: Penn State Press, 1996), p. 33.

[5] Plato, *The Republic of Plato*, trans. Allan Bloom (New York: Basic Books, 1968), 491d–e.

king." As Socrates puts it in the *Republic*:

> Unless . . . the philosophers rule as kings or those now called kings and chiefs genuinely and adequately philosophize, and political power and philosophy coincide in the same place, while the many natures making their way to either apart from the other are by necessity excluded, there is no rest from ills for the cities . . . nor I think for humankind . . .[6]

Plato's idea of the philosopher-king sounds outlandish at first. But it is not merely a thought-experiment in the *Republic*. Plato thought that philosopher-kings could actually exist. Plato makes this clear in his own voice in his *Seventh Letter*, which explains why he became involved with politics in Syracuse.[7]

Philosopher-kings may be unlikely, but they are not impossible. Indeed, there are two ways to create them: to make philosophers into kings and to make kings into philosophers.

Granted, most philosophers lack the urbanity and prudence necessary for political careers. The image of Thales gazing at the stars and falling down a well immediately springs to mind. But, as G.R.F. Ferrari has noted, Plato himself knew of philosophers who became lawgivers and rulers, including the sophist Protagoras of Abdera and the Pythagorean Archytas of Tarentum.[8]

But, as a rule, turning existing kings into philosophers seems the likelier path to success. And, since what is essential is one-man rule, Plato's Athenian Stranger points out in the *Laws* that a tyrant will do just as well as a king, provided that he is "young, with a good memory, quick to learn, courageous, and by nature high-minded."[9] In fact, because tyrants are less beholden to laws and traditions than kings, they are even better positioned

---

[6] Plato, *Republic*, trans. Bloom, 473c–d.

[7] Plato, Seventh Letter, 326a–b.

[8] Plato, *The Republic*, ed. G.R.F. Ferrari, trans. Tom Giffith (Cambridge: Cambridge University Press, 2000), p. xx. Archytas may have been the basis for Plato's depiction of the Pythagorean philosopher-statesman Timaeus.

[9] Plato, *Laws*, trans. C.D.C. Reeve (Indianapolis: Hackett, 2022), 709e.

to effect radical change.

By making a tyrant into a philosopher, we simultaneously make him into a king, for Platonic kings and philosophers both live virtuously and aim at the common good. But how can a tyrant become a king? He can become a king instantaneously simply by vowing to rule for the common good, not his own personal interest. But such a decision is possible only if the tyrant's character has not been irredeemably corrupted.

How could one become a tyrant without being corrupt? The most likely route is simply to *inherit* tyranny, preferably when one is relatively young and unformed, then come under the tutelage of a Platonic philosopher. Clearly, this is what Plato hoped for when he sought out Dionysius II of Syracuse. But Plato found that he had already been hopelessly corrupted by sensuous self-indulgence and the flattery of courtiers.

In sum, both Socrates and Plato regarded tyranny as a disease of the soul and society at large. Thus they had no sympathy for tyrants or tyranny as such. However, they invested great hope in the kingship of the wise and virtuous, which at least at the start can be mistaken for tyranny. Moreover, they saw tyrants as men of rare ability. They believed that such men could be turned toward good or evil, depending upon how they were educated. Thus when Socrates and Plato encountered able men with tyrannical ambitions, they sought to turn them toward the good. Finally, as Plato's voyages to Syracuse showed, he was willing to take great personal risks to influence existing tyrants toward lawful rule.

Plato describes his own interactions with tyrants in his *Letters*.[10] Plato depicts Socrates' interactions with tyrants and would-be tyrants in a number of dialogues. Alcibiades appears in the *Greater Alcibiades*, *Lesser Alcibiades*, *Protagoras*, and *Symposium*.[11] Critias and Charmides appear in the *Charmides*, and

---

[10] For extensive discussions of the *Letters* and their historical context, see James Romm, *Plato and the Tyrant*. See also *Plato's Letters: The Political Challenges of the Philosophic Life*, ed. and trans. Ariel Helfer (Ithaca: Cornell University Press, 2023).

[11] Xenophon's, *Memorabilia*, book I, ch. 2, also contains useful information on Socrates' relationships with Alcibiades and Critias.

Critias may appear in the *Timaeus* and *Critias* as well.[12] In the *Gorgias*, Socrates squares off against Polus and Callicles, both of whom praise the tyrannical life.

Plato's most extensive critique of tyranny is found in the *Republic*, where Socrates battles the sophist Thrasymachus, who is an apologist of tyranny. But the main focus of the *Republic* is the education of Plato's older brother Glaucon, a highly spirited and politically ambitious youth who sought to harangue the Athenian assembly before he came of age at twenty. (Even Alcibiades was willing to wait until he turned twenty.)[13]

In this volume, I offer detailed commentaries on the *Greater Alcibiades* and the *Gorgias*. The ancient Neoplatonists placed these two dialogues at the start of their Plato curriculum, and with good reason.[14] Together, they are an excellent introduction to Plato. First of all, the *Greater Alcibiades* is not just an introduction to Platonic philosophy but to philosophy as such. It belongs to the genre known as the "protreptic" speech, the purpose of

---

[12] Warman Welliver argues that the Critias in the *Timaeus-Critias* is actually the grandfather of Critias the tyrant. But his argument hinges on two questionable assumptions. First, he assumes that the setting of the *Timaeus-Critias* is a specific year, but this is not necessarily the case. For instance, dialogues like the *Gorgias* and the *Lesser Alcibiades* are set anachronistically over a span of decades. Second, he assumes that Critias the grandfather of the tyrant is lying about his memories without considering the possibility that it would be perfectly in keeping with the character of Critias the tyrant to tell even more blatant lies about his memories. See Warman Welliver, *Character, Plot, and Thought in Plato's Timaeus-Critias* (Leiden: E.J. Brill, 1977), pp. 50–57.

[13] See my lecture, "Introduction to Plato's *Republic*," in *From Plato to Postmodernism* (San Francisco: Counter-Currents, 2019). According to Xenophon's *Memorabilia* III.6., Glaucon's family and friends were unable to dissuade him from politics, but Socrates was. Plato's *Republic* can be read as an enormous extension of the brief conversation that Xenophon relates.

[14] Iamblichus (c. 245–c. 325 CE) placed the *Greater Alcibiades* and the *Gorgias* at the head of his curriculum, followed by the *Phaedo, Cratylus, Theaetetus, Sophist, Statesman, Phaedrus, Symposium,* and *Philebus*. This canon was followed for more than two centuries by thinkers like Proclus (412–485 CE) and Olympiodorus (c. 495–505, died after 565 CE).

which is to convert the listener to a new way of life. Second, the *Greater Alcibiades* and the *Gorgias* offer an overview of the central themes of Platonic moral philosophy.

These dialogues, moreover, dramatize historically significant encounters. The *Greater Alcibiades* is the first conversation of Athens' most famous philosopher and her most infamous traitor. The *Gorgias* depicts Socrates' first encounter with the great philosopher and rhetorician Gorgias.

Beyond that, the *Greater Alcibiades* and the *Gorgias* are the best introduction to Plato's treatment of tyranny. The *Gorgias*, in particular, reads like a preliminary sketch of the *Republic*, where Plato gives his fullest treatment of tyranny.

In the *Greater Alcibiades*, Alcibiades is just shy of twenty, the age when he can embark upon a political career. We learn that Socrates has been observing young Alcibiades for years. But he never spoke to him until he noticed a change in Alcibiades' character. Formerly, Alcibiades was notable for his smug self-satisfaction and complacency. He did not need anything from anyone. This is a deeply apolitical character. Indeed, in his self-sufficiency, Alcibiades more resembles a philosopher of the purely contemplative type. Like Aristotle's Unmoved Mover, Alcibiades was the object of other people's desires but needed nothing from them.

But now Alcibiades is possessed by an immense and boundless longing which is deeply political. He wishes to be known and honored by all nations as a leader. He wishes to seize their acclaim by force of personality and force of arms. In short, Alcibiades wishes to become a tyrant, first over Athens and then over all the known world.

Alcibiades is the scion of an aristocratic family in a democratic society. As an aristocrat, he has inherited high expectations and the genes and connections necessary to realize them. As a democrat, he has grown up with an ethos of self-indulgence, saying and doing whatever pops into his head.[15] But his education has been shockingly neglected, which is particularly dangerous, for as Socrates says in the *Republic*: ". . . unless a man has

---

[15] Plato, *Republic*, 561c–d.

a transcendent nature, he would never become good if from earliest childhood his play isn't noble and all his practices aren't as well."[16] This wasn't a problem while Alcibiades was focused entirely on himself. But now that his gifts are paired with the ambition to make a mark on the world, for good or ill, Socrates has come forward to help guide him toward the good.

Socrates does not approach Alcibiades as a philosopher but as a political advisor. Socrates unfolds the full measure of Alcibiades' ambitions and then tells him: you can't do this without me. Alcibiades won't admit to tyrannical ambitions, but he is intrigued. He wants to know more.

Socrates is acting as a good citizen when he offers his guidance to Alcibiades. For without guidance, Alcibiades' natural gifts, social connections, and overweening ambition are a danger to Athens. But Socrates has a secondary patriotic motive: if Alcibiades can be turned into a philosopher-statesman, he can be a great blessing to Athens. Alcibiades had grown up to be a powerful force. Depending on who influenced him, he could do great good or great evil.

Unfortunately, these philanthropic aims are only clear to those who think about what Socrates is doing. The vast majority of readers, however, are superficial. And at first glance, Socrates simply appears to be a friend and teacher of tyrants. Indeed, he might even be seen as implanting tyrannical ambitions in a previously apolitical youth. Corrupting him, as it were. This case of mistaken identity ultimately cost Socrates his life. Thus Plato depicts Socrates as innocent of the charge of corrupting the youth, but he also shows why it was virtually inevitable that he would be accused and convicted of this crime anyway.[17]

---

[16] Plato, *Republic*, trans. Bloom, 558b.

[17] The *Greater Alcibiades* and the *Gorgias* both give ample evidence that Socrates did not follow the gods of Athens, thus he was guilty of impiety by the letter of the law. However, if the purpose of legislating piety is to protect the city, Socrates' heterodox religion is in keeping with the spirit of the law because it promotes virtue, whereas the ancestral gods of Athens were actually quite vicious: guilty of parricide, adultery, theft, and a host of other crimes and vices. See my lecture on Plato's *Euthyphro* in *The Trial of Socrates* (San Francisco: Counter-

Socrates patiently and methodically demonstrates to Alcibiades that he doesn't know anything about politics. He doesn't know what justice means. He doesn't even know what expediency means. But Alcibiades isn't convinced that he needs to know such things to win power, because his Athenian rivals aren't any better educated than he is, so he thinks he can beat them simply based on looks and connections. To counter this complacency, Socrates lauds the careful cultivation and vast wealth of Alcibiades' true rivals: the kings of Sparta and the Great King of Persia.

Ultimately, Alcibiades' problem is a lack of self-knowledge. He's not just ignorant of justice or the power of Athens' enemies, he's ignorant of his own ignorance. Once Alcibiades recognizes the need to pursue self-knowledge, Socrates identifies self-knowledge with moderation (*sophrosyne*). This makes sense, because to know oneself is to know one's limits. But knowing one's limits reins-in one's ambitions and desires. Oligarchy, democracy, and tyranny are inherently unstable systems because they are built on the sands of infinite desire. Alcibiades has infinite desires because he doesn't yet know his limits. The philosophical quest for self-knowledge and virtue is thus anti-tyrannical at its core. Alcibiades places himself in Socrates' tutelage, but Socrates knows that he has a powerful rival pulling Alcibiades in the opposite direction, namely the people of Athens. In the end, the city triumphed over Socrates and Alcibiades alike.

In the *Gorgias*, Socrates's approach is very different. Alcibiades is inarticulate and philosophically naïve. Thus the *Greater Alcibiades* is primarily an exhortation to pursue philosophy. The *Gorgias*, however, is a philosophical discussion from the start.

Socrates is in the company of accomplished intellectuals. Gorgias is a renowned philosopher and sophist. Polus is a student of Gorgias and a sophist in his own right. Callicles is a wealthy Athenian student of the sophists. He has political ambitions as well as a tough-mindedness and radicalism that point to a philosophical soul.

Both Polus and Callicles are articulate defenders of tyranny.

Currents, 2023).

Callicles, moreover, actually offers philosophical arguments for the superiority of the tyrannical life to the philosophical life. Socrates' old friend Chaerephon is also present, along with an unknown number of men who have gathered to hear Gorgias speak. Typically, such men would be drawn from the Athenian elite, with a preponderance of ambitious young men on their way up.

The core of the *Gorgias*' critique of tyranny is Socrates' long conversation with Callicles. Polus praises tyranny, but he is not a potential tyrant, certainly not in Athens, where he is a foreigner. Callicles, however, is a citizen of Athens. He is, moreover, wealthy, ambitious, and obviously highly intelligent. He could be a threat—or an asset.

The *Gorgias*, like the *Republic*, focuses on the question of which life is the most choiceworthy: in this case, the philosophical life or the tyrannical one. This binary choice is framed by Callicles. It makes sense given who is debating. Socrates merely works within that frame. Neither the *Gorgias* nor the historical record indicate which option Callicles chose in the end.[18]

But perhaps it was best that Plato left that question unanswered, because contemplating the enigma draws us into the conversation, and ultimately what matters most is not the fate of Callicles but our own fateful encounters with the ideas he debates with Socrates.

Some readers will choose philosophy, others will choose tyranny, but the most philosophical will question the whole framework. Doesn't Callicles leave out a range of non-tyrannical political options? Beyond that, doesn't he ignore the possibility of a synthesis: the philosopher-statesman? Socrates works within Callicles' framing, but along the way, he offers plenty of clues that it might be inadequate. Callicles, however, never picks up on them.

Callicles' idea of philosophy is distinctly "pre-Socratic." In fact, his depiction of Socrates owes a lot to the "pre-Socratic" Socrates of Aristophanes' *Clouds*: a politically naïve student of

---

[18] Plato mentions several associates of Callicles—Demos, Tisander, Andron, and Nausicydes—who are corroborated by other historical records, but Callicles is not.

nature.[19] This is a highly questionable conception of philosophy. We shall see, moreover, that Callicles himself shares many ideas with the Socrates of the *Clouds*. These ideas should be questioned as well.

Working within Callicles' private and apolitical vision of philosophy, Socrates paints a very bleak picture of the possibility of a philosopher attaining power in a democratic society without fundamental moral compromises. Of course this leaves out the other possibility: a statesman becoming philosophical. But how could a statesman attain power in a democracy without becoming hopelessly corrupt and thus incapable of becoming a philosopher? Of course this is more an argument for rejecting democracy than the idea of a philosopher-king. Non-democratic regimes might be more amenable to the rise of philosopher-statesmen.

Callicles' image of Socrates as essentially private and apolitical is belied by the action of the dialogue. At the beginning of the *Gorgias*, we learn that Socrates missed an indoor speech by Gorgias by tarrying outdoors in the agora.[20] Now, outside Gorgias' lecture hall and in the presence of many members of the audience, Socrates engages in a philosophical battle with Gorgias, Polus, and Callicles. Gorgias' audience is full of ambitious young men like Callicles, who aim to make their mark on public life. Socrates throughout the conversation is grandstanding to this crowd. In short, this is a very public and political way to philosophize. And, because of Plato's artistry, Socrates' audience and influence will continue to grow as long as his works survive.

In the *Gorgias* as in the *Greater Alcibiades*, the key to Socrates' critique of tyranny is the virtue of moderation, through which reason imposes order on the infinity of desire and thus establishes its sovereignty in the soul. But Socrates' arguments in the *Gorgias* go well beyond a critique of ancient Greek tyranny. Indeed, the *Gorgias* offers a critique of all forms of desire-based politics, including modern liberalism.

---

[19] See my extensive discussion of the *Clouds* in *The Trial of Socrates*.

[20] Compare this to Xenophon's claim in *Memorabilia* I.1.10 that Socrates was always in public. Cf. *Memorabilia* I.6.14 for what appear to be more private goings on.

In the *Gorgias*, we learn that sophistry is not just the art of persuasion, for in a democracy, persuasion is the route to political power. The Greek word for "art" here is "*techne*," from which we get such words as technique, technology, and technocracy. Once one has political power, one can literally enslave the practitioners of all the other arts. Thus sophistry is a master art, encompassing and subordinating all other arts to those who wield it.[21] This master art, moreover, is value neutral. It is a means to many ends, good or evil. Here we have the precursors of the modern liberal idea of the state as a morally neutral technocracy.

For Socrates, however, all of life should be ruled by wisdom. Wisdom is like art insofar as it is also practical. But unlike art, wisdom is not morally neutral. Indeed, wisdom is about the *right use* of all other things, including arts like persuasion and politics. Every true statesmen, therefore, is guided by knowledge of the good.

In the *Gorgias*, Polus and Callicles defend a very liberal and modern-sounding idea of freedom as *doing what one pleases*. This is what modern liberals call "negative liberty." Socrates, by contrast, defends what we call "positive liberty," which is *doing what one really wants*.

To understand the difference, we must know what Socrates means by "what we really want." According to Socrates, we all want the same thing, namely to attain happiness or well-being. The fact that so many of us fail to do so means that we can be mistaken about what makes us happy. Thus we can do *what we please* but fail to do *what we really want*. Negative liberty is basically acting on *opinions* not *truths* about what leads to happiness.

For Socrates, we are not free if we are not doing what we *really* want, even though we *think* we want it and *feel* free when we pursue it. A simple example is drug addiction. It feels like happiness, but in fact it leads to misery. It feels like freedom, but in truth it leads to slavery. Indeed, if we are forced not to take drugs, that makes us freer, because it makes it easier to do what we really want. In short, we can be forced to be free.

The sophists were moral subjectivists, meaning that the good

---

[21] In Plato's *Protagoras*, the great sophist Protagoras claims that he teaches "*politike techne*" and "how to make men good citizens" (318e).

is whatever we say it is. Even Callicles, who speaks of what is "right by nature," simply means that the strongest people by nature are the ones who get to declare arbitrarily what is right and wrong for the rest of us. In short, he believes that "might makes right." Socrates, by contrast, held that the good is objective, thus propositions about the good are established by showing that they correspond to reality, not by winning an arm-wrestling contest.

Unsurprisingly, Callicles also defends hedonism: the idea that pleasure is the good. Hedonism is rife in modern society as well, even though Socrates destroyed it as a philosophical thesis in the *Gorgias*.

For Callicles, the purpose of life is not just pleasure, but unlimited pleasure: the unending pursuit of one desire after another that ceases only in death. The Greeks called the desire for ever more stuff *pleonexia*. It too is one of the foundations of modern liberalism. Socrates, by contrast, believed that the purpose of politics is inculcating virtue, which is founded on the limitation of desire.

Callicles put a huge premium on vulgar success—wealth and power—over and above the cultivation of moral character. He justified injustice and vice, as long as they produce wealth and power. Socrates, by contrast, measured everything by the effect that it has on one's character. He thought it was a bad deal to lose one's soul, even if one gains the whole world.

Callicles constantly harps on self-preservation, even at the expense of one's honor. He thinks a long and comfortable life is the most important thing. This is basically the bourgeois value system that reigns today. Socrates, however, is an eloquent exponent of the aristocratic ethos that puts a virtuous life above mere life. Thus, when forced to choose between death and dishonor, he prefers death.

If Socrates offered powerful responses to all these sophistical views, why do we live in a world where sophistry seems to have triumphed? One reason, surely, is that people don't know enough about dialogues like the *Greater Alcibiades* and the *Gorgias*. Let us now remedy that together.

THE GREATEST PICK-UP LINE OF ALL TIME

"This dialogue is the beginning of all philosophy, as indeed is the knowledge of ourselves; and for this reason scattered throughout it is the exposition of many considerations of logic, the elucidation of many points of ethics and such matters as contribute to our general investigation concerning happiness, and the outline of many doctrines leading us to the study of natural phenomena and even to the truth concerning divine matters themselves, in order that, as it were, in outline in this dialogue the one, common, and complete plan of all philosophy may be comprised, being revealed through our actual first turning towards ourselves. It seems to me that this is why the divine Iamblichus gives it the first position among the ten dialogues in which he considers the whole of Plato's philosophy is embraced, their whole subsequent development having been, as it were, anticipated in this seed."

—Proclus on Plato's *Greater Alcibiades*[1]

PLATO'S WEIRDEST DIALOGUE

In the *Greater Alcibiades*, an ugly stalker who looks like a dirty bum tries to seduce a wealthy and handsome young man by claiming to have the power to realize his greatest ambition, namely to become tyrant over his own people and conqueror of the known world—and it works.

The young man was the infamous Alcibiades, who lived in Athens in the latter half of the fifth century BCE.

Alcibiades was tall and handsome. He was also rich and well-connected. Alcibiades's father, Cleinias, was a wealthy and powerful Athenian with ties to Sparta. His mother, Deinomache,

---

[1] Proclus, *Alcibiades I: A Translation and Commentary*, trans. William O'Neill, second edition (Dordrect: Springer, 1971), <11>, pp. 7–8.

was from the prominent Alcmaeonid family. Her first cousin was Pericles, the most powerful man in Athens for more than 30 years, who brought Athens to the peak of its glory and then sent it on its way to decline and utter devastation, which he did not live to see. Cleinias died in the Battle of Coronea in 447 BCE, so Alcibiades was actually raised by Pericles. In short, Alcibiades was a real catch. So naturally he attracted many suitors.

When Alcibiades became a teenager, older men started taking a sexual interest in him, as was common in his time and social class. But Alcibiades ran off most of his suitors in short order. In ancient Greece, pederastic relationships between adult men and teenaged boys had a transactional dimension. The ancient Greeks put a very high value on youth and beauty. If you were young and beautiful, everybody wanted you. But if you wanted a younger partner to overlook the ravages of time, you'd better have something else to offer: knowledge, skills, money, social connections, etc. But Alcibiades had it all. He felt that other people had nothing to offer him, and as his suitors learned this, they dropped away, one by one.

By the time Alcibiades was about to turn twenty, only one suitor remained, and, to put it bluntly, he didn't have a chance. He was about eighteen years older than Alcibiades. He was ugly. He was poor. And, frankly, he was creepy, more of a stalker than a suitor. He was the first to show interest in Alcibiades. He had been lurking around ever since Alcibiades hit puberty, watching him from a distance, and in all those years, *he never once spoke to Alcibiades*. His name was Socrates, and he had an evil reputation for investigating the secrets of nature, denying the local gods, swearing oaths by foreign deities, and corrupting the youth. Then, a few days before Alcibiades turned twenty, Socrates finally broke his silence. Plato's *Greater Alcibiades* is their conversation.

I regard the *Greater Alcibiades* as one of the best introductions to Plato.[2] I also think it is one of Plato's greatest philosophical

---

[2] In ancient and medieval times, the *Greater Alcibiades* was used as an introduction to Plato's writings The earliest known recommendation of the *Greater Alcibiades* as an introduction to Plato is from the

dramas. I agree with Paul Friedländer that the *Greater Alcibiades* maintains a dramatic tension unequaled in Plato.³ It also executes Plato's most dramatic reversal of roles. At the start, Alcibiades is a would-be master of the world. At the end, he pledges to be Socrates' slave. At the beginning, Socrates approaches Alcibiades as a seducer. At the end, it is Alcibiades who pursues Socrates.

The *Greater Alcibiades* is longish, but for me at least, it reads quickly enough. The arguments are mostly straightforward, although it is somewhat padded by a lot of tedious "yes" and "no" exchanges.

THE DRAMATIC DATE, SETTING, & CHARACTERS

Since the *Greater Alcibiades* is a play, let's begin with the dramatic date, the setting, and the characters.

The dramatic date of the *Greater Alcibiades* is about 432 BCE. The two main characters are Alcibiades (c. 452–404 BCE) and Socrates (c. 470–399 BCE). Alcibiades' guardian, Pericles, is mentioned as being alive, so the dialogue cannot be set later than his death in 429 BCE. Alcibiades was at least 20 in 432 BCE when he fought at the Battle of Potidaea, where Socrates saved his life. This conversation takes place before Potidaea because this is their first conversation. We can infer the date of around 432 BCE

Middle Platonist Albinus (fl. c. 150 CE), who in his *Introduction to Plato's Dialogues* recommended reading the *Greater Alcibiades, Phaedo, Republic,* and *Timaeus* as a series.

The Neoplatonist Iamblichus (c. 245–c. 325 CE) placed the *Greater Alcibiades* at the head of his curriculum, followed by the *Gorgias, Phaedo, Cratylus, Theaetetus, Sophist, Statesman, Phaedrus, Symposium,* and *Philebus*. This curriculum was followed by other Neoplatonists for more than two centuries.

In the Middle Ages, Alfarabi (c. 870–c. 951) begins his *Philosophy of Plato* with the *Greater Alcibiades*, but after that, his curriculum completely differs from the Neoplatonists. See Alfarabi, *The Philosophy of Plato and Aristotle*, trans. Muhsin Mahdi (Ithaca: Cornell University Press, 2001), pp. 53–54.

³ Paul Friedländer, *Plato*, vol. 2, *The Dialogues: First Period*, trans. Hans Meyerhoff (New York: Pantheon, 1964), p. 232.

from the fact that the dialogue itself says that Alcibiades is "not yet twenty" (123d) but soon will be, allowing him to speak in the Athenian Assembly and fight abroad at Potidaea. Socrates was born around 470 BCE, so he was about 38 at the time of this conversation.

The settings of Platonic dialogues are either public or private places. This is important, because people often speak less candidly in public than in private. Of course, even in private conservations, one's level of candor needs to be adjusted to the character of one's partner in conversation. This dialogue is in a private setting, for at one point Socrates says "we two are alone" (118b).

Socratic dialogues can also be divided into those in which Socrates or someone else initiates the conversation. In this case, Socrates has chosen the time and place of the meeting.

As for the characters, Socrates and Alcibiades are an exceedingly odd couple.

Alcibiades was highly favored by fortune, yet somehow he turned out to be a very bad and unhappy man.

Socrates really is the opposite paradigm. Socrates was highly intelligent and had a craggy charisma of his own. But he wasn't good-looking. He wasn't rich. He wasn't from a prominent family. Nevertheless, Socrates generally played his cards well and was a very good and happy man.

Alcibiades came of age shortly before the Peloponnesian War (431–404 BCE), which encompassed, defined, and consumed the rest of his life.[4] Alcibiades had enormous political ambitions,

---

[4] The two most important primary sources on Alcibiades are Thucydides, *The Peloponnesian War* and Plutarch's *Alcibiades* in his *Lives*. Thucydides (c. 460–c. 400 BCE) was a contemporary of Alcibiades. Plutarch (c. 40–120s CE) wrote centuries later but drew on other sources now lost. He also clearly drew upon the *Greater Alcibiades*. Jacqueline de Romily, *The Life of Alcibiades: Dangerous Ambition and Betrayal in Athens*, trans. Elizabeth Trapnell Rawlings (Ithaca: Cornell University Press, 2019), is an excellent contemporary biography, written by an accomplished classicist who does not get lost in the weeds of scholarly minutiae. The career of Alcibiades is also central to Mark Munn's *The School of History: Athens in the Age of Socrates*.

and war was one of the primary ways would-be Athenian leaders could distinguish themselves.

Alcibiades' ambitions, however, were frustrated in March of 421 BCE, when Athens and Sparta signed the Peace of Nicias, which ended hostilities for fifty years. According to Thucydides,[5] Alcibiades was offended that he was left out of the negotiations conducted by two senior generals and political leaders, Nicias and Laches. When forced to choose between the peace of Athens and his own political ambitions, Alcibiades chose ambition. Thus he hatched an elaborate plot to destroy the peace. The war resumed and lasted until 404 BCE, ending with Athens' utter defeat and ruin.

In 415 BCE, Alcibiades opened a new front in the Peloponnesian War. He was the principal promoter of Athens' expedition to conquer Syracuse, a powerful Greek city state in Sicily. It was an enormous venture, bigger than anything undertaken by Pericles. After two years of fighting, the Athenian expedition was crushed. Some 200 ships were destroyed or captured. At least 10,000 Athenian men were killed or captured from a population estimated at between 20,000 and 30,000 male citizens, i.e., between one half and one third. Athens never recovered. The Sicilian disaster was the turning point in the war, although it was nearly a decade before the city's final defeat.

Although Alcibiades was the architect of the Sicilian expedition, he did not end up commanding it. First of all, many Athenians did not trust him, so the expedition was put under the command of three generals: Alcibiades, Nicias, and Lamachus. Second, on the morning the expedition was to sail, Athens awoke to find that the city's Herms, guardian statues with the head and genitals of Hermes, had been mutilated in the night. After his departure, Alcibiades was accused of this sacrilege, as well as profaning the Eleusinian Mysteries. He was called back to Athens to face trial but chose instead to defect to the Spartans.

Alcibiades advised the Spartans to send help to Athens' enemies in Sicily, thus contributing to the destruction of the Athenian expeditionary force. He also recommended that the Spartans

---

[5] Thucydides, *The Peloponnesian War*, 5.43.

build a fortress at Decelea, within sight of Athens herself, cutting the Athenians off from land trade, their silver mines at Laurium, and their religious site at Eleusis. The Spartan garrison at Decelea also played an important role in Athens' ultimate defeat.

But Alcibiades was incapable of loyalty to the Spartans as well. First, Alcibiades seduced and impregnated Timaea, the wife of King Agis II. Then in 412 BCE, when his attempts to broker an alliance between Sparta and the Persian empire broke down, Alcibiades defected to the court of the Persian satrap Tissaphernes, with whom he ingratiated himself. Alcibiades then began plotting with oligarchical elements in Athens to overthrow the democracy and reinstate him as citizen and general. He promised Persian money and aid. When the democracy was overthrown, however, Alcibiades sided with the mutinous Athenian fleet which wanted to sail home and reestablish the democracy. But Alcibiades then dissuaded them from sailing. Eventually, a more moderate oligarchy was formed.

Alcibiades remained with the Athenian fleet, which he led to a number of important victories. But he feared returning to the city and did not do so until 407 BCE, when he received a hero's welcome. But the following year, Alcibiades was defeated by the Spartans in the Battle of Notium. He returned to exile, supported himself as a pirate, and in 404 BCE was assassinated on Persian territory at the instigation of the Spartan king Lysander with the help of the Persian satrap Pharnabazus.

Alcibiades, more than any other individual, was responsible for Athens' defeat in the Peloponnesian War and destruction as a great power, largely because he was more concerned with his own glory than service to his homeland. In the end, he was loyal only to his own ambition.

Even though Socrates and Alcibiades were from different social worlds, ancient Athens was a small place, and they were brought together by common intellectual interests. The life of the mind, then and now, has the power to bridge social classes. But it also meant that just as Socrates made some powerful and influential friends, he also made some powerful and influential enemies. Friends like Alcibiades, Critias, and Charmides all aspired, more or less successfully, to become tyrants over Athens.

Such associations eventually led to Socrates' trial and execution for impiety and corrupting the youth.

SOCRATES' GOAL & PLATO'S

But at the time of the *Greater Alcibiades*, Alcibiades' sordid career and unhappy end were far in the future. In this dialogue, Alcibiades is all potential, enormous potential. However, the greater your potential to do good, the greater your potential to do evil as well, thus the greater your need for moral education. Fortune can give us many advantages and disadvantages. But our happiness depends on *how well we use them*. Wisdom for Plato is the ability to make *right use* of fortune's gifts, both good and bad.[6]

Socrates' aim in approaching Alcibiades is frankly to seduce him. But not in the way you think. Socrates wishes to seduce Alcibiades into pursuing philosophy as a way of life. Plato wrote this dialogue to seduce you as well.

As we will see, Alcibiades was on the path to becoming a tyrant. In this conversation, Socrates' basic agenda is to convince Alcibiades that, if he wishes to become a tyrant, he must pursue philosophy as a necessary means to tyranny. But, once Alcibiades begins to pursue philosophy, Socrates then argues that tyranny is not a worthy aim and that Alcibiades should instead pursue philosophy as an end in itself. Does Socrates want Alcibiades to become a philosopher? Probably not. But, on the assumption that a politician who studies philosophy is something different from a tyrant pure and simple, we can at least say that Socrates is trying to deflect Alcibiades from becoming a tyrant.

Plato's agenda in the *Greater Alcibiades* is threefold. First, Plato is presenting his and Socrates' philosophy. Plato and Socrates had some philosophical differences, but none of them are present here. Second, Plato is presenting a case for philosophy *as such*. Third, Plato is defending Socrates from his accusers.

---

[6] On the Platonic concept of wisdom as the ability to make right use of all things, see my essay "The Relevance of Philosophy to Political Change," in *New Right vs. Old Right* (San Francisco: Counter-Currents, 2014).

It was easy for Socrates' enemies to paint him as the villain who corrupted Alcibiades, but in the *Greater Alcibiades*, Plato gives us a very different picture. Here Socrates is trying to turn Alcibiades away from politics. But another corrupter was pulling Alcibiades toward politics: the people (*demos*) of Athens. This seducer ultimately proved stronger than Socrates, probably because it aligned with Alcibiades' tyrannical ambitions. Thus, according to Plato, Socrates tried to prevent Alcibiades from becoming a menace to Athens, but the Athenians themselves turned him into a monster, then made Socrates the scapegoat for their own folly.

SOCRATES BREAKS THE ICE
Socrates' first words are "Son of Cleinias, I suppose you wonder why it is I, who was the first to become a lover of yours, alone persist in it now that the others have left off" (103a). Addressing Alcibiades as the "Son of Cleinias" emphasizes that Socrates is of an older generation, a peer to Alcibiades' father, and intimates his pederastic intention, which resembled the father-son relationship in terms of age differences and mentoring. The word for "wonder" here is *thaumazein*, which for Plato[7] and Aristotle[8] is the pathos that gives rise to philosophy, which is the topic of this dialogue.

Socrates apparently was the first to show interest in Alcibiades when he became a teenager. However, as becomes clear later, he didn't actually *speak* to him until now, when he is just about twenty and will soon take part in public life. Socrates claims that he was held back by his famous "*daimonion*," a guardian spirit. In *The Trial of Socrates*, I argue based on Plato's *Theages* that Socrates equates the *daimonion* with his knowledge of "the erotic things."[9] *Eros*, of course, was personified as a *daimon*: a spirit that partakes of both human and divine nature and

---

[7] Plato, *Theaetetus*, 155d.

[8] Aristotle, *Metaphysics*, book I, chapter 2, 982b11–21.

[9] See Plato, *Symposium*, 177d, where Socrates, who supposedly denied knowing anything, claimed to "know nothing but the erotic things [*ta erotika*]."

shuttles between them as a messenger. In the *Symposium* the human soul itself is said to be *daimonic*, partaking of both human and divine nature and occupying the intermediate realm between them.[10] Thus knowledge of erotic things is equated to knowledge of the human soul. Thus the *daimonion* is Socrates's personification of his knowledge of human nature and ability to act prudently based on that knowledge.[11]

Interestingly enough, the alternative title of the *Greater Alcibiades* is "On the Nature of Man," which encompasses knowledge of human nature in general as well as knowledge of human individuals, specifically self-knowledge. As we shall see, this is an important theme throughout the dialogue.

This reading is consistent with Proclus, who claims that Socrates' *daimonion* corresponds to the realm of human nature (namely body and soul joined together), as opposed to the soul alone or the intellect (*nous*) understood in Neoplatonic terms. "Hence when the inquiry centers around the nature of man, no mention will be made of intellect, but Socrates will remind the youth of the providence of the spirit, sometimes calling it a 'spirit' [the *daimonion*] and other times 'a god.'"[12] It is important to bear in mind that Socrates explicitly identifies the *daimonion* with a god, because whenever he speaks of "god" or "a god" throughout this dialogue, he is referring to the *daimonion*.

Thus when Socrates says his *daimonion* held him back, he means his sense of Alcibiades' character.

Alcibiades' response is rather chilly, as one might expect when dealing with a creepy "nuisance" (104d). But he is willing to listen.

Pride & Magnanimity

Socrates remarks that Alcibiades has attracted many "proud" (*megalophronon*) suitors, but every one of them left because they found his pride too much for them. "*Megalophronon*" is derived

---

[10] Plato, *Symposium*, 202e–203a; 209e–212a. .

[11] See Greg Johnson, *The Trial of Socrates*, where I discuss the *daimonion* in the chapter on Plato's *Theages*.

[12] Proclus, *Alcibiades I: A Translation and Commentary*, p. 29.

from "*megalo,*" which means great, and "*phren,*" which refers both to the mind and to the diaphragm muscle in the chest that allows us to breathe. The *phren* is thus associated with *thumos* or "spiritedness," which resides in the chest. Hence W.R.M. Lamb translates *megalophrona* as "high-spirited." It could also be translated as "great-spirited." A more down to earth reading is "thinking oneself great" or "thinking highly of oneself." Thus I favor David M. Johnson's translation of "pride." Plato chooses this word to evoke Alcibiades' highly competitive nature and swaggering masculine arrogance.

In the *Symposium*, Socrates says that Agathon's "manliness [courage] and pride" (*andreian kai megalophrosunen*) is the root of his confidence on the stage.[13] In *Republic* book VII, Socrates claims that certain forms of advanced mathematical research need state patronage, but such patrons are rare, and if one did find leaders with the ability to understand the importance of such research, under current conditions, they would not listen because they are "proud men" (*megalophronoumenoi*).[14] It is hard not to hear an echo here of Plato's failed attempt to teach geometry and philosophy to Dionysius II, the tyrant of Syracuse.[15] In *Republic*, book VIII, Socrates observes that tyrants fear the manly/courageous (*andreios*) and proud (*megalophron*) and thus must purge them from their cities.[16]

"*Megalophrona*" is related to the more commonly used Greek word "*megalopsychia.*" "*Psyche*" means "soul." So "*megalopsychia*" literally means "greatness of soul." The Latin equivalent is "magnanimity," which is an English word as well. Another translation is "high-mindedness."

Megalopsychia is the supreme virtue of the aristocrat. The canonical treatment of the idea is in book IV of Aristotle's *Nicomachean Ethics*. Magnanimity is a higher-order virtue. It presupposes all-round excellence, including the possession of the other virtues. Magnanimity, moreover, involves *awareness* of

---

[13] Plato, *Symposium*, 194b.
[14] Plato, *Republic*, 528c.
[15] See Romm, *Plato and the Tyrant*, chs. 4 and 8.
[16] Plato, *Republic*, 567b–c.

one's excellence. The magnanimous man feels entitled to recognition for his achievements. But magnanimity is more than justified pride. It is also ambition. The magnanimous man sets great goals, because small goals are not worthy of him.

Magnanimity also encompasses how superior individuals at the top of the social hierarchy get along with the rest of society, which consists mostly of their inferiors. Magnanimity lubricates social interactions in a hierarchical society, preserving the dignity of the inferior and the status of the superior. Magnanimous people recognize that most people are not their equals and adjust their expectations accordingly. When confronted with the failings of others, they are tolerant, forgiving, and "big." When we compliment a person for being "mighty big," we are referring to the "magna" in magnanimity. Great-souled men have a quality of aloofness and unflappability. They don't trifle over small things.

Magnanimous individuals also refrain from calling attention to their superiority. One way to do this is false modesty, what the Greeks called "irony" (*eironeia*). For Aristotle, it is the only virtuous form of lying. The magnanimous man conceals his superiority to spare the feelings of others.

The opposite of magnanimity is *mikropsychia*, sometimes translated as "pusillanimity" or "small-mindedness." The small-minded man loves to make lesser men feel inferior, generally because he is gnawed by feelings of inferiority to still greater men. Pusillanimous men are the strivers, the greasy pole climbers, whose basic motto is "suck up and kick down." They will seize on any petty advantage if it allows them to hoist themselves up and put others down.

Aristotle's *megalopsychia*, however, is very much an urbane and courtly refinement of *megalophrona*, which connotes the back-biting, one-upping, head-butting pride of highly thumotic young men.

Socrates offers a simple explanation of Alcibiades' overwhelming and off-putting pride. Alcibiades' would-be lovers have nothing to offer him, for he makes it clear that he is their superior in beauty and build, in his distinguished family and powerful friends, and in his wealth "on which he prides himself the least" (104b). This last remark is meant ironically, for Alcibiades was famous for flaunting his wealth. Which means that his pride in his family, physique, and appearance was truly hyperbolic. He's so full of himself, so smugly self-satisfied, that he needs nothing from anyone.

THE GREATEST PICK-UP LINE OF ALL TIME

But then Socrates launches into a speech arguing that Alcibiades was either completely wrong about himself or he has changed dramatically. According to Socrates, Alcibiades is deeply dissatisfied with his life and will always want more. (This idea of unlimited desire is articulated by Callicles, a student of the sophists and defender of tyranny, in Plato's *Gorgias*.[17]) Because Alcibiades is so needy, he needs Socrates, for only Socrates can help him satisfy himself:

> It seems to me that if one of the gods were to say to you—"Alcibiades, would you wish rather to live having what you now have or to die at once if it were not permitted you to acquire more?"—you would choose, it seems to me, to die.[18] But as to what hope it is you now live on, I shall tell you. You believe that if you come shortly before the people of Athens—and you believe this will occur within a very few days—upon coming forward you would prove to the Athenians that you are deserving of being honored more than Pericles or anyone else who has ever existed and, having proved this, that you will have very great power in the city, and that if you are very great here that you will be so among the other Greeks and not only among the Greeks but also among the barbarians who share the mainland with us. [The Macedonians, among others.] And if the same god were again to say to you that you must hold sway here in Europe but

---

[17] Plato, *Gorgias*, 491e–492c.

[18] Xenophon says that if a god offered Alcibiades or Critias the choice of dying or living as modestly and self-sufficiently as Socrates, they would have preferred death (*Memorabilia*, II.2.15–16).

will not be permitted to cross into Asia or to interest yourself in affairs there, it seems to me that you would again be unwilling to live on these terms alone without being able to fill with your name and your power all mankind, so to speak. And I suppose you believe that apart from Cyrus and Xerxes, no one deserving of mention has ever existed. That this is the hope you have, then, I know very well—I am not guessing. (105a–c)[19]

First of all, this "one of the gods" that is reading Alcibiades' character is probably Socrates' *daimonion*.

Alcibiades thinks very highly of himself, and he wants his fame to spread throughout the entire world. He has the character of great conquerors like Alexander the Great or Julius Caesar. For the ancients the pre-eminent route to glory was politics and conquest. He wanted to create an empire.

The greatest empire that existed at that time, and that had ever existed, was the Persian Empire. Cyrus was its founder. Xerxes brought the empire to its greatest expanse. He also tried to conquer Greece. He was noted for his insane hubris. When the waves were too choppy for him to cross into Greece, he sent men down to the sea to beat it into submission. Even nature itself would have to submit to Persia's emperor. He was somewhat mad, but modest people don't try to conquer the world. Alcibiades, of course, failed, but it wasn't a very long time before Alexander the Great succeeded.

Alcibiades wants to conquer the world, and Socrates uses this enormous ambition to try to sell him on philosophy. He continues:

> Perhaps then, since you know I speak the truth, you will say, "What has this to do then, Socrates, with the account you said you would give of why you don't abandon me?" I will tell you, dear son of Cleinias and Deinomache, it is not possible for all these things you have in mind to be

---

[19] Plato, *Alcibiades I*, trans. Carnes Lord, in *The Roots of Political Philosophy: Ten Forgotten Platonic Dialogues*.

brought to a completion without me. So great is the power I suppose myself to have regarding your affairs and you, and I suppose this is why the god [clearly this is the *daimonion*, and probably the god posing the question at the start] did not allow me to converse with you for so long, and I waited for him to permit it. . . . I too hope to have the greatest power with you after having proved that I am invaluable to you and that no guardian or relative or anyone else is capable of bestowing the power you desire apart from me, though with the help of the god. (105d–e)

Socrates is saying, 'You want to conquer the world, my boy? You can't do it without me.[20] Not only will you rule the world, but I will do it right along with you.' These are extraordinary claims. For one thing, this is precisely how the great sophists hocked their wares to ambitious young men: 'Attend my lectures, learn rhetoric and political science, and you can attain political power.'

When you pair these sorts of arguments with Socrates' frequent public demonstrations of clever argumentation and speech-making, it is easy to understand why Socrates was often mistaken for a sophist.

But Socratic philosophy is different from sophistry. In fact, the sophists are Socrates' greatest rivals. But what differentiates them are their ends. On the surface, they use many of the same means. Hence to the superficial observer—and that's most people—Socrates is indistinguishable from a sophist.

Note that Socrates is clearly referring to his *daimonion* here as "the god." This must be borne in mind throughout the rest of the dialogue. Socrates then goes on to explain why his *daimonion* has now allowed him to speak to Alcibiades: "When you were

---

[20] Elizabeth Belfiore, *Socrates' Daimonic Art: Love for Wisdom in Four Platonic Dialogues* (Cambridge: Cambridge University Press, 2012), notes that, "Proclus 156.10–13 makes the insightful observation that Socrates does not say that Alcibiades will attain his goals with Socrates' help, but only that he could not attain them without this help" (p. 37, n16).

younger and not yet teeming with so much hope, the god, it seems to me, would not permit our conversing, in order that I not converse to no point." Socrates was watching Alcibiades for a long time. But Socrates only thought it necessary to speak to Alcibiades when he showed signs of tyrannical hubris.

In the *Theages*, the *daimonion* tells Socrates that the young Theages is not a good candidate for philosophical education. Does this mean that the *daimonion* thinks that Alcibiades has the potential to be a good student? Not necessarily. Alcibiades' ambitions may simply constitute an emergency, and Socrates must do his best to curb them, whether Alcibiades is receptive or not. If this is the case, one can't even say that Socrates was wrong about Alcibiades. He may have had entirely realistic expectations. He may have done his best in a bad or even impossible situation. But the city defeated him—and itself—in the end.

Alcibiades has never heard a come-on like this and is clearly intrigued. He says, "You now appear even more outlandish [*atopoteros*] to me, Socrates, now that you have begun to speak than when you followed in silence" (106a).[21] His sense of wonder is awakening. Alcibiades will not admit to tyrannical ambitions, but neither will he deny them, saying that Socrates would not believe him anyway. But "if" he does have such ambitions, he wants to know why he needs Socrates to help fulfill them.

---

[21] Cf. Plato, *Greater Alcibiades*, 116e, discussed below at pp. 41–42.

THE QUESTION OF JUSTICE

Before Socrates explains why his advice is necessary for Alcibiades' world-shaking ambitions, Socrates asks if he expects a "long speech... of the sort you are accustomed to hear" (106b).

Long speeches, like those heard in a legislative assembly or a law court, were a focus of the sophistical education sought out by ambitious young men like Alcibiades. Interestingly enough, there is no record of Alcibiades studying with the sophists, though he had the requisite money and ambition. However, in Plato's *Protagoras*, which is set not too long after the *Greater Alcibiades*, Alcibiades is at the house of Callias where three prominent sophists—Protagoras, Prodicus, and Hippias—have gathered to display their talents.[1]

Socrates, unlike the sophists, specializes in dialogue. He will instruct Alcibiades by asking questions. (Socrates also insists on dialogue rather than speech-making in his discussions with the sophists Gorgias, Polus, and Callicles in the *Gorgias*.)

As soon as he comes of age, which will be quite soon, Alcibiades wants to go before the Athenian assembly to advise them. But of what? Surely Alcibiades would only advise them about things that he knew, specifically things that he knew better than the men in the assembly. One can give advice only about the things one knows. One will be listened to only if one knows better than one's audience.

Socrates suggests that there are two kinds of knowledge: things one discovers oneself and things one learns from others. Alcibiades agrees. But maybe he was too hasty. Socrates seems to have an empirical model of knowledge in mind here, namely all knowledge can be traced to experience, either one's own or that of another. By assuming that premise, he can then show that Alcibiades has not learned anything that would qualify him to advise the city. But are there other forms of knowledge that are not derived from experience? For instance, isn't it possible that

---

[1] Plato, *Protagoras*, 309b, 316a.

we are simply *born* with some kinds of knowledge? Socratic argument actually presupposes that we *already know* what we are trying to define. Maybe we *always already know* some things.[2]

Socrates also proposes that Alcibiades would not have pursued knowledge unless he was aware that he lacked it. Alcibiades agrees. Self-knowledge, specifically knowledge of one's own ignorance, seems to be a necessary condition for pursuing knowledge of other things.

Socrates then lists the things that Alcibiades has studied: reading and writing, cithara playing, and wrestling—but not the flute. Note that there's no mention of sophistry. How does Socrates know this? Apparently because he had stalked Alcibiades' every move for years. Socrates knew Alcibiades studied wrestling, because he followed him to and from the wrestling school. We moderns are not comfortable with this. But I think it was supposed to seem creepy to the ancients as well.

So does Alcibiades plan to advise the assembly about spelling, cithara playing, or wrestling, since these are things he knows? Obviously not. What about house-building, divination, or medicine? Obviously not. Athenians would only listen to experts in those fields.

Socrates also points out that looks, breeding, and wealth really don't matter when it comes to technical expertise. This is Socrates slyly voicing what Alcibiades is really depending upon: not *what he knows* but *who he is*, not *what he has learned* but *what he was born with*.

There might be something to this. There may be more to leading the city than possessing the requisite knowledge and technical expertise. Looks, breeding, and wealth really do matter to politics. But Socrates keeps the discussion firmly focused on knowledge, specifically different forms of technical expertise.

The Athenians might well give Alcibiades a hearing based simply on his looks, breeding, and wealth. But when he opens his mouth, he had better have something of substance to say. He needs to *know* something. But what does he know? What is his

---

[2] See my "Notes on Philosophical Dialectic" in *From Plato to Postmodernism*.

area of expertise?

Alcibiades answers that he will advise the citizens about "their own affairs." But again, Socrates finds this vague. He wants something more concrete. Will Alcibiades advise the Athenians about building ships, for instance? Obviously not, since he has no expertise in shipbuilding. That would be for shipbuilders to discuss.

So Alcibiades gets more specific. He will advise the Athenians "when they are deliberating on war or on peace or some other of the city's affairs" (107d).

Socrates thinks this is promising. He asks if this means that they are deliberating about whom it is *better* to fight, when it is *better* to fight, and how long it is *better* to fight. Alcibiades agrees. Here Socrates is introducing the concept of the *good*. He is turning the discussion toward moral philosophy. For Socrates, philosophy is about wisdom, and wisdom is the ability to make *right* use of all things, which means it is intrinsically connected to the good.

But then Socrates does something surprising. He argues that questions of the good are subordinate to technical expertise. Wrestling coaches know the better and worse in wrestling. Musicians know the better and worse in music. Thus, as a general rule, "what is correct is surely what comes about according to art [*techne*]" (108b).

Is the good merely a technical question, a matter of know-how? On the one hand, an expert is the best judge of how skillfully an art is performed. But there's more to the good than being good at wrestling or playing music or any other skill.

A skilled wrestler would also be a skilled assassin. A skilled musician would also be adept at torturing people with unbearable noise. A pharmacist has the ability to cure or to kill. The difference is merely a matter of dose. A surgeon also has the power to cure or to kill. A surgeon would probably be the best torturer, but being the best at torturing people is not the same as being good in the moral sense.

The mere possession of a technical ability does not guarantee that it will be used *rightly*. That requires something over and above knowledge or skill. It requires wisdom, which directs the skill toward good ends and away from bad ones. But as far as Socrates is concerned here, there seems to be nothing above knowledge, specifically technical knowledge.

Socrates argues that we would call the better in wrestling the "gymnastic" and the better in music the "musical." This is somewhat confusing, however, for we use "gymnastics" to refer to one particular form of athletic activity and "music" to refer to one particular form of artistic activity. Socrates, however, uses "gymnastic" to refer to all athletics and "music," which refers to the Muses, who are the patronesses of all the arts, to refer to all the arts. So it would be less confusing to say that an excellent wrestling performance is "athletic" and an excellent musical performance is "artistic." Alcibiades agrees, but it takes a good deal of prodding before Socrates can elicit the concept of the arts, which may indicate that Alcibiades is not particularly bright.

Why does Socrates wish to place wrestling in the broader category of athletics before speaking about its excellence? Why does he place music in the broader context of the arts before speaking of its excellence? Because Socrates wants to place war and peace and other affairs of the city in a common context before asking Alcibiades the word we use for performing them well. But when asked, Alcibiades draws a blank: "Nothing occurs to me" (109e).

Socrates mocks this as shameful. Alcibiades doesn't need to be a doctor to know that the better in medicine is health. Yet he would advise the Athenians on war and peace without knowing the word for the better regarding war and peace.

Socrates prods Alcibiades by asking what people fight wars about. He responds: "we say we have been deceived, or done violence to, or deprived of something" (109b). Socrates then asks how we are affronted in such cases. This question finally gets Alcibiades to the right answer: "do you mean justly [*dikaios*] or unjustly [*adikos*]?" And Socrates says, "This very thing!" When matters of war and peace are handled well, we call that justice (*dike*). It isn't a complete account of justice, but it is a start.

ALCIBIADES KNOWS WHAT JUSTICE IS AFTER ALL

Socrates continues to shame and bully Alcibiades for not

knowing what justice is, even though he plans to advise the city on matters of justice and injustice.

Even more shamefully, Alcibiades made no provisions to learn about justice: "Or did it escape me that you were learning and going to a teacher who taught you to recognize the more just and the more unjust? And who is this, who is your teacher in this matter? Tell me as well, so you can introduce me, and I too can become his pupil" (109d). It is slightly absurd that the ward of Pericles himself has studied wrestling and music but nothing of politics and its highest value, justice.

Alcibiades is a spirited young man, and at this point, he accuses Socrates of mocking him, which Socrates denies with an oath to Zeus. (He is clearly lying, so his oath is an act of impiety.)

Alcibiades asks if he could not have learned about justice and injustice in a different way, i.e., not from a teacher. This is a pertinent question. Socrates immediately responds: "Yes . . . if you discovered it" (109e). But this, as we have noted, is not the only option.

Socrates says that Alcibiades could discover the just if he investigates it. But "I do think you could investigate this if, that is, you supposed you did not know." This is classic Socrates: you will only search for knowledge if you know that you don't know something. If you're unaware of your own ignorance, you'll never search for knowledge.

Socrates continues to hammer away at Alcibiades for being ignorant of justice, and ignorant of his ignorance. Socrates asks Alcibiades if there was ever a time when he didn't think he knew what justice is: "When did you learn the just and the unjust things? Three or four years ago when you were still a child?" (110a–b). Alcibiades can't remember a time when he thought he was ignorant of justice. Socrates is insinuating, of course, that Alcibiades is deluded that he always knew about justice. But Alcibiades is not eager to accept this claim.

Socrates points out that when Alcibiades was a child playing dice or other games with his fellow children, he did not act like he was ignorant of justice. In fact, he would declare loudly and confidently that other children were behaving unjustly toward him. 'No fair!' How many times have you heard little kids say that? Even as children, we think we know what justice is.

Alcibiades replies, "But what was I going to do, Socrates, when someone was behaving unjustly towards me?" (110b). Except protest 'No fair!'

And Socrates replies, "What should you do, you mean, if you happened at that time to be ignorant of whether you were being unjustly treated or not?" If Alcibiades didn't know what justice is, Socrates insinuates, perhaps he should have remained silent.

Alcibiades' response is interesting. He says, "By Zeus! I was not ignorant but knew clearly that I was being treated unjustly." His oath indicates indignation. He is pushing back angrily at Socrates.

Socrates says, "You suppose, therefore, you had knowledge of the just and the unjust things even as a child, as it appears."

Alcibiades stands his ground: "I did, and I did have the knowledge" (110c).

WHEN & HOW DID ALCIBIADES LEARN ABOUT JUSTICE?

When Alcibiades claims he knows what justice is, Socrates asks *when* he discovered it. Alcibiades can't remember when he discovered it. Socrates then reminds Alcibiades that he said that he didn't learn it either. Socrates is inviting Alcibiades to consider that there might be other possibilities besides discovering what justice is himself or learning it from others, such as innate knowledge. But Alcibiades immediately flips back to the other side of the false dichotomy, affirming that if he didn't discover it, he must have learned it from someone. Socrates asks from whom. To which Alcibiades gives a surprising answer: "from the many" (110e), i.e., from the people of Athens.

Socrates is initially dismissive. He responds that the many are not very serious teachers. They couldn't competently teach him to play a child's board game, much less something important like justice. But Alcibiades stands his ground, arguing that the many *are* capable of teaching important things: "for instance it was from them I learned to speak Greek" (110e). If you've ever studied Greek, you know that's no mean thing. But Alcibiades learned Greek as a child, and he learned it from the people of Athens.

Socrates admits that the many can teach Greek. But that's only because they *know* it. You can only teach what you know.

Socrates then introduces the idea that agreement is a sign of knowledge. If two people know something, they would say the same things about it. This is true of language, for speakers use the same words to mean the same things. But when it comes to justice, the many disagree. They even fight wars about it. Isn't this evidence that they don't know what justice is?

Alcibiades agrees, but again he might be too hasty. If, for instance, we all had innate knowledge of justice, we might still disagree about it, if we articulate this innate knowledge in different ways. We might also disagree about the application of this knowledge in particular situations.

However, because Alcibiades accepts that disagreement indicates the absence of knowledge, Socrates easily convinces him that the many cannot know what justice is, because the many are constantly disagreeing about justice. And if the many don't know what justice is, they could not have taught it to Alcibiades.

When Alcibiades draws the conclusion that the many did not teach him justice, he attributes this conclusion to Socrates. But Socrates reproaches him for speaking badly. Socrates did not draw the conclusion that Alcibiades does not know what justice is. Socrates only asked questions. Alcibiades is the one who drew the conclusion. Thus he learned it from himself, not from Socrates.

But if Alcibiades learned this truth from himself, doesn't that imply that the truth was *already* in him, in an implicit fashion, and all he needed to access it was the right questions? Indeed, that is true. But the deeper Socratic teaching is that actually Alcibiades *does* know what justice is, but it is innate knowledge, which he neither learned from others nor discovered outside himself. All he needs is the right questions to access it.

Then Socrates states the practical implication he's been driving at with this line of questioning: it would be mad for Alcibiades to go before the people of Athens to teach them things he does not know. Alcibiades is not yet ready for politics. First he must study philosophy.

JUSTICE & EXPEDIENCY

Alcibiades admits that he doesn't know what justice is. But he thinks he's found a way around Socrates' objection, since politics doesn't really deal with justice (*dike*). Instead, it deals with the expedient or advantageous (*sympheronta*). The just and the expedient are different things, since one can benefit from unjust acts and be harmed by just acts.

Socrates suggests the example of a man who suffers injury or death by risking his life to save his kinsman or countryman in battle. This is a just and courageous act, even though one is harmed by it. Conversely, if one avoids injury or death by being cowardly, one is benefitted by injustice. Therefore, the just and the advantageous are different things.

It is important to note that this example operates within a definition of justice that Socrates rejects in the *Republic*: justice as helping one's friends and harming one's enemies.[1] It is also important to note that just a short time after the setting of this conversation, Socrates risked his life to save Alcibiades at the Battle of Potidaea.

The difference between justice and expediency was a commonplace idea in ancient Greece. Socrates deals with just such claims at length in the *Gorgias* and the *Republic*, where he takes great pains to argue that, properly understood, there is no distinction between justice and expediency. But these arguments depend on two premises: (1) the distinction between the soul (*psyche*) and the body (*soma*) and (2) the superiority of the soul over the body, meaning that our true self is the soul, not the body.

For Socrates, the soul is perfected by virtue and marred by vice. Therefore, when a man suffers death or injury while acting courageously, his body may be harmed but his soul is benefitted, and the soul is the most important part. (This argument need not assume that the soul survives the death of the body.)

---

[1] Plato, *Republic*, 331e–336a.

Conversely, if a man prolongs his life through dishonest acts, he sacrifices something of greater value (his soul) for something of lesser value (his body). However, Socrates does not make this sort of argument, because the concept of the soul has not been introduced at this point in the *Greater Alcibiades*.

Socrates challenges Alcibiades to prove that he knows that the just and the expedient are different. Alcibiades hesitates, but Socrates presses the argument. If Alcibiades proposes to stand before the assembly and speak about the just vs. the expedient, then there is nothing to stop him from standing before Socrates and saying the same things. After all, a mathematician can persuade one man or many about numbers.

Alcibiades accepts this argument, but he is too hasty. Is it really true that the same things can be taught to one man or many? Doesn't this presuppose that the audience is all basically equal? Doesn't this undermine the need for distinguishing between exoteric and esoteric forms of speech? Obviously, some things that can be taught to intelligent individuals cannot be taught to large crowds, which contain people of different levels of intelligence. Socrates, being a tougher sell than the assembly, might be much harder to persuade. Such objections do not, however, occur to Alcibiades, who instead accuses Socrates of being hubristic. This is odd, because Socrates is actually placing himself on the level of every other Athenian. But Alcibiades is merely objecting to being defeated in argument.

Socrates proposes to persuade Alcibiades that the just and the advantageous are the same. Again, Alcibiades wants a speech, but Socrates insists on a dialogue. Socrates first establishes that Alcibiades thinks, "Of the just things, some are advantageous and some not" (115a). Socrates wishes to argue that justice is always advantageous.

First Socrates establishes the premise: "All the just things are also noble [*kalon*]" (115a). Then Socrates establishes that Alcibiades holds that "some noble things are bad [*kakos*]" and "some shameful [*aischros*] things are good [*agathos*]" (115a). Socrates illustrates the "noble but bad" with the example of the courageous man who goes to the aid of his comrade in battle and suffers wounds or death. An example of the "shameful but good" would be the coward who saves his own skin by leaving his comrade behind.

But Socrates points out that "Coming to the aid of friends is not . . . noble and bad in the same respect . . ." (115c). It is morally noble but physically disadvantageous. Likewise, abandoning one's friend might be morally ignoble but physically advantageous.

At this point, Socrates has set the stage for distinguishing between the soul and the body. We can be both noble and suffer at the same time, but not in the same respect. Part of us is noble, and a different part of us suffers. The soul can be noble or ignoble. The body suffers or is spared physical death or wounds. But Socrates does not make this distinction explicit until later in the dialogue.

Socrates, however, turns to the question of whether courage is good or bad. He asks Alcibiades if he prefers good or bad things for himself? Alcibiades, of course, prefers the good, indeed, the best (115c). This is standard Socratic ethics, the thesis that 'All men pursue the good.' Having established that Alcibiades wants the best for himself, Socrates asks him about courage (*andreia*): "For what price would you be deprived of it?" (115d).

Alcibiades replies, "I wouldn't choose to live if I were a coward" (115d). To which Socrates replies that cowardice (*deilia*) is equal to death, that "And life and courage are most opposed to death and cowardice" (115d); and that "courage is among the best things . . . and death among the worst" (115e). Alcibiades agrees with all of these claims.

But, again, this seems hasty. By saying that death is one of the worst things, Socrates implies that death is never choiceworthy, since we always choose the best option available to us. But Alcibiades has already said that he would choose death over dishonor if forced to choose between the two.

Socrates continues by asking if Alcibiades thinks that rescuing one's friends in battle is noble because it produces good effects by means of courage. Alcibiades agrees. Then Socrates asks if it is also bad because it produces the bad effect of death. Alcibiades agrees with this as well. Socrates then establishes the premise that either act—rescuing or failing to rescue—might be deemed good if it produces good results, evil if it produces evil results. Alcibiades agrees with that as well. Then Socrates proposes a surprising conclusion: "Then in saying that the rescue of one's friends in battle is noble and yet evil, you mean just the same as if you called the rescue good but evil" (116a).

Socrates seems to be claiming that Alcibiades has contradicted himself. But has he? Hasn't Socrates already provided an answer to this sort of objection? Is rescuing one's friend good and evil *in the same respect*? Why not say that rescuing one's friend is good because it is the courageous thing to do (which is becoming for the soul), but it is also evil because of the wounds or death suffered by the body?

Socrates then offers a summary: "So nothing noble, insofar as it is noble, is evil, and nothing base, insofar as it is base, is good" (116a). But to say that nothing noble is evil, just insofar as it is noble, does not rule out the possibility that a noble deed might lead to evil consequences, like dying in battle while rescuing a friend. And to say that nothing base is good, just insofar as it is base, does not rule out the possibility that it has good consequences, for instance that cowardice might prolong one's life.

The final phase of Socrates' argument at 116c–d is somewhat jumbled and difficult to follow. This is my reconstruction:

> "Whoever does nobly, does well [*eu prattein*] . . ."
> By acting nobly and well, we acquire good things.
> By acquiring good things, we attain well-being or happiness (*eudaimonia*).
> Therefore, those who act nobly enjoy well-being.

The trouble with this argument is that there is no guarantee that by acting nobly and well, we will acquire the external good things that Socrates says lead to well-being. Beyond that, we can think of many cases in which we can secure external goods by acting ignobly and badly. This is why the Greeks distinguished expediency from justice (and all the other virtues). The only way to argue that there is a necessary connection between virtue and well-being is to make virtue itself a sufficient condition for well-being, regardless of external goods. Socrates makes such arguments in the *Gorgias* and *Republic*, but not in the *Greater Alcibiades*.

Socrates continues:

"Noble and good are the same thing."
The just things are noble.
Therefore, the just things are the same as the good things.

The good things are the same as the just things.
The good things are advantageous.
"Hence the just things, Alcibiades, are advantageous."

But the conclusion does not follow with necessity, because, based on the examples we have examined, sometimes acting justly leads to bad consequences, and sometimes acting unjustly leads to good consequences. Alcibiades should reject this argument, but he agrees.

If the just is the expedient, and Alcibiades does not know the just, then Alcibiades is again in no position to advise anyone about politics, whether they be the Athenians or Peparethians. Peparethus was a tiny island off the coast of Thessaly. If Athens is the most important place in Greece, Peparethus might be the least. It was the Greek equivalent of Podunk or Peoria: the paradigm of provincialism. We don't know if "Peparethus" sounded funny to the Athenians. But if it did, Plato's contrast might be the equivalent of contrasting Washington, D.C. with Walla Walla, Washington. (Some classicists think they can date the composition of the *Greater Alcibiades* to when Peparethus was "in the news." But that would undermine the whole contrast. The point is that Peparethus is not famous at all.[2])

ALCIBIADES' PLIGHT

Alcibiades is quite distressed. Whereas Socrates seemed "outlandish" to Alcibiades at the beginning of their conversation (106a), now Alcibiades feels equally outlandish or unsettled

---

[2] Denyer, *Alcibiades*, p. 152; Renaud and Tarrant, *The Platonic Alcibiades I*, p. 267.

(*atopos*) (116e). He felt he knew what justice is, then Socrates changed his mind. He felt he knew what expediency is, then Socrates changed his mind.

Socrates argues that we don't change our minds about things that we actually know. If we change our minds about something, that is a sign that we don't know it. This is a version of the earlier argument that disagreement (in this case, disagreement with oneself) is a sign of ignorance. But this is a false premise, because it is one thing to know something, another to put it into words, and just as two people who know the same thing might say it differently, the same person might articulate the same knowledge in different ways at different times.

Not only do we not contradict ourselves on matters that we know, Socrates argues that we don't contradict ourselves on matters about which *we know that we are ignorant*. We only contradict ourselves on matters that we mistakenly *think* that we know about, but we actually don't. Mere ignorance is not the problem. The real problem is *ignorance of our own ignorance*. When we know that we are ignorant, we simply defer to those who know. When we don't know that we are ignorant, we make fools of ourselves by talking about things we do not know.

Alcibiades is not just ignorant. He's not just ignorant of his ignorance. He's also ignorant of the most important things: "the just, noble, good, and advantageous" (118a). Socrates sums it up bluntly: Alcibiades is guilty of "stupidity. . . in its most extreme form" (118b). At this point, Alcibiades takes the need for education seriously, and he is ready to follow Socrates as his teacher.

But Socrates does not close the deal. Instead, he overdoes it. He gets hubristic. He decides to gild the lily, to lay on the paint a bit too thickly. And in overreaching, he almost loses Alcibiades.

Socrates' mistake is to point out that Alcibiades may be stupid, but he's in good company. Most of the statesmen of Athens are clueless about justice too, perhaps even Pericles.

Alcibiades points out that Pericles actually sought the counsel of wise men: Pythocleides, Anaxagoras, and Damon. Anaxagoras was a natural philosopher. In the *Phaedo*, Socrates admits to reading him avidly when he was younger, only to be disappointed.[3] According to Protagoras in Plato's dialogue of that name, Pythocleides was a wise man who disguised his wisdom as music.[4] He was a teacher of Pericles and Sophocles. Damon was a music theorist and teacher.

But Socrates doubts that Pericles learned much from them, for the simple reason that if one learns a particular topic, one can also teach it. But Pericles did not make his two sons wiser. So how could he be wise himself? This is a classic Socratic argument found in the *Theages* and *Meno* as well.[5] But Alcibiades pushes back against it.

He excuses Pericles's failure to educate his sons by pointing out that the lads were simpletons. What about Pericles' failure to educate Alcibiades' own brother, Cleinias? Alcibiades excuses this by pointing out that Cleinias is mad.

Well, what about his failure to educate Alcibiades himself? Alcibiades suggests that maybe he is at fault for not paying attention to Pericles. But Socrates persists. Is there any evidence that Pericles made anyone wiser by associating with him? Alcibiades cannot think of a single example.

Obviously, Alcibiades has been poorly educated, especially given his political ambitions. Socrates thinks that Alcibiades is now ready for the conclusion he has been driving for: Alcibiades must put himself in Socrates' hands to be educated.

But Alcibiades draws a completely different but still reasonable conclusion from Socrates' argument: if the majority of Athenian statesmen are ignorant, then Alcibiades need not be educated to compete with them, for he has another advantage over them. He is confident that he can beat them based simply on his own *natural* superiority.

---

[3] Plato, *Phaedo*, 97b–99d.
[4] Plato, *Protagoras*, 317e.
[5] Plato, *Theages*, 128a–b, and *Meno*, 92e–94e.

Raising the Stakes

Socrates has convinced Alcibiades that he is ignorant of justice. Therefore, he should not go into politics until he is educated. But Socrates undermines his argument by pointing out that none of the other eminent Athenians, even Pericles himself, knows what justice is. From this, Alcibiades concludes that if his rivals for power are equally ignorant, he has no need to waste time on education, because he is confident that he can beat them based on his superior nature.

Socrates is defeated by his own argument. But he is unflappable. Immediately he changes course. Instead of continuing the dialogue, he makes a speech. The content of his speech is a story; the Greek word for "story" is "*mythos*." The purpose of the myth is to shame Alcibiades. It is highly effective.

Socrates laments that Alcibiades's idea that he can simply glide through life on his looks and connections is "unworthy" of him (119c). Alcibiades has a strong sense of pride, so he is eager to know in what way he is not living up to his potential. Then Socrates pulls the old 'I'm not mad, son, just disappointed' routine. Socrates is disappointed that Alcibiades is only concerned with competing with his fellow Athenians. When Alcibiades asks, 'With whom, then?' Socrates shames him again, saying that the question is "unworthy of someone who thinks of himself as proud [*megalophrona*]" (119c). Socrates is trying to inflame Alcibiades' pride and competitiveness against his complacency.

Socrates uses a beautiful analogy to prod Alcibiades to raise his sights. If Alcibiades were to captain a warship, it would be small-minded to preen about his superiority to the men serving under him, because the true question is whether he is superior to the captains on the other side. Likewise, if Alcibiades were to lead Athens, he should compare himself not to the men he rules over, but to the rulers of Athens' great rivals: Sparta and Persia. Alcibiades agrees with this. But he still doesn't think that the Spartans and the Persians are all that special.

Socrates first offers a pragmatic response. If Alcibiades thinks the Spartans and Persians are formidable enemies, he will try to improve himself to be a worthy opponent. Self-improvement is never a bad thing. Thus dismissing the superiority of the Spartans and Persians would be bad because it promotes complacency rather than self-improvement. Note that this is not an argument for the *truth* of Socrates' claims about the Spartans and the Persians. It is merely for the usefulness of his claims. It also indicates that Socrates has ample incentive to exaggerate just how formidable they really are.

Socrates characterizes his second argument as probabilistic: "it is probable that noble races should produce better natures" (120e). The well-born, if well-raised, will "probably be perfected in virtue." Then Socrates argues that the Spartan and Persian kings are of noble descent by citing myths about their divine origins. The Spartan kings descend from Hercules; the Persian kings stem from Perseus the son of Zeus. It is hard to credit Socrates with taking these arguments seriously, but clearly he hopes that Alcibiades will.

Again, though, Socrates falls into his own trap, for Alcibiades responds that he is not inferior to the Spartan and Persian kings due to his descent from Eurysaces, son of Zeus. As if to throw in the towel, Socrates responds that even he is descended from Zeus, which almost reduces his argument to absurdity. For the Greeks, being descended from Zeus may have been about as common as being descended from Adam, i.e., it puts us all on equal footing. It does not establish that some are better than others.

But Socrates changes tack. The point is not descent but upbringing. Socrates and Alcibiades may descend from Zeus just as much as the Spartan and Persian kings. But their upbringings differ. Spartan and Persian kings come from long lines of kings, and they are raised to carry on their dynasties. By contrast, Socrates and Alcibiades are merely private persons, the sons of private persons for generations back, and have been raised to be private persons.

Socrates says that if Alcibiades were to cite his lineage and upbringing and wealth in order to impress the Great King of Persia, Artaxerxes I, he would be laughed at. This is designed to inflame Alcibiades' *thumos*. "I am afraid," says Socrates, that "we are quite outdone by those persons in pride of birth and upbringing altogether" (121b).

A ROYAL TALE

Then Socrates launches into a speech lauding the family lives, upbringing, education, and wealth of the Spartan and Persian kings. First Socrates mentions how both royal lines assure their continuation and the legitimacy of their offspring.

In Sparta, the queens are closely guarded by the ephors to prevent cuckoldry. One wonders who guards the ephors, however, since they were not eunuchs. Beyond that, when Plato wrote these words, he knew what was in Alcibiades' future. After defecting to the Spartans in 415 BCE, Alcibiades did not find any insurmountable barriers to seducing Timaea, the wife of King Agis II. Alcibiades fathered a son with Timaea, Leotychides of Sparta. She did not hide his paternity from King Agis. Thus the throne passed to Agis' brother, Agesilaus II.

As for the Persians, Socrates says that their king is so feared that none of them would dare cuckold him. If this were true, however, then the Great King would have no need of the army of eunuchs who attended him.

In short, an informed reader in Plato's time and ours would see the farcical and contradictory elements of Socrates' speech and rapidly conclude that Socrates is trying to fool Alcibiades. Indeed, he's testing Alcibiades to see how gullible he may be.

According to Socrates, when a Persian heir is born, his birthday becomes a holiday throughout the empire, whereas in Athens not even the neighbors notice their births. The Persian princes are cared for by eunuchs. When they are seven, they learn to ride and hunt. When they are 14, they are turned over to four royal tutors, eminent men of mature age, renowned as the wisest, most just, most temperate, and most courageous men in the empire. Wisdom (*sophia*), justice (*dikaiosyne*), temperance (*sophrosyne*), and courage (*andreia*) are the four cardinal virtues of Plato's *Republic*.

The wisest tutor teaches the Magian lore of Zoroaster, the worship of the gods, and everything connected to kingship. This has little to do with *sophia* (theoretical wisdom) as Plato understood it. The just man teaches truthfulness; the temperate man, mastery of the appetites; and the brave man, mastery over fear.

Pericles, by contrast, gave Alcibiades only one tutor: an elderly and otherwise useless servant, Zopyrus the Thracian. But nobody really cares about the education of young Athenians, unless they are lucky enough to find a lover like Socrates who is interested not in their bodies but in their souls.

Socrates also points out that the fabulous wealth and luxury of the Persians puts Alcibiades to shame, even though Alcibiades was quite wealthy by Athenian standards. Socrates would not have made this point if he really believed that Alcibiades didn't think much of money.

The Spartans too have enormous wealth, despite their reputation for austerity and toughness. But it is their virtues—which include "temperance, orderliness, coolness, even-temperedness, magnanimity, discipline, courage, endurance, and love of toil, victory, and honor" (122b)—that most put Alcibiades to shame.

Socrates then underscores the wealth and luxury of the Persians by reporting the story of a Greek who travelled to the court of the Great King, passing through districts whose entire revenue was dedicated solely to creating single items of clothing for the Persian queen. Socrates lauds the wealth of the Persians and Spartans because he knew very well that Alcibiades loved wealth, pomp, and display.

Then Socrates' argument takes a strange turn. As in the *Symposium*, where Socrates relates the speech of the priestess Diotima, and in the *Menexenus*, where Socrates relates a speech of Aspasia, the mistress of Pericles, Socrates here speaks through two women who were both wives and mothers of kings: Amestris of Persia and Lampito of Sparta.

Amestris was the queen of Xerxes I, who reigned from 486 to 465 BCE, who invaded Greece in 480–479 BCE, and who was defeated at Salamis. Amestris was the mother of Artaxerxes I, who succeeded Xerxes I and ruled from 465 to 424 BCE. Lampito was married to Archidamus II, king of Sparta from c. 469 to c. 427 BCE. She was mother of King Agis II, who reigned c. 427–400 BCE. Given that the dramatic date of the *Greater Alcibiades* is

432 BCE, it is anachronistic to say that Lampito was the mother of a king, although she was the mother of the king's heir who later did become king.[1]

If someone were to tell Amestris that the "son of Deinomache," i.e., Alcibiades, wished to challenge her son Artaxerxes, she would scoff at Deinomache's paltry wardrobe and Alcibiades' tiny estates. But, interestingly enough, despite her snobbery, she would not dismiss Alcibiades out of hand, for she knows that other factors may counterbalance wealth and power, namely "taking pains [*epimelesthai*] and wisdom [*sophia*], for these are the only things of any account among the Greeks" (123d).

According to Nicholas Denyer, referring to Alcibiades simply as the "son of Deinomache" was "utterly extraordinary."[2] This strange locution was dictated by the analogy that Socrates wished to establish between Alcibiades, Artaxerxes I, and Agis II.

But why does he speak of the mothers of Athens' rival kings rather than their fathers? Surely their fathers had just as much, if not more, influence on the upbringings of their sons. Is it because Alcibiades was not raised by his father but by his mother together with his guardian Pericles? Would, therefore, the contrast between different styles of mothering have been more poignant and meaningful to Alcibiades? Did Socrates decide to put words in the mouths of enemy women because he thought that Alcibiades would be extra ashamed if his mother were bested by foreign women? Did Socrates think that it would be especially humiliating for Alcibiades himself to be looked down upon by women, especially foreign women?

SELF-CULTIVATION & WISDOM

Let's now turn to the concepts of self-cultivation and wisdom. The word *epimelesthai* can be translated as care, concern, taking trouble, taking pains. It plays an important role in the *Greater Alcibiades*. Alcibiades uses this word at the beginning when he

---

[1] Even though Lampito was the wife and mother of kings, Spartans did not style the wives of kings as queens.

[2] Plato, *Alcibiades*, ed. Denyer, p. 187

describes Socrates' stalking behavior as "always taking such trouble [*epimelestata*] to show up where I happen to be" (104c).³ The primary sense of *epimelesthai* in the dialogue is, however, taking care of oneself (*epimelesthai sautou*), because Socrates' goal is to shake Alcibiades from his complacency and accept Socrates as his teacher. Thus his mouthpiece, the Persian queen, fears Greek self-cultivation, for it will even the odds against her son.

Although the queen uses "*sophia*," the word for theoretical wisdom, here it is clear that she is thinking about practical wisdom or *phronesis*.

The Socratic idea of wisdom is the ability to make *right use* of *all things*. The goal of life is well-being or happiness (*eudaimonia*). To achieve happiness we need certain external things and conditions. But mere *possession* of even the greatest wealth and power is not enough for happiness, because goods must be *used*. If goods are used rightly, i.e., wisely, they are conducive to happiness. If they are used badly, i.e., foolishly, they are not conducive to happiness. (I say "conducive," because there are no guarantees in a world where fortune plays a role.)

In fact, great wealth and power without wise use are worse than poverty and powerlessness, for great wealth and power afford enormous opportunities for self-destruction. But the reverse is also true: the poor and powerless can lead happy lives through wise use of whatever modest opportunities fortune dispenses. Wisdom, therefore, is a great equalizer of fortune: the wise but unfortunate can rise; the fortunate but foolish can fall.

Thus Amestris is not immediately dismissive of Alcibiades for his lack of wealth, for if through self-cultivation he acquires wisdom, he may have the ability to overcome her son's advantages.

This brings to mind a fragment from another dialogue called *Alcibiades*, by Aeschines of Sphettus. When Darius of Persia invaded Greece, the Athenians turned to Themistocles to save them. When Themistocles compared the forces of the Persians to

---

³ On *epimelesthai* in the *Greater Alcibiades*, see Gary Alan Scott, *Plato's Socrates as Educator* (Albany: SUNY Press, 2000), ch. 3, "The *Alcibiades I*: Socratic Dialogue as Self-Care."

those of the Greeks, he found the Greek forces far inferior.

> [B]ut he knew that unless that man [the Great King] excelled him in giving advice, all these other things, great as they were in magnitude, would not be of any great help to him. . . . [W]hichever people had men more worthy and excellent overseeing their affairs, it was their side that was usually victorious.[4]

A great army, foolishly commanded, may be defeated by a smaller army, wisely commanded.

However, if Amestris were to learn that Alcibiades does not see fit to cultivate himself to pursue wisdom, but instead thinks he's fine as he is, she would conclude that Alcibiades is simply mad to challenge Artaxerxes. Socrates points out that Lampito of Sparta would feel the same way.

Then Socrates draws his conclusion: Isn't it shameful that mere women, the wives and mothers of their enemies, "should have a better idea of the qualities that we need for an attempt against them than we have ourselves?" (124a).

Shaming is a way to make people conscious of themselves, specifically of their inadequacies. Hence Socrates bids Alcibiades to "listen to me and the Delphic motto 'Know thyself'" and take to heart that "only self-cultivation [*epimeleia*] and art [*techne*]" will allow Alcibiades to exceed his real rivals and win the renown he seeks (124d–e).

Alcibiades is convinced. He has to raise his sights. He has to cultivate himself and pursue wisdom.[5] So he asks Socrates for advice. But Socrates is not going to give another speech. Socrates says that they will work *together* to figure out how to be as excellent as possible, for Socrates claims that he too is in the same predicament as Alcibiades, with only one advantage: Socrates'

---

[4] Plato and Aeschines of Sphettus, *Socrates and Alcibiades: Four Texts*, p. 95.

[5] Xenophon notes that Alcibiades and Critias stopped following Socrates as soon as they believed that his instruction had made them better than their rivals. See *Memorabilia*, II.2.16 and 47.

daimonion is a better guardian to him than Pericles is to Alcibiades.

Here Socrates refers to the *daimonion* simply as "god" (*theos*) (124c). Other references to god in the dialogue should also be read this way. The *daimonion* is Socrates' personification of his knowledge of "erotic things" (*ta erotika*). By "erotic things," Socrates means human nature, particularly the nature of the human soul, which is charged throughout with eros. Recall that the ancient subtitle of this dialogue is "On the Nature of Man." Socrates says that his *daimonion* tells him what not to do or say. I gloss this as Socrates' ability to regulate his actions and speech based on his ability to assess human nature. In Plato's dialogues, the *daimonion* manifests itself in the context of philosophical conversations. Thus we can say that the *daimonion* is Socrates' philosophical prudence.

Socrates claims that "the god" has told him that Alcibiades will attain the renown he seeks "through no other man but me" (124c). Alcibiades brushes this off as a joke, and Socrates allows that "perhaps" he's right. But then immediately Socrates emphasizes the practical situation that—god or no god—human beings in general need to take care of themselves, especially Socrates and Alcibiades, for the greater our talent and the greater our ambition, the greater our need for wisdom.

EXPERTISE VS. COMMON KNOWLEDGE

BACK TO DIALOGUE

To borrow a term from classical music, the *Greater Alcibiades* has a "sonata" form: ABA. The first part (A[1]) consists of Socrates' initial dialogue with Alcibiades. Part B is the speech about the Persian and Spartan queens. The third part (A[2]) is a return to the dialogue form. Socrates and Alcibiades first return to the idea of justice. Then they discuss self-knowledge.

Socrates establishes that we wish to become as excellent (*aristoi*) as possible (123e). In particular, Alcibiades wishes to acquire the excellences of the Athenian gentlemen (*kaloi kagathoi*), the ruling stratum of society. Gentlemen are characterized as having practical wisdom or prudence (*phronesis*) rather than being imprudent. Prudent men are good. Imprudent men are bad.

But prudent in what sort of affairs? Athenian gentlemen are not prudent in specialized arts and crafts like training horses, making shoes, or healing the sick. Instead, their prudence is comprehensive: they rule over the whole city, i.e., the whole of social life. Moreover, the citizens are citizens in virtue of something in *common*. They "share in the city as fellow citizens and do business with one another" (126d).

Socrates wants to know what the art of the gentleman is. If the pilot's art rules over sailors, and the chorister's art rules over singers, what art rules over all the citizens? Obviously, this is the political art, what Aristotle called the "architectonic art."[1] Alcibiades answers: the art of "good advice" (*euboulia*). Good advice is equivalent to practical wisdom or *phronesis*.

FRIENDSHIP & AGREEMENT IN THE CITY

But what is good counsel *for*? What is its end? Alcibiades answers: "for the better management and preservation of the city"

---

[1] Aristotle, *Nicomachean Ethics*, book I, chapter 1, 1094a14–18, 1094a26–b11.

(126a). What does better management produce for the city, and what negative effects are felt from its absence? Alcibiades responds: "friendship [*philia*] with one another will be there, while hatred and faction will be absent" (126c). The opposite of faction, of course, is unity. Thus the political art produces *unity* and *friendship*. The unspoken assumption here is that unity and friendship constitute *justice*, for justice is the *sine qua non* of the well-managed and well-ordered city.

But what sort of "unity" is the opposite of faction? Socrates pursues this question by asking if friendship produces "agreement" or "oneness of mind" (*homonoia*). Alcibiades says yes. But what sort of agreement is this? Mathematics creates agreement about numbers between individuals, within individuals (consistency), and for the city as a whole. The same is true with the arts of measurement and weighing. If the political art produces friendship, and friendship produces agreement, what is this agreement *about*? And is this agreement the same within and between individuals as well as for the city as a whole?

Alcibiades responds, "I suppose I mean the friendship and agreement you find when a father and mother love their son, and between brother and brother, and husband and wife" (126d). The model is the shared ideas and mutual affection that bind families together.

Socrates focuses on the connection between agreement and friendship. He seeks to shatter it by focusing on specialized arts and crafts. Within the household, for instance, women specialize in spinning and weaving, and men specialize in soldiery. Each of these tasks has its own body of knowledge and skill. Yet men know nothing of spinning and weaving, and women know nothing of soldiery. There is a division of labor and expertise within the family and within society as a whole. We are not of "one mind" on such matters. We are experts in some and amateurs or ignoramuses in others.

From this Socrates makes the following argument:

Friendship is agreement.
There is no agreement between men and women about their tasks.

> Therefore, there is no friendship between men and women in the family. (127a)

The same argument can be applied to the whole of society:

> Friendship is agreement.
> There is no agreement between experts within the city about their differing fields of expertise.
> Therefore, there is no friendship between different experts in the city. (127a)

This raises a question about the causal relationship between friendship and agreement. At first Alcibiades implies that the political art produces friendship and unity. Then Socrates implies that friendship produces unity in the sense of agreement. Now, Socrates is assuming that friendship and agreement are the same. Thus a lack of agreement means a lack of friendship. Friendship and agreement are thus produced simultaneously by the political art.

Then Socrates asks if "states, therefore, are not well-ordered insofar as each person does his own business?" (127b). For if each person merely minds his own business, there is no agreement; thus, there is no friendship; thus, society is not well-ordered.

EXPERTISE VS. ONENESS OF MIND

There's a problem with Socrates' argument. Alcibiades is correct to think that the art of politics is *comprehensive*. It deals with the *whole* of the society. And society is a whole in virtue of things that are held in *common*: common ideas and mutual affection.

But by focusing on the division of labor within the family and society, Socrates is implicitly reducing the common and social to the private and economic. The division of labor is an economic concept. Specialized knowledge is the opposite of comprehensive knowledge. Specialized arts are the opposite of the architectonic art. Once Socrates has reduced the social to the private, common knowledge to specialized knowledge, it is no surprise that he can't make sense of social life.

Alcibiades should say that, yes, insofar as we are merely minding our own business, practicing our specialized crafts in the economic realm, there is no agreement, no friendship, and no justice. But there's more to life than economics, private interests, and specialized knowledge and techniques. Above work, there is leisure. Above private interests, there is the common good and the common life of society. Above expertise, there are forms of knowledge and practice that all can take part in. This is the realm where we find the affections and oneness of mind that bind societies together.

The concept of *homonoia* is derived from *"homo"* (same) and *"nous"* (mind). It is a specifically political concept, referring to the unity of a city or a culture based on being of one mind. Greeks were one people because of *homonoia*. Barbarians, however, were not of one mind with Greeks. The concept took on increasing importance under the reigns of Philip II and Alexander the Great, whose imperial ambitions required thought about the sources of social unity. The concept remained central to Greek and Latin political thinking throughout antiquity. There was even a temple to the goddess Homonoia in Ephesus. (The Roman equivalent of *homonoia* was *concordia*, which was also deified as a goddess.)

Ideal objects (*noeta*) are metaphysically different from material objects. If I give you a material object, I no longer possess it. If I give you an idea, I still possess it. Material objects must be divided to be shared among humans. The more people who share in my birthday cake, the thinner the slice each individual gets. Material objects are thus finite. Ideal objects, however, need not be divided to be shared by many individuals. My share of an ideal object is not, moreover, decreased by additional people sharing in it. I can't share my cake with all of humanity, but I can share the recipe. Moreover, when I share my cake, each individual material slice is different and unique. But when I share the recipe, it remains the same. It is the same ideal object, whether printed in ink, carved into stone, or committed to memory a million times over. As Heraclitus marveled, "the *logos* [another word for the intelligible structure of things] is common to all" (Fragment 2).

But even though ideas can in principle be shared with everyone, human finitude makes it impossible for us to learn everything, and human inequality makes it impossible for some ideas to be *understood* by everyone. This is why Socrates' focus on expert knowledge makes genuine *homonoia* impossible. The basic form of *homonoia* is language. The Greeks have one mind because they have one language. This is what separates them from the barbarians. As Rudyard Kipling wrote in his poem, "The Stranger":

> The Stranger within my gate,
> He may be true or kind,
> But he does not talk my talk—
> I cannot feel his mind.

Other important forms of *homonoia* are shared aesthetic, religious, and athletic spectacles: recitations of Homer, tragic and comic dramas, choruses, religious rites and festivals, civic rites and festivals, public buildings and monuments, and athletic competitions like the Olympic Games.

Why Justice Isn't "Minding Your Own Business"

Alcibiades does not reject the bias against *homonoia* built into Socrates' appeals to expert knowledge and division of labor. Instead he suggests that friendship arises among people precisely to the extent that they do their own work (127b). Thus such a society can be well-ordered. This is basically the classical liberal view that public benefits can arise as the unintended consequence of people pursuing their private interests. Nobody likes it when others step on their toes or interfere with their work. But this is hardly an adequate foundation for social solidarity. There is much more to friendship than gratitude for being left alone.

Socrates quickly forces Alcibiades to abandon this position simply by restating his argument. Friendship cannot arise without agreement, and there is no agreement when people merely mind their own business (127c).

Socrates then reintroduces the concept of justice into the discussion, asking "are they doing what is just or unjust, when each man does his own business?" (127c). Compare this to the discussion of justice at *Republic* 433a: "Justice is minding one's own business and not being a busybody." Alcibiades agrees that this is justice. Then Socrates asks if justice leads to friendship. Alcibiades agrees. But if justice is minding one's own business, which does not produce agreement, then how could it produce friendship, since agreement and friendship are the same?

Alcibiades is flummoxed: "By the gods, Socrates, I do not even know what I mean myself, and I fear that for some time I have lived unawares in a very disgraceful condition" (127d). Alcibiades has now attained knowledge of his own ignorance. Socrates comforts him by pointing out that he is learning this at a good time, because he is still young enough to correct it. If he were fifty, it would be harder to cultivate himself.

Alcibiades asks what he needs to do, and Socrates responds: "Answer my questions, Alcibiades. If you do that, then, god willing, if we are to trust in my divination, you and I will be in a better state" (127e). Socrates wishes to continue the dialogue and claims that if Alcibiades perseveres, they may both benefit. The god is Socrates' *daimonion*, i.e., his knowledge of human nature. Socrates' power of divination is his ability to predict human action based on that knowledge. Alcibiades promises to answer, and Socrates then leads him through the final part of the dialogue, on the question of self-knowledge.

Knowing the Self

The final part of the *Greater Alcibiades* deals with the self and self-knowledge. Most ancient commentators held this discussion to be the core of the dialogue.

From Self-Cultivation to Self-Knowledge

Socrates has finally gotten Alcibiades to admit that he needs to pursue self-cultivation. But what is self-cultivation? We must answer that question lest we mistakenly cultivate something other than ourselves. Socrates asks, "When a man cares for what belongs to his feet is that the same as caring for his feet?" (128a). Shoemakers take care of shoes, but we need another art to take care of our feet. Socrates adds that the same art that improves the feet improves the body as a whole. Let's just call it care of the body. There is a difference between caring for the body and caring for the body's things. They are different fields, so they require different arts.

What kind of art cultivates the human being as opposed to his things? To answer this question we must know the nature of man, hence the subtitle of the dialogue "On the Nature of Man." Socrates asks, "Is it easy or hard to follow the Delphic injunction 'Know thyself'?" (129a). Alcibiades is not sure. Socrates replies that, easy or not, with self-knowledge we can practice self-cultivation; without self-knowledge we cannot.

The Soul as the Self

Socrates then asks a strangely worded question: "In what way might the itself itself [*auto to auto*] be discovered? Maybe this is the way to find out what we ourselves are—maybe it's the only possible way" (129b). There is a great deal of debate about how to understand "*auto to auto*." Some favor "the itself itself."[1] Others favor "the self itself."[2] Some even question

---

[1] I prefer "the itself itself" interpretation, following the arguments of Denyer (*Alcibiades*, p. 211) and Christopher Gill, "Self-Knowledge in Plato's *Alcibiades*," *Reading Ancient Texts*, vol. 1., *Presocratics and Plato*,

whether this is really Plato's text. For instance, W.R.M. Lamb amends the Greek as "*auto tauto*" and translates it as "the same-in-itself,"[3] whereas François Renaud and Harold Tarrant render "*auto tauto*" as "the self itself."[4]

Generally when Plato speaks of "*auto to* x" or "the *x* itself," he is referring to his Forms or Ideas in abstraction from the things of which they are Forms. Thus when Socrates wishes to know what "piety itself" is, he is not talking about particular pious deeds, but about the essential traits that all pious deeds have in common. Accordingly, if Socrates refers to "the itself itself" or "the same-in-itself" he is referring to the Form of Forms, the Idea of Ideas, Form as such. If Plato is referring to "the self itself," he is referring to the Form of the self, selfhood, or the self as such.

If Socrates is indeed talking about the Form of Form or the Form of the self, how exactly would such a Form help us "find out what we ourselves are"? First of all, a Form is not simply the answer to the question "Who is Alcibiades?" or "Who is Socrates?" There are not Forms of individuals. The Form of the self would be the same for Alcibiades and Socrates. So simply by knowing the Form of the self, Alcibiades would not know himself from Adam.

If Forms are not the objects of self-knowledge, perhaps they are a *tool* of self-knowledge. Perhaps the Form of the self could help Alcibiades distinguish between his real self and things he mistakes for himself.

Interestingly, the Neoplatonists did not think that "*auto to auto*" refers to the Forms. Instead, Olympiodorus accepts the earlier interpretations of Proclus and Damascius who hold that it is the soul.[5] For Proclus, "*auto to auto*" is the "rational soul"

---

ed. Suzanne Stern-Gillet and Kevin Corrigan (Leiden: E.J. Brill, 2007).

[2] See David M. Johnson's translation in *Socrates and Alcibiades*, p. 45; Carnes Lord's translation in *The Roots of Political Philosophy*, p. 211; and D.S. Hutchinson's translation in Plato, *Complete Works*, p. 587.

[3] Loeb Classical Library, vol. XII, pp. 194–95.

[4] Renaud and Tarrant, *The Platonic* Alcibiades I, p. 58.

[5] Olympiodorus, *On Plato First Alcibiades, 10–28*, trans. Michael Griffin (London: Duckworth, 2016), 202, p. 127.

as opposed to the embodied soul.[6] For Damascius, the "self" is the "civic soul," i.e., the embodied soul we meet in society, which uses the body as an instrument. He calls "the self itself" the "purificatory and contemplative soul" which no longer uses the body as an instrument. Thus for the Neoplatonists, the self itself is the soul (*psyche*) considered in separation from the body (*soma*). But the Neoplatonists recognize that in the *Greater Alcibiades*, Socrates proposes an easier path to self-knowledge than knowing the soul in abstraction from the body, which is based on knowing what each individual self is, i.e., the embodied "civic" human being.

Whether we translate *"auto to auto"* as "the itself itself" or "the self itself" — whether we think it refers to the Forms or souls — there is no question that we are getting into some deep metaphysical waters here. Philosophers and philosophy professors have been scratching their heads at Socrates' meaning for more than two thousand years.

Imagine then the effect on the nineteen-year-old Alcibiades, who has been pretty much convinced that all his dreams hinge on self-knowledge, then hears that somehow knowing whatever *"auto to auto"* means might be the *only* way to achieve it. His heart must have sunk even more than ours did when we first encountered that phrase.

Of course, if knowing *"auto to auto" might* be the only way to know the self, then it also *might not*. Imagine Alcibiades' relief, then, when Socrates reveals that maybe we have an easier route to self-knowledge, which bypasses *"auto to auto"* entirely. Perhaps we can approach self-knowledge through (*dia*-) words (*logoi*). In short, perhaps we can attain self-knowledge by means of dialogue (*dialogos*).

This is very much like what scholars call Socrates' "flight to the *logoi*" and "second sailing" in the *Phaedo*. The first sailing, namely knowledge of ultimate causes — in the case of the *Phaedo*, knowledge of the immortality of the soul — might be difficult or impossible. But fortunately, there is a second best route:

---

[6] Olympiodorus, *On Plato First Alcibiades*, 10–28, 204–205, pp. 128–29.

starting with common sense and the world we perceive around us, then working our way forward through dialogue. The results might be merely probable, but they might be good enough. In any case, they are the best we can do.[7] This also parallels the distinction between the "correct account" (*orthos logos*) and the "likely account" (*eikos logos*) in the *Timaeus*.[8]

Socrates draws attention to the fact that he and Alcibiades are having a conversation with each other. The means they are using is language. From this he derives the general truth that "The user and the thing he uses are different" (129c). We use our bodies to do things. Thus "Man is different from his own body" (129e). If man is different from his body, man is "the user of the body" (129e). The user of the body is the soul. Therefore, man is the soul.

Socrates offers a second argument. We can be body, soul, or the two together. We are not the body, as already established. We are not the two together, for the body plus the soul does not rule the body. Therefore, man is the soul. But we must not forget that this conclusion has been drawn by two embodied souls speaking to each other.

Alcibiades is convinced, but Socrates is more cautious:

> SOCRATES: If it is tolerably though not exactly proved we are content. Exact knowledge will be ours later, when we have discovered the thing that we passed over just now because it would involve much consideration.
> ALCIBIADES: What's that?
> SOCRATES: What we mentioned just now, that we should first consider what *auto to auto* is. Now instead of it we were investigating what each individual is [*auto hekaston*]. Perhaps that will suffice, for surely nothing has more authority over us than the soul. (130c–d)

It is important to note that the soul here must be the *individual* soul of Alcibiades. Knowledge of the soul as conceived by

---

[7] Plato, *Phaedo*, 85c–d, 99d–e.
[8] Plato, *Timaeus*, 29b2–c3.

the Neoplatonists—a soul as denuded of individuality as the Forms—would be entirely useless to Alcibiades, who needs to understand his own particular self if he is to live his own particular life well.[9]

Thus self-knowledge means knowledge of the individual soul, which is the true self. Knowledge of our individual bodies is knowledge of something we own, something we use, but not of ourselves.

Trainers and physicians as such know the body but not the soul. Farmers and craftsman as such don't know the body so much as the things owned by the body. There is thus a threefold distinction here between the soul, what belongs immediately and directly to the soul (the body), and the things that belong to the body (and thus indirectly to the soul).

There is, however, a sense in which the Forms still play a role in this dialogue between Socrates and Alcibiades. As I have argued elsewhere, Platonic dialectic presupposes that we somehow *already* know what we are investigating.[10] This is particularly plausible when we are investigating ourselves. But

---

[9] In an influential paper, Julia Annas argues that self-knowledge in the *Greater Alcibiades* and other "early" Platonic dialogues refers to knowledge of social roles and duties, not the psychology of an individual. See Julia Annas, "Self-Knowledge in the Early Plato," *Platonic Investigations*, ed. Dominic J. O'Meara (Washington, D.C.: The Catholic University of America Press, 1985).

This sort of "impersonal" self-knowledge is entirely useless to Alcibiades and ignores the whole context of the dialogue, which begins because Socrates has discerned a change in Alcibiades, namely his complacency has been replaced by an immense longing.

Sara Ahbel-Rappe's *Socratic Ignorance and Platonic Knowledge in the Dialogues of Plato* (Albany: SUNY Press, 2018) offers a fundamentally Neoplatonic and impersonalist reading of self-knowledge in the *Greater Alcibiades*.

For a corrective to impersonalist readings of self-knowledge, even in the Neoplatonists, I highly recommend Kevin Corrigan's *Love, Friendship, and the Good: Plato, Aristotle, and the Later Tradition* (Eugene, Oregon: Cascade Books, 2018).

[10] Greg Johnson, "Notes on Philosophical Dialectic," *From Plato to Postmodernism*.

this knowledge is implicit and inarticulate, not explicit and articulate. This is why philosophical dialectic is experienced as a process of *recollection*, which in the *Meno* Socrates explains with the myth of the soul beholding the Forms before embodiment, forgetting them due to embodiment, then recollecting them through philosophical dialectic.[11]

Socrates and Alcibiades can pursue knowledge of their individual selves because, in some sense, they already know the what it is to be a self, including selfhood in general or the Form of the self. Even though they are not reflecting on and articulating this knowledge, it is still *operative* in their discussion, thus making it possible for Socrates and Alcibiades to distinguish between the self and not-self. The Forms thus function as a *means* for understanding concrete individuality. They are not the *object* of the quest for self-knowledge. We look *through* them, not *at* them, to know ourselves.

SELF-KNOWLEDGE & MODERATION

Socrates' next move is to introduce the premise that self-knowledge is the same thing as the virtue known as moderation (*sophrosyne*) (131b). The Delphic injunction "Know thyself" was accompanied with another injunction "Everything in moderation." Hence the equation of self-knowledge and moderation was common among the ancient Greeks up to the time of Plato.

But what is the connection between self-knowledge and moderation? If one knows oneself, one must necessarily also know one's *limits*. Knowing one's limits allows one to impose measure on one's desires, which left to their own can run to infinity. Infinite desire is one of the traits of tyrants, as we see in the *Greater Alcibiades* and the *Gorgias*.[12] Thus self-knowledge — understood as knowledge of one's limits — allows one to moderate one's desires, to rule over them rather than be ruled by them.

Because self-knowledge and moderation are related, Socrates

---

[11] Plato, *Meno*, 81a–d.
[12] Plato, *Gorgias*, 491e–492c, 493a–494a. Cf. *Republic*, 571d–576b, 588b–589b.

points out that he who tends the body and the body's things is "not moderate in respect of his art" (131b). Thus such arts are held to be "base" (*banausoi*) and beneath good men.

This sounds terribly snobbish, but Socrates has a point here. Why doesn't art (*techne*) make one moderate? Because *techne* is morally neutral. *Techne* gives you the power to change the world, but it can't tell you "Enough is enough." The arts that service the whole realm of desire can be infected with the boundlessness of desire itself. And just as unbounded desire is slavish, the arts that cater to such desires are slavish as well. To make the right use of art, we need a higher order knowledge that can direct art to good rather than bad ends. This is wisdom, which consists of the whole suite of virtues, including moderation.

TRUE LOVE

At this point, Socrates turns to the nature of love. Those who are focused on caring for their bodies and property are not practicing self-cultivation. Those who love bodies do not love the true person, namely the soul (131c). The lover of the body will quit when the body loses its beauty. The lover of the soul will stick around. Thus Socrates has been Alcibiades' only true lover. The rest merely loved his body, which now, at the ripe age of almost twenty, is losing its boyish charm.

But Socrates does not love Alcibiades unconditionally, for his soul must be worthy of love, which is why he must cultivate himself, i.e., adorn his soul with virtue. Socrates fears that Alcibiades' soul might become "blighted and deformed" by "becoming a lover of the people [*demos*]" (132a).

The Athenian people look handsome on the outside, unlike Socrates. But if you could see their souls stripped of their bodies, they would be an ugly sight, unlike the beautiful soul of Socrates. (The stripping of the body to view the soul is also a theme in the *Gorgias*.[13])

To maintain Socrates's love, Alcibiades must try to learn what he must know before entering politics. This knowledge

---

[13] Plato, *Gorgias*, 524a–b.

will protect him from the corrupting charms of the city, which would seduce him to demagoguery and tyranny.

Alcibiades agrees and asks Socrates to explain how they can cultivate themselves. Socrates says they have made a good start, for by distinguishing the soul from the body and its things they are unlikely to cultivate something other than their true selves. We can allow others to tend our bodies and our possessions while we tend to ourselves. But now they must deal with the nature of the soul.

THE MIRROR OF THE SOUL

THE MIRROR OF THE BODY

How does one apply the Delphic injunction "Know thyself" to the soul? To illustrate this, Socrates uses a physical analogy. Imagine if the eye were told to "See itself." How would it do so? It must look into a mirror. Isn't there something mirror-like in the eye? That would be the pupil. The pupil is also the best part of the eye, for that is where the power of sight dwells. Thus an eye, looking into the pupil of another eye, will see itself. But, Socrates says, if an eye looks anywhere else, in man or nature, it will not see itself.

But is that true? Why does the eye need another eye and not simply a mirror? Wouldn't a mirror be much better for viewing the eye, and the whole body for that matter, than squinting at one's tiny image in the eye of another?

There are two reasons why Socrates insists on this idea.

First, Socrates wishes to uphold the principle that "like knows like," i.e., it takes one to know one, which he uses as his argument unfolds.

However, the best kind of mirror is not like the object it reflects. The best mirror has no determinate look or appearance of its own. If it did, this would interfere with reflecting other things. Thus the best mirror is entirely blank and indeterminate, so that it can accurately capture and reflect the appearances of other things. Aristotle makes this point about intellect (*nous*) in *De Anima*: intellect can know all things because it itself is indeterminate.[1]

Second, it is in keeping with the erotic nature of the dialogue. We are to imagine two lovers gazing intently into one another's eyes. The Greek for pupil is *"kore."* The Latin is *"pupilla."* Both terms refer to little dolls, such as small votive statues of a god or goddess that were left as offerings at shrines. Thus if Alcibiades were to lean in close to Socrates' eyes, he

---

[1] Aristotle, *De Anima*, book III, ch. 4.

would see himself as Socrates sees him: namely as a godlike object of adoration.

This reading accords with Plato's *Symposium*. In Olympiodorus's exposition of this passage he uses the phrase "*theia agalmata*" (divine images).[2] This alludes to Alcibiades' description of Socrates in the *Symposium* as a Silenus figure, which, when opened up, is found to contain an image of a god.[3] And indeed, if Alcibiades were looking at Socrates, he would see a Silenus-like figure: bald, paunchy, snub-nosed, big-lipped. But, if he were to lean in close and peer into Socrates' somewhat protruding eyes, he would see a godlike little statue, namely a statue of himself. Socrates offered this image as a gesture of adoration. But for Alcibiades to affirm it reeks of narcissism.

Of course, at the same time Alcibiades sees himself in Socrates' eyes, Socrates sees himself in Alcibiades' eyes. Thus when Socrates looks at Alcibiades, he sees a beautiful young man. But when he leans in, he sees an ugly old Silenus. Of course if we liken the image to the soul—and knowing the soul is the whole point of the discussion—there's a lesson here: just as an ugly body can conceal a beautiful soul, a beautiful body can conceal an ugly soul.

The Greeks believed that objects cause vision by emitting images of themselves which enter our eyes. So Alcibiades' likeness is not just on the surfaces of Socrates' pupils. It is *inside* them, inside *him*. This is why Socrates can call up Alcibiades' image in his memory.

But this works both ways. As Alcibiades leans in and admires his own image in the pool of Socrates' eyes, Socrates' image is entering Alcibiades as well. Soon, Alcibiades will be able to call up Socrates' image in his absence. And, as, Crito's son Critobulus tells Socrates in Xenophon's *Symposium*, ". . . the sight of [Cleinias, his beloved] in person has the power to delight . . . whereas the sight of the image [*eidolon*] does not give pleasure, but implants a craving for him."[4]

---

[2] Olympiodorus, *On Plato First Alcibiades, 10–28*, 217, p. 139.

[3] Plato, *Symposium*, 115b.

[4] Xenophon, *Symposium*, trans. O.J. Todd, Xenophon, vol. IV, Loeb

This is Socrates' art of seduction (*erotike techne*[5]) at work. By getting Alcibiades to look into Socrates' eyes, Socrates is slipping his image into Alcibiades' soul. This will implant a longing for Socrates. As we will see, this longing is already taking effect by the end of the dialogue. In Xenophon's *Symposium*, Socrates likens the effect of a kiss to a spider's bite that produces madness (*mania*).[6] In Plato's *Symposium*, Alcibiades compares the effect of Socrates' seduction to being bitten by a snake, which produces pain and *mania*:

> ... What happens to a man who is bitten by a snake happened to me as well. They say that one who has experienced this is unwilling to speak of it except to those who have themselves been bitten, since they alone will understand if he brought himself to do and say anything because of the pain. I was bitten by a more painful thing and in a more painful spot than anyone could be bitten, for I was struck and bitten in the heart, or the soul, or whatever one should call it, by philosophical words, which take fiercer hold of one than a serpent, whenever they get a hold on a soul that is young and not without natural gifts, and make one do or say anything. . . . You've all shared in the madness and frenzy of philosophy, so you will all hear what I've got to say. [7]

If Socrates' image enters Alcibiades' soul through his eyes, how then do Socrates' philosophical words enter his soul? Through (*dia*) words (*logoi*): i.e., dialogue.

Classical Library (Cambridge: Harvard University Press, 1923), iv, 22, pp. 574–75. I have been inspired by a somewhat different treatment of these texts by Victoria Wohl, "The Eye of the Beloved: *Opsis* and *Eros* in Socratic Pedagogy," *Alcibiades and the Socratic Lover-Educator*, ed. Marguerite Johnson and Harold Tarrant (London: Bloomsbury, 2012).

[5] Plato, *Phaedrus*, 257a7–8.

[6] Xenophon, *Symposium*, iv, 28.

[7] Plato, *Symposium*, 117e–218b, translated by David M. Johnson, *Socrates and Alcibiades*, p. 84.

THE MIRROR OF THE SOUL

If the self is the soul, and "like knows like," then to know oneself, one must find another soul as a mirror. This is what Socrates and Alcibiades are doing through their dialogue: they are using words to "gaze" into one another's souls, hoping to catch a "glimpse" of their own. And just as the eye sees itself best in the best part of another eye, the soul sees itself best in the best part of another soul:

> SOCRATES: So, my dear Alcibiades, if a soul is to know itself, it must look into a soul, and particularly into that region of it in which the excellence of the soul, wisdom [*sophia*], resides, and to anything that this [wisdom] is similar to?
> ALCIBIADES: So it seems to me, Socrates.

Socrates then offers examples of what *sophia* is similar to:

> SOCRATES: Can we say that anything in the soul is more divine [*theoteiron*] than that which is concerned with knowing [*eidenai*, which is related to *eidos*, the word for Form] and prudence [*phronein*, practical wisdom]?
> ALCIBIADES: We cannot.
> SOCRATES: So it is to the god that this aspect of soul is similar, and one looking to this [the best part of the soul], and knowing all that is divine [*pan to theion gnous*], both god and prudence [*phronesin*], would in this way also most know himself.
> ALCIBIADES: It appears so. (133b–c)

This passage has also vexed interpreters for centuries. François Renaud and Harold Tarrant group the interpretations into *anthropocentric* and *theocentric* readings.[8] The dispute is

---

[8] Renaud and Tarrant, *The Platonic* Alcibiades I, pp. 64–71. Renaud and Tarrant helpfully rehearse the evidence for an anthropocentric reading, but ultimately they try to maintain that both readings are correct in different ways ("Alcibiades has an anthropological interpreta-

about the meaning of "the god" to which the highest aspect of the soul is similar. My reading is entirely anthropocentric, because I hold that here "the god" refers to the *daimonion*, which is Socrates' personification of his knowledge of human nature and the prudence that springs from this knowledge. Let's review the evidence.

THE *DAIMONION* AS "THE GOD"

At the very beginning of the dialogue, Socrates explicitly states that his "*daimonion*" held him back from conversing with Alcibiades until that point (103a).

We should note that immediately after introducing the *daimonion*, Socrates tells Alcibiades "you will be told of its power [*dunamis*] later as well." Whatever Socrates is promising here, it is more than just *mentioning* the *daimonion* again. He is going to say something about what it can do. We should bear this in mind, because the best candidate for this explanation of the *daimonion*'s power is the passage we are examining at 133b–c.

A little later, at 105a, Socrates states that if "some god" asked Alcibiades if he would be satisfied with his current life and lot, it makes sense to identify the god with the *daimonion*, for this god, like the *daimonion*, is merely a mask for Socrates' own understanding of Alcibiades' character.

A few lines later, at 105a, Socrates says that if "this same god" told Alcibiades that he could only rule in Europe, not Asia, Alcibiades would reject it.

Then, a bit later, in the same speech, Socrates says, "It will be impossible for you to accomplish all the things you have in mind without me, so great is the power that I think I have regarding

---

tion of this conversation; Socrates, if he is serious, would seem to adhere to a theological one" [p. 78]) because they do not see that throughout the dialogue "the god" refers to the *daimonion*, and the *daimonion* is the personification of Socrates' knowledge of human nature.

In "Self-Knowledge in Plato's *Alcibiades*," Christopher Gill also tries to maintain both readings by claiming that there is a triangular relationship between Socrates and Alcibiades as well as the god. On my reading, it is a two-term relationship because there is ultimately no difference between the god (*daimonion*) and Socrates' wisdom.

your affairs and you. And this is why, I think, the god I was waiting to allow me to speak with you did not allow me to speak for so long" (105d). Here it is clear that "the god" and the *daimonion* are one and the same.

Then, near the end of the same speech, Socrates says that only he can help Alcibiades achieve his ambitions, "with the help of the god" (105e). There is no reason to think that Socrates is now referring to another god, and if the *daimonion* represents insight into human nature, it would be a powerful tool for an aspiring tyrant.

Socrates then concludes the speech by saying, "In your younger days, to be sure, before you had built such high hopes, the god, as I believe, prevented me from talking with you . . . Now he has permitted it" (105e). Again, what Socrates refers to as "the god" here is what he called the *daimonion* at 103a.

At 124c, Socrates claims that his "guardian" is "better and wiser [*belistos . . . kai sophoteros*]" than Alcibiades' guardian, Pericles. When asked who this guardian is, Socrates replies, "The god, Alcibiades, who until this day would not let me converse with you." Again, this is clearly the *daimonion*.

At 127e, Socrates says, "Answer the questions, Alcibiades, and if you do this, the god willing—if one should at all trust in my divination [*manteia*]—both you and I will be better off." Here the god is identified with Socrates' ability to divine future human actions, which is the function of the *daimonion*.

OTHER REFERENCES & OATHS TO GODS

Does Socrates make reference to any other gods in the *Greater Alcibiades* that would be candidates for "the god" in question? Not really. Socrates alludes to but does not name Apollo five times in connection with his oracle at Delphi (124a, 129c, 130e, 132c, 132d). Socrates also mentions the Muses to elicit the concept of music from Alcibiades (108b-d). Socrates asks Alcibiades if he plans to advise the city on divination at 107b. Finally, Socrates mentions Zeus three times at 120e-121a in connection with mythical genealogies.

Although Socrates speaks much more than Alcibiades, he swears only three oaths by any of the gods, as opposed to seven oaths by Alcibiades. Socrates swears two oaths by Zeus, referring to him by name at 129b and as Friendship at (109d). In oaths, Friendship is a name of Zeus. This is followed by the phrase "mine and yours" (*ton emon te kai son*). What does this modify? The most natural reading is that it refers to the mutual friendship of Socrates and Alcibiades. But when friendship is the object of an oath, it refers to the *god* of friendship. Thus "mine and yours" implies that Socrates and Alcibiades have *different* gods of friendship. In Alcibiades' case, it is presumably Zeus. But in Socrates' case, it may refer to the *daimonion*, which is clearly governing Socrates' initial friendly overtures toward Alcibiades. Socrates also swears an oath "by the gods" at 132c.

By contrast, Alcibiades swears oaths "by Zeus" six times (107a, 110c, 112a, 119a, 130c, 133d) and an oath "by the gods" once at 116e.

None of these mentions of deities are candidates for "the god" at 133c, where Socrates says that the best part of the soul is akin to "the god."

THE POWER OF THE *DAIMONION*

Given the evidence reviewed above, there is no reason to think that Socrates is speaking of anything other than the *daimonion* at 133c. Recall that the best part of the soul is where *sophia* (theoretical wisdom) resides. Socrates also counsels us to look to things akin to *sophia*, namely knowing and thinking, which he says are "divine."

Given all this, does it make sense to say that the highest part of the soul (wisdom, knowing, thinking) is akin to the *daimonion*? Yes, for the *daimonion* personifies Socrates' knowledge of human nature (which would include the faculties of wisdom, knowing, and thinking), as well as the practical wisdom in human affairs that follows from being a good judge of character. Given that the goal here is self-knowledge, an understanding of human nature would be extremely useful in this quest.

Socrates continues: "one looking to this [the best part of the soul], and knowing all that is divine [*pan to theion gnous*], both god and prudence [*phronesin*], would in this way also most know himself" (133c).

If the god here is the *daimonion*, then Socrates equates "all that is divine" (*pan to theion*) with the *daimonion* and prudence. This implies that nothing else is divine, including all the Greek gods, which is subtle confirmation of the charge that Socrates did not believe in the gods of Athens.

I believe that "theocentric" readings of "the god" here are based simply on the failure to note that throughout the dialogue, references to "the god" point back to the *daimonion*. Furthermore, if one does not understand the *daimonion* as equivalent to knowledge of the soul or human nature, then it is hard to see how it belongs in the company of *sophia*, knowing, and *phronesis*.

In the final chapter, I will show how other references to the god are consistent with this reading.

A Christianizing Interpolation (133c)

How far back does the "theocentric" interpretation of the *Greater Alcibiades* go? At least to the third century CE, for at this point we find an interpolation into Plato's text that seems to be motivated by a specifically Christian theocentric reading of 133c.

Eusebius of Caesarea (c. 260/265–339 CE) was a Christian theologian, historian, and bishop. Joannes Stobaeus (fl. 5th-century CE) compiled an anthology of extracts from Greek authors. In both writers there is a quote from the *Greater Alcibiades* that includes an interpolation that is not present in any of the six complete manuscripts of the dialogue. This passage reads as follows:

> SOCRATES: Then just as mirrors are clearer than the reflection in the eye as well as purer and brighter, so the god happens to be purer and brighter than what is best in our soul?
>
> ALCIBIADES: It would seem so at least, Socrates.
>
> SOCRATES: In looking to the god, therefore, we shall treat him as the finest mirror, and in human things we shall look to the virtue of the soul. In this way, above all, we may see and know ourselves.
>
> ALCIBIADES: Yes. (133c)

Just as a big mirror is better for seeing an eye than the pupil of another eye, so a bigger soul is a better mirror for the human soul. That bigger soul is "God," in the big-"g" Christian sense.

Now, the mere fact that this passage is not found in the complete manuscripts of the *Greater Alcibiades*, but only in quotations from it, is no reason to dismiss it as inauthentic. Elsewhere in the *Greater Alcibiades* itself, there are two other passages that are also present only in quotes from the dialogue but not the main manuscripts (115e, 128a).

There are two basic reasons to reject such passages as inauthentic: if either (1) the language or (2) the ideas are inconsistent with the rest of Plato. In the cases of the passages at 115e and 128a, neither of these problems pertain. If the passages are inauthentic, it is likely that they are simply glosses on what has already been said in the dialogue.

In the case of 133c, however, there are both linguistic and doctrinal problems. Nicholas Denyer points out five linguistic problems in his commentary on the Greek text.[9] But for me, the decisive problem with 133c is that it is inconsistent with the rest of the dialogue.

First of all, it rejects Socrates' premise that a pupil is the best mirror for the eye. This may be a highly questionable premise, but it is necessary for Socrates' argument that the best mirror for a soul is another soul.

Second, 133c is also inconsistent with the usage of "god" throughout the dialogue to refer to the *daimonion*.

Third, a deeper problem with the idea of God with a big-"g" as the mirror of the soul is that such a God is metaphysically rather remote from human beings, much like whatever "*auto to auto*" means. Socrates would allow that the absolute best way to know the self would be to know its ultimate causes: "*auto to auto*" or God. But such knowledge is difficult, perhaps impossible, to attain.

Fortunately, it is also unnecessary, because there is a second-best route. We can know our souls in dialogue with other souls. Moreover, it is precisely through the back and forth of

---

[9] Denyer, *Alcibiades*, pp. 232-33.

philosophical dialogue that we can articulate our innate knowledge of Ideas like justice and moderation. And by reading these dialogues actively and critically, we too can know ourselves and awaken the virtues within us.

Why would a later writer insert this passage into Plato? The author could very well have believed that his ideas were implicit in Plato, or at least consistent with him. It could even have been a marginal gloss on a manuscript that a later copyist somehow worked into the body of the text. But it is more likely simply a bit of pious fraud, an attempt to graft a specifically Christian idea to the trunk of Plato's dialogue. John Dillon has documented other such emendations to Plato's texts.[10]

---

[10] John Dillon, "Tampering with the *Timaeus*: Ideological Emendations in Plato, with Special Reference to the *Timaeus*," *The American Journal of Philology*, vol. 110 (1989), pp. 50–72.

VIRTUE VS. TYRANNY

Having established that the true self is the soul and defended philosophical dialogue as the best path to self-knowledge, Socrates wraps up his argument.

STATESMANSHIP & MODERATION
First, Socrates returns to the premise that self-knowledge is the same as moderation (*sophrosyne*). Without *sophrosyne* we cannot know what belongs to us, "evil [*kaka*] or good [*agatha*]" (133c). Moderation, being a virtue, i.e., a form of knowledge of the good, is inherently able to distinguish between good and evil. Moreover, without *sophrosyne* we cannot know what belongs to the things we own. Nor can we know the things that belong to others. Alcibiades agrees.

But why is knowledge of ourselves necessary to know the things belonging to *other* people? Why can't we simply know those other people? The answer is that Socrates does not just envision *knowing* things but *making right use of them*, specifically moderate use of them. Because self-knowledge is the same as moderation, self-knowledge allows us to make moderate use of our property and the property of others as well. This is useful knowledge for someone who wishes to rule over others.

What is true of the property of other individuals is also true of the things of the city. To *merely know* the things of the city we should know the city itself. But to *make right use* of the things of the city, we must know ourselves. Specifically we need to know our limits.

Because the goal is right use of human things, Socrates says, "It seems to be the function of one man and one art [*techne*] to discern all three things: himself, his belongings, and the belongings of his belongings" (133d). Later Socrates notes that the man who lacks this knowledge/art "can never be a statesman [*politikos*]" (133e). Nor can he be a good manager of a household. Thus we must have *sophrosyne* to have the political art.

Men who lack *sophrosyne* make mistakes. Mistakes cause

unhappiness for oneself and others. "Thus it is impossible to be happy [*eudaimon*] if one is not moderate and good" (134a). Bad men are unhappy.

Socrates also adds that wealth does not lead to happiness, but moderation does. The pursuit of wealth is in principle endless. Moderation imposes limits. As Socrates argues in the *Euthydemus*, the more money you have, the greater the means you have of ruining yourself. If you are a fool, you are better off poor and powerless.[1] This is true of all worldly goods. Only wisdom can reliably secure happiness.

From this, Socrates draws a powerful conclusion: "Thus it is not walls or warships or arsenals that cities need, Alcibiades, if they are to be happy, nor numbers nor size without virtue [*arete*, also translated as 'excellence']" (134b).

Alcibiades wants to be a tyrant. Tyranny is characterized by unbounded desire, which leads to the worship of numbers and size. Tyranny is opposed to moderation, which imposes measure, order, and finitude. Thus the political art, which is based on self-knowledge and leads to moderation, is anti-tyrannical.

Socrates is not saying that cities don't need walls, warships, arsenals, or numbers and size. He is saying that none of these things, alone or together, is *sufficient* to produce happiness unless one also has the virtue necessary to *use them rightly*. In fact, great power used badly is more dangerous for a city than lesser power if well-managed.

Socrates continues: "And if you are to manage the city's affairs finely and correctly, you must impart virtue to the citizens" (134b). But one cannot give what one does not have. Therefore, "You must first acquire virtue yourself" (134c), as must anyone who takes care of things, public or private.

Two Concepts of Freedom

The appeal of tyranny is that one can do whatever one pleases. Thus Socrates attacks this concept of freedom: "It is not license or authority for doing what one pleases that you must secure for yourself or the state but justice and moderation"

---

[1] Plato, *Euthydemus*, 281b–c.

(134c-d). As is made clearer in the *Gorgias*, Socrates is here contrasting two concepts of freedom: freedom as "doing what one pleases" versus freedom as "doing what one wants."[2]

What is the difference? Socrates claims that all men strive for well-being or happiness (*eudaimonia*). That's *what we really want*. But if all men are striving for happiness, why are so many unhappy? Clearly, they are mistaken about what will make them happy. They pursue happiness in the wrong way. They do *what pleases them*—which does not make them happy—instead of doing *what they really want*, which would make them happy. So doing what pleases us is not necessarily the same thing as doing what we really want.

Consider, for instance, an alcoholic. It pleases him to drink, but it doesn't make him happy, because it leads to bad decisions, bad health, and broken relationships. Thus doing what pleases him is not doing what he really wants.

If *true* freedom is doing what we really want, then the freedom to do what *merely pleases us* is incompatible with true freedom. Society provides us many pleasing alternatives to happiness and calls this freedom. But for Socrates, it is not real freedom, because we are not doing what we really want. It is only apparent freedom, because it pursues false images of happiness. Indeed, it is often a form of slavery to desire: bad habits, addictions, vices. Thus, by restricting our freedom to do what we please—by imposing moderation on the infinity of desires—we can actually become freer to do what we really want.

HUMAN NATURE AS DIVINE MODEL

Socrates says, "If you and the state act justly and moderately, you will act so as to please the god" (134d). Again, one can read the "god" here as being Socrates' *daimonion*. To act with moderation and justice is, after all, consistent with human nature. As for the claim that acting this way is "pleasing" to the god, this is an appeal to a conventional idea of piety, namely the idea that the pious is what is pleasing to the gods. In Plato's *Euthyphro*, Socrates makes mincemeat of this idea of piety, so

---

[2] Plato, *Gorgias*, 466c–468e.

we know that he is using it only ironically or exoterically.[3] But this is in keeping with the concept of the *daimonion*, which is also an exoteric way of speaking about knowledge of human nature.

Socrates continues: "As we were saying in what went before, you [both you and the city] will act with your eyes turned on what is divine [*theion*] and bright [*lampron*] . . . And looking thereon you will behold and know both yourselves and your own good . . . and so you will act correctly [*orthos*] and well [*eu*]" (134d). Alcibiades agrees on all points.

Here Socrates is using the "divine" in the sense of the *daimonion* to refer to looking to human nature as a model. He uses "bright" because he is speaking of the Idea of human nature at the very least and perhaps the entire realm of intelligible Forms, and Forms are the light in which we see things as they are.

Socrates says that if Alcibiades and the city act in this way, he is "prepared to guarantee you will be happy" (134d). This is a very strong knowledge claim from Socrates. Note that it is also a knowledge claim about the future, which the Greeks would naturally liken to divination as practiced by augurs or oracles. But Socratic divination is based on a knowledge of human nature, which Socrates personifies as his personal oracle, the *daimonion*.

Socrates continues: "But if you act unjustly [*adikos*] with your eyes on the godless [*atheon*] and dark [*skoteinon*], it is likely that your acts will resemble those through ignorance of yourselves" (134e). If the divine and bright are the truth about human nature, then the godless and the dark are falsehoods, half-truths, and illusions about human nature. If you turn away from human nature, you will not know yourself, therefore you will not act virtuously and are unlikely to attain well-being. Again, Socrates is speaking of both Alcibiades and the city.

Some readers claim that the use of "bright" (*lampron*) and "dark" (*skoteinon*) here are a reference back to the "pure and bright" mirror of God in the Christianizing interpolation at

---

[3] See my lecture on the *Euthyphro* in *The Trial of Socrates*.

133c and treat it accordingly. For instance, Antonio Carlini, who rejects 133c, excises the passage where bright and dark appear (134d1–e7) as a later interpolation as well,[4] even though it is present in all the manuscripts and attested to by the Neoplatonic commentators.[5] D.S. Hutchinson does the same in his translation.[6] Nicholas Denyer also declines to comment on the passage.[7] David M. Johnson, by contrast, uses the "bright" and "dark" passage to argue for the authenticity of 133c, in support of his strongly theocentric reading of references to "the god" throughout the dialogue.[8]

I, however, see no reason to accept the premise both camps share, namely that the two passages stand or fall together. If one deletes 133c and keeps 134d–e, the only objection one can raise is that this is the first occurrence of *"lampros"* in the text. But that argues for the excision of every word that occurs for the first time in any of Plato's dialogues. Must a word always refer back to something already mentioned in a dialogue to be retained? What then of the first word of every dialogue?

Plato's opposition between the divine and bright on the one hand and the godless and dark on the other makes sense in its own terms, and in the context of the dialogue, without the interpolation at 133c.

THE FINAL CRITIQUE OF TYRANNY

At this point, Socrates drives home his critique of tyranny:

> If a man is at liberty to do what he pleases but lacks mind [*nous*], what is the likely outcome for himself or the city? For instance if he is sick and at liberty to do what he pleases without a medical mind and with a tyrant's power that

---

[4] Antonio Carlini, "Studi sul testo della quarta tetralogia platonica," *Studi italiani de filologia classica*, vol. 34 (1963): 169–89, pp. 169–74.

[5] See Renaud and Tarrant, pp. 76–77. Cf. Olympiodorus, *On Plato First Alcibiades, 10–28*, 229, p. 148

[6] Plato, *Collected Works*, p. 594.

[7] Denyer, *Alcibiades*, p. 241.

[8] David M. Johnson, "God as the True Self: Plato's *Alcibiades I*," *Ancient Philosophy* 19 (1999): 1–19, p. 13.

prevents anyone from criticizing him, what will be the result? Isn't it likely his health will be ruined? (134e–135a).

Tyranny is a dangerous system because it concentrates all power in a single individual. To make rational decisions, one needs accurate information. But because people fear the tyrant's disapproval and seek his approval, they have every incentive to conceal bad news and tell him flattering lies. It is no way to run a society or one's individual life.[9] Alcibiades agrees, so Socrates concludes: "Then my good Alcibiades, if you are to be happy it is not tyrannical power that you need for yourself or the city but virtue" (135b).

Socrates argues that those who lack virtue, whether adults or children, are better off being governed by the virtuous than by themselves. The better is the nobler. The nobler is the more appropriate. "Thus it is appropriate for a bad man to be a slave, since it is better" (135b).

In what sense is Socrates talking about slavery? He is not talking about chattel slavery, the buying and selling of human beings. Slaves are simply people who cannot govern themselves. Just as children, the mentally retarded, the senile, and the crazy cannot make their own decisions and are better off being governed by others, so too are vicious people. Vice is appropriate to slaves. Virtue is appropriate to free men. Thus anyone who would be free must shun slavishness and acquire the virtues needed to govern himself.

THE CONCLUSION

Alcibiades agrees, so Socrates confronts him with the question of which condition *he* is in.

Alcibiades is mortified.[10] Socrates spares Alcibiades' feelings by not naming his slavish state, which is disgraceful for such a

---

[9] See my lecture, "Freedom of Speech," in *Toward a New Nationalism*, 2nd ed. (San Francisco: Counter-Currents, 2023).

[10] At *Symposium* 216b, Alcibiades claims that Socrates is the only man who made him feel ashamed of himself, which sometimes caused him to wish that Socrates were dead.

"fine [or noble, *kalon*] man" (135c). Instead, Socrates asks Alcibiades if he knows how to escape his condition. Alcibiades basically says that it is up to Socrates to save him. But Socrates says it will be by the will of god (the *daimonion*) which is really just Socrates' knowledge of human nature and the prudence that springs from it (135d).

Alcibiades says that he and Socrates should switch roles. Instead of Socrates pursuing Alcibiades, Alcibiades will pursue Socrates.[11] Socrates finds this a pleasing prospect: "Then my love for you, my well-born friend, will be just like a stork. After hatching a winged love [*eros*] in you, it will be cared for by it in return" (135e). The Greeks depicted Eros (Cupid) as a winged baby armed with a bow and the arrows of desire. Here, however, Socrates identifies Eros with a different sort of winged creature, the stork, specifically a baby stork, which the ancient Greeks believed sustained their elders. This passage is dramatic foreshadowing of Alcibiades' famous speech in the *Symposium*, in which he describes his unsuccessful attempts to seduce Socrates.[12]

Alcibiades vows to begin morally cultivating himself immediately.[13]

This is a very hopeful ending, but we all know what happened: Alcibiades became a monster, and Socrates' close association contributed to his trial and death. Thus Plato gives Socrates these final, prophetic words: "Yet I'm afraid—not because I distrust your nature, but because I know how powerful the

---

[11] In the *Symposium*, Alcibiades says of Socrates, "He deceives us by acting as if he is in love, but he becomes the one who is loved instead of the one who is in love" (222b), trans. David M. Johnson, *Socrates and Alcibiades*, p. 88.

[12] Plato, *Symposium*, 217a–219e.

[13] Alcibiades was a quick study. Xenophon recounts a "Socratic" dialogue in which Alcibiades refutes Pericles about law. Xenophon dates it to shortly before Alcibiades' twentieth birthday, i.e., shortly after the conversation of the *Greater Alcibiades*. However, Alcibiades does not demonstrate any moral cultivation. In fact, he is quite disrespectful, making it easy to see why the Athenians regarded Socrates as a corrupter of the youth. See *Memorabilia*, II.2.40–46.

city is—lest it overcome both me and you" (135e). This is Socrates' art of divination at work: predicting human action based on knowledge of human nature.

In the end, Athens destroyed both Socrates and Alcibiades. Socrates was accused of harming Athens by corrupting youths like Alcibiades. Plato's depiction of the relationship of Socrates and Alcibiades inverts those charges. Athens itself stoked Alcibiades' tyrannical ambitions, whereas Socrates tried to rein them in. Socrates tried to be a good influence on the young Alcibiades. But Alcibiades' true corrupter, the city of Athens, proved stronger in the end. Then, after the Athenians ruined Alcibiades and were ruined in return, they blamed Socrates for their own folly and punished him as a scapegoat.

* * *

It is easy to see why the ancients regarded the *Greater Alcibiades* as an ideal introduction to Plato.[14] It has a little bit of everything found in the more widely read dialogues.[15]

The dialogue touches on key elements of the life and character of Socrates. It features Alcibiades, Socrates' most infamous

---

[14] The most perverse argument for rejecting the authenticity of the *Greater Alcibiades* is offered by A.E. Taylor: "The work has the qualities of an excellent manual, and this is the strongest reason for denying its authenticity," for Taylor just doesn't think Plato would have created such a "text-book." But this is an arbitrary assumption. Moreover, the *Greater Alcibiades* is better characterized as a "synoptic" dialogue, which is not the same thing as a "text-book." See A.E. Taylor, *Plato: The Man and his Work*, 6th edition (London: Methuen, 1949), p. 522.

[15] Classicists have observed that linguistically, the *Greater Alcibiades* resembles Plato's later dialogues. However, in terms of style, the *Greater Alcibiades* resembles Plato's earlier, so-called Socratic dialogues. This has been offered as evidence that the dialogue is not genuine. (See Taylor, *Plato*, p. 522.) But there is no reason to assume that in his later years, Plato would not have composed a "Socratic" dialogue reflecting his more mature style and thinking, especially if he wanted to create a synoptic work. Perhaps the ancients regarded the *Greater Alcibiades* as an ideal introduction to Plato because Plato intended it to be just that.

and fateful friend. It features Socrates' *daimonion*. It speaks extensively of *eros*. It alludes to Socrates' trial and implicitly defends him against his accusers.

The dialogue also displays three central Socratic forms of discourse: the dialogical refutation of bad ideas, the dialogical midwifery of good ideas, and speechmaking, specifically mythologizing.

The *Greater Alcibiades* focuses on central ideas in Socratic-Platonic moral and political philosophy. Socrates defends the theses that all men are pursuing the good life and that moral wisdom is crucial for attaining the good life. He offers analyses of such important virtues as justice and moderation. He argues for the importance of self-knowledge and self-cultivation. He criticizes the idea of liberty as doing what one pleases as an impediment to true liberty, which is doing what one really wants, namely attaining the good life. Socrates also applies this argument to distinguish between tyranny and true statesmanship.

The *Greater Alcibiades* also touches upon metaphysical issues. Socrates argues that the true self is the soul. He also alludes to the Ideas. Finally, he introduces the distinction between approaching the Ideas directly and through the mediation of dialogue. Thus the *Greater Alcibiades* offers a defense of Platonic philosophical dialogue as a means to attain self-knowledge and knowledge of the Ideas.

Finally, the *Greater Alcibiades* is an excellent protreptic speech to turn us toward the philosophical life. Socrates convinces Alcibiades that if he wants to rule the world, there's nothing more important than pursuing wisdom. Even if you just wish to rule yourself, you are well-advised to follow the same path.

"WAR & BATTLE"

An ancient commentator on Aristotle tells a story about a farmer who got ahold of Plato's *Gorgias* and was so stunned that he gave up the life of farming, trudged to Athens, looked up Plato, and put his soul in Plato's care.[1]

Like the *Greater Alcibiades*, the *Gorgias* offers a wonderful argument for pursuing the philosophical life. But there are differences. The *Gorgias* is more than twice as long as the *Greater Alcibiades*. Instead of speaking to a naïve young man, Socrates faces three formidable opponents, including one of the greatest of all sophists, Gorgias of Leontini, for whom the dialogue is named. But in the end, philosophy wins. Sorry for giving away the ending, but did you imagine it would turn out any other way given that Plato is our author?

THE DRAMATIC DATE

Like the *Greater Alcibiades*, the *Gorgias* is a play. So let's analyze it first in terms of the dramatic date, characters, and setting.

The *Gorgias* is a very strange text for a number of reasons.

First of all, it's impossible to assign a single dramatic date to it. The death of Pericles in November of 429 BCE is mentioned as a recent event (503c), which would place the discussion about three years after the setting of the *Greater Alcibiades*. But Gorgias first set foot in Athens in 427 BCE. So, there's a two-year discrepancy there. Callicles is said to be in love with Demus, the son of Pyrilampes (481d). Aristophanes mentions that young Demus was the talk of the town in his play *Wasps*, which premiered in 422 BCE. Archelaus is mentioned as having recently become the king of Macedon (470d), but that happened in 413 BCE. Callicles quotes a play by Euripides, *Antiope* (485e), which premiered in either 411 or 408 BCE. And Socrates refers to his opposition to the condemnation of the Athenian

---

[1] Themistius (317–c. 388 CE), *Orations*, 295 c–d.

generals in 406 BCE as "last year" (473e), so that gives us the year 405 BCE. Now, the *Gorgias* is one of Plato's longer dialogues, but the conversation does not last 25 years.

Plato, of course, couldn't have done this through accident or lack of historical sense. It's got to mean something.

The first word of the *Gorgias* is "*polemos*" or "war." The dramatic dates span the years 429 to 405 BCE. It is noteworthy that 431 to 404 BCE were the years of the Peloponnesian War, the greatest event in the life of Socrates and all his contemporaries. The whole discussion is bounded by the Peloponnesian War, minus the very beginning and the very end. This is significant, for if he wanted to, Plato could have found a way to broaden the dates to include the whole of the war. Dramatically speaking, the dialogue is comprehended by the war. It does not comprehend it. Beyond that, the central themes of the dialogue touch on war and power politics. The participants talk about city walls, arsenals, and battleships.

Another possible reason Plato set the *Gorgias* over a period of 25 years is to oppose one of the main features of the sophists' teaching, which is the primacy of the ever-changing, ever-passing moment. Gorgias was the first theorist of rhetoric who emphasized timeliness, *kairos*, the moment. Benjamin Disraeli once claimed that timeliness can overcome even great learning, even very rigorous arguments. If you give the right argument in an untimely manner, it will fall deadborn from your lips, whereas a specious argument or a mere arbitrary exhortation, if delivered at the right time, hits home and changes people's minds.

One philosophical assumption of the sophists is the centrality of time and change, especially the variability of conventions and opinions, which are the media of persuasion. You can't have a dialogue outside of time, of course. The closest you can get is *untimeliness*. Thus perhaps the strange untimeliness of the *Gorgias* is at least a gesture toward a metaphysics that's deeply anti-sophistical.

THE CHARACTERS

There are five characters in the *Gorgias*.

Socrates is, of course, the main character. He's a citizen of Athens, where he is known as a good-for-nothing philosopher.

Chaerephon (c. 469–c. 399 BCE) has a small speaking part but an important role in the dialogue. He also speaks in Plato's *Charmides* and the *Halcyon*, a Socratic dialogue by an unknown author. He is mentioned in Plato's *Apology of Socrates*.

Chaerephon is also mentioned in Aristophanes' *Clouds*, *Wasps*, and *Birds*, and in Xenophon's *Apology* and *Memorabilia*. He was a citizen of Athens and one of Socrates' old friends. He was known for his manic energy and his high, squeaky voice, for which he was known as "the bat." In the *Clouds*, he is described as the cadaverous and unhealthy-looking sidekick of Socrates, whom Aristophanes depicts as a natural philosopher, an atheist, and a sophist.[2]

In Plato's dialogues, Chaerephon is a networker, a connector, a bridger of gaps. Olympiodorus the Neoplatonist describes Chaerephon as a recruiting agent through whom Socrates "hunts the youth," since Chaerephon is "young and familiar to them."[3] But this is a mistake, for they were friends from Socrates' youth, so Chaerephon could not have been that much younger.[4]

In the *Apology*, Socrates mentions that Chaerephon, his old friend and comrade in philosophy, was the one who asked the oracle of the god Apollo at Delphi, "Is there anybody wiser than Socrates?" To which the oracle said, "No."[5] Socrates said that this got him started as a philosopher.

Socrates also pointedly mentions that Chaerephon was part of the democratic faction that went into exile in 404–403 BCE during the reign of the Thirty Tyrants. Socrates was not a

---

[2] See my chapter on Aristophanes' *Clouds* in *The Trial of Socrates*.

[3] Olympiodorus, *Commentary on Plato's Gorgias*, p. 67. This description has an unsavory connotation, as if Chaerephon is a procurer or pimp. Olympiodorus seems to be under the impression that Chaerephon was much younger than Socrates, which makes no sense if they were friends from their youth.

[4] Debra Nails, *The People of Plato: A Prosopography of Plato and Other Socratics* (Indianapolis: Hackett, 2002), p. 86.

[5] Plato, *Apology*, 20e–21b.

member of their faction and did not share their exile. In fact, he was chosen by the Thirty to be part of their much-limited franchise. Socrates points this out because many of the exiled democrats were now sitting in judgment of him, in large part because of his association with the Thirty, especially Critias and Charmides. Thus Socrates thought it helpful to stress that he and the democrats had a mutual friend in Chaerephon.

Chaerephon also plays an intermediary role in Plato's *Charmides*, which is set in 431 BCE, immediately after Socrates' return from the Battle of Potidaea, at the beginning of the Peloponnesian War. When Socrates showed up at his old haunt, the wrestling school of Taureas, Chaerephon greeted him eagerly, asked him for news of the battle, then led him over and seated him next to none other than Critias the son of Callaeschrus, the very Critias who became one of the leaders of the Thirty Tyrants when the war ended in 404 BCE (153c). Chaerephon's relationships truly encompassed all extremes.

In the *Gorgias*, Chaerephon is a friend of both Socrates and Gorgias and thus an intermediary between them.

Gorgias (c. 485–380 BCE), a visitor from Leontini, lends his name to the dialogue. Leontini was a Greek city-state in Sicily, and Gorgias was one of its most prominent citizens. Gorgias was sent to Athens in 427 BCE as an ambassador to seek a crucial alliance against Syracuse. He lived either 105, 108, or 109 years. (Reports vary.) He was reputedly a student of Empedocles the Pythagorean, but there is nothing particularly Pythagorean about his philosophy, which was deeply anti-metaphysical and skeptical. Gorgias was one of the most impressive and influential sophists. Gorgias is very much a gentleman, which in part means being unwilling to do or say shameful things. During his time in Athens, Gorgias made a powerful impression on the locals with his rhetorical skills. He apparently returned many times and may even have settled there.

Polus (dates unknown) was a visitor from the city of Acragas in Sicily. He was an actual historical figure who authored a book on rhetoric. But little is known about him outside the *Gorgias*.[6]

---

[6] Plato also mentions Polus in the *Theages* (127e–128b) and *Phaedrus*

Based on the dialogue, we can say that he was a student of Gorgias who traveled with his teacher. Like Gorgias, Polus was a sophist. The name "Polus" means "colt," and there is something coltish about his depiction in the *Gorgias*. He's young and enthusiastic. He was less of a gentleman than Gorgias and thus more willing to say shameful things. He actually upbraids Gorgias for allowing Socrates to use his sense of shame to defeat him in argument.

Callicles (dates unknown) was a citizen of Athens and the host of Gorgias and Polus. He is depicted as the consummate Athenian aristocrat, which is reflected in his very name, which is compounded from the roots *kalon*, the beautiful, fine, or noble, and *kleos*, meaning "fame" or "glory." He is known only from the *Gorgias*, but there's no reason to think that he was not a historical figure. Callicles is, however, depicted as a somewhat decayed or degenerate aristocrat, for he is a student of sophistry, an advocate of cynical power politics, and prides himself on his ungentlemanly lack of shame and his willingness to speak frankly about ignoble things. But this decadence is also the mark of a philosophical temperament.

Callicles is even more shameless than Polus. So, there's a downward trajectory in the *Gorgias* that illustrates the negative influence of the sophists. The sophists believed that morality is conventional, and conventions are mutable. Increasingly, conventions were seen as hindrances to one's freedom and as tools to manipulate others. Thus with the passage of time and the weakening of conventions, the sophists become increasingly shameless and immoral.

Gorgias is the most gentlemanly but the least effectual against Socrates. Polus is less gentlemanly and more challenging to Socrates. Callicles is the least gentlemanly and the most difficult for Socrates to defeat. This is why fully three-fifths of the dialogue is devoted to the conversation with Callicles.

Socrates defeats Gorgias and Polus by appealing to their sense of right and wrong. Callicles has no sense of right and

---

(267b), and Aristotle mentions him in his *Rhetoric* (book II, chapter 23, 1400b20) and *Metaphysics* (book I, chapter 1, 981a4).

wrong. At least he thinks he doesn't. Thus he's a tougher opponent. But if there's even the tiniest bud or shoot of moral sensibility in Callicles' soul, Socrates will try to find and nurture it, because that's how he's going to defeat him. But to truly overcome Callicles, Socrates must place morality on natural rather than conventional foundations.

THE SETTING

The setting of the *Gorgias* is Athens, but where precisely is unclear. Socrates and Chaerephon arrive at a building in which Gorgias has given a speech and held a question-and-answer session before a crowd. Outside the building, they meet Callicles, who is the host of Gorgias and Polus, who emerge from the building, at which time the discussion takes place. It is not even clear whether the building is public or private, or if the space outside it is public (for instance, a street or square) or private (for instance, an enclosed courtyard or garden).

WHAT GORGIAS TAUGHT

Gorgias wrote two books, but it is hard to say what he taught, because only two complete speeches and a few fragments and testimonia survived the collapse of the ancient world.

The first book was a collection of his show speeches. Gorgias was renowned as a speechwriter for all occasions. But he was most famous for writing and performing some speeches simply as show pieces. Only two survive: his *Encomium of Helen*, which is a defense of Helen of Troy from her accusers, and the *Apology* or *Defense of Palamedes*, a character in Homer who was unjustly accused and put to death by Odysseus. (The *Defense of Palamedes* is interesting for readers of Plato, because some of the rhetoric is echoed by Plato's *Apology of Socrates* and *Crito*.)

The second book is called *On Non-Being*, which argues for three theses:

1. [Anything you might mention] is nothing.
2. If it were something, it would be unknowable.

3. If it were something and knowable, it could not be made evident to others.[7]

So, there is nothing, and if there were something we couldn't know it, and if we could know it, we couldn't communicate it to anybody else.

Is Gorgias trying to communicate that we can't communicate? Is he trying to communicate that he doesn't exist, that we don't exist, that these facts can't be known, and that he has a really good argument why none of us exist, which we can't know, and he can't communicate? That hardly seems likely. So what is a more plausible interpretation?

I think Gorgias is attacking the notion of objective reality *as some philosophers conceived it*, and if that fails he's attacking the notion that you can *know* objective reality, and if that fails he falls back and attacks the notion you could ever *communicate* objective truth.

What does Gorgias put in place of objective reality? Probably the changing things that we see around us. What does he put in place of objective truth? Probably opinions (*doxa*) about the changing things around us. Opinions are beliefs that change as well. Gorgias wants to argue that "Opinion is king," just as Herodotus argued that "Custom is king," which amounts to the same thing. Opinion is always shifting and changing. Opinion is relative to time and place. Opinions vary from person to person. A single person's opinions change from day to day and from hour to hour and from place to place.

What art is most suited to govern a world of shifting opinions? The art of rhetoric, because rhetoric is an art of manipulating opinions and appearances in order to get one's way. So, the rhetorician, the persuasive man, is king in the land of opinion. Beyond that, the best kind of rhetoric pays attention to timeliness. In a world of change, rhetoric must develop a sense for the right moment. Thus Gorgias' philosophy serves as a foundation

---

[7] Gorgias, *On Non-Being*, in *Early Greek Political Thought from Homer to the Sophists*, ed. and trans Michael Gagarin and Paul Woodruff (Cambridge: Cambridge University Press, 1995), p. 206.

for his rhetorical teachings.

Gorgias was primarily a teacher of rhetoric, which he defined as a value-neutral technique of persuasion. But there was more to it than that. Gorgias was fundamentally a good man and thus believed that he made his students better men. Gorgias, who was quite rich, dedicated a golden statue of himself in Olympia. The statue, alas, is lost, but the inscription on the base remains, probably the words of Gorgias himself: "No mortal has yet found a finer art [*techne*] than Gorgias to train the soul for the contests of virtue [*arete*, also translated as "excellence"]. This statue stands in the vale of Apollo, a tribute not to wealth but to the piety of his character."[8]

As we shall see, however, Socrates finds a contradiction between the idea that rhetoric is a value-free technique and the idea that studying rhetoric makes us better men.

What are Gorgias' innovations in rhetoric?

He was the first to thematize the whole issue of timeliness: the right word at the right time makes all the difference.

In one fragment, Gorgias claims, "One must defeat the seriousness of one's opponents with laughter and their laughter with seriousness."[9] This is a nice illustration of what an artful wordsmith Gorgias is. Beyond that, it illustrates how a supple pragmatism copes with ever-changing situations. Precisely opposed actions—seriousness or humorousness—can produce victory in different situations.

Gorgias also was the first to discuss the necessity of always accommodating one's speeches to one's audience, which is a basic principle of rhetoric that Plato would certainly accept.

Gorgias was one of the first rhetoricians to pay attention to ornamenting speeches. He used metaphors, poetic turns of phrase, dramatic antitheses, and measured repetitions. He carefully crafted clauses of the same length. He was also attentive to the rhythm of speech. Gorgias' speeches dazzled his plain-

---

[8] Gorgias, fragment 14, *Early Greek Political Thought from Homer to the Sophists*, p. 205.

[9] Gorgias, fragment 9, in *Early Greek Political Thought from Homer to the Sophists*, p. 204.

spoken contemporaries, like a peacock spreading his tail for the first time amid a muster of dowdy peahens. He was eagerly imitated. But to later generations, his style came to seem contrived: jangling, ornate, and sing-songy.

I am no classicist, so I can't evaluate Gorgias' style in Greek. Thus I will turn to the great Irish classicist E.R. Dodds:

> His art was in fact the art of verbal magic. . . . And the extant samples of his writing . . . fully support that view. They make the impression of a dazzling insincerity, an insincerity so innocently open as to be (except in the funeral oration) entirely void of offence. They are the work of an indefatigable stylist, a man who polished painfully every sentence that he wrote, caring passionately about its form, but . . . very much less about its relationship to the truth. For him fidelity to fact is a subsidiary matter. . . . The style seems to us, as it did to later antiquity, affected and boring: the well-drilled words execute *ad nauseam* the same repetitive maneuvers with the mechanical precision of a platoon on a barrack square. But Gorgias' contemporaries were bewitched by it, perhaps just because it was so easily imitable, a style that could be taught and learned. We can still see for ourselves that men as diverse in their gifts and interests as Thucydides, Antiphon, and Isocrates succumbed in varying degrees to the fascination.
>
> Plato did not.[10]

Gorgias was also a master of extemporaneous speaking. He would speak on any topic nominated by his audience. He also invented the question-and-answer session.

Finally, just as Socrates was a master of persuading people that philosophy was the most important thing in the world, Gorgias was a great salesman for rhetoric, lauding it for its almost supernatural powers.

Let's look at a few passages from the *Encomium of Helen*, in

---

[10] Dodds, pp. 8–9.

which Gorgias seeks to absolve Helen of Troy of all blame for going to Troy: "Either she did what she did because of the will of fortune and the plan of the gods and the decree of necessity, or she was seized by force, or persuaded by words, [or captured by love]."[11] No matter why Helen went to Troy, Gorgias argues that you can't blame her for it. She's a victim.

Let's look at his discussion of persuasion by words:

> If speech [*logos*] persuaded and deluded her mind, even against this it is not hard to defend her or free her from blame, as follows. Speech is a powerful master and achieves the most divine feats with the smallest and least evident body. [By the "smallest and least evident body," Gorgias is referring to the invisible material vibrations of speech.] [Speech] can stop fear, relieve pain, create joy, and increase pity....
>
> Poetry [*poiesis*] as a whole I deem and name speech with meter. To its listeners, poetry brings a fearful shuddering, a tearful pity, and a grieving desire, while through its words the soul feels its own feelings for good and bad fortune in the affairs and lives of others. [It produces sympathy, "suffering with."] ...
>
> Sacred incantations with words inject pleasure and reject pain, for in associating with the opinion of the mind, the power of incantation and chants persuades and alters it through bewitchment. The twin arts of witchcraft and magic have been discovered, and these are illusions of mind and delusions of judgment.
>
> How many men on how many subjects have been persuaded, and do persuade how many others, by shaping the false speech! For if all men and all subjects had memory of the past, understanding of the present, and foresight into the future, speech would not be the same in the same way. But as it is, to remember the past, to examine the present, or to prophesy the future is not easy, and so most men on

---

[11] Gorgias, *Encomium of Helen*, in *Early Greek Political Thought from Homer to the Sophists*, p. 191.

most subjects make opinion an advisor to their minds. But opinion is perilous and uncertain and brings those who use it to perilous and uncertain good fortune.[12]

This is an argument for the sovereignty of opinion in human life. If we knew better—if we had good memories, if we understood what was happening in front of us, if we had genuine insight into the future—we would have knowledge and not opinion. But because we don't know better—because we have faulty memories, because we have deranged or slow wits, because we usually understand things in hindsight, if we understand them at all, and because the future is all just a matter of conjecture—we live in a world ruled by opinion. That means we live in a world ruled by opinion-makers and opinion-shapers. And that means a world ruled by sophists, rhetoricians, and orators.

Why, then, did Helen not just go as unwillingly under the influence of speech as if she were seized by the violence of violators? For persuasion expelled her thought—persuasion which has the same power but not the same form as compulsion [*ananke*]. A speech persuaded a soul that was persuaded and forced it to be persuaded by what was said and to consent to what was done.

The persuader, then, is the wrongdoer, because he compelled her, while she who was persuaded is wrongly blamed because she was compelled by the speech.

To see that persuasion when added to speech indeed molds the mind as it wishes, one must first study the arguments of astronomers who replace opinion with opinion, displacing one but implanting another, and make incredible, invisible matters apparent to the eyes of opinion.[13]

Here Gorgias rejects the basic idea of natural philosophy and natural science, namely that they replace opinion with

---

[12] Gorgias, *Encomium of Helen*, pp. 192–93.
[13] Gorgias, *Encomium of Helen*, p. 193.

knowledge. Induction on the basis of past experience shows that science has a long history of plausible yet failed theories, and if the past is a good guide to the future—which all scientists presume—then present-day theories, which we regard to be as well-founded and as true as anything, will be replaced as well. So science is just the replacement of one opinion—however well-founded—with other opinions, albeit still better-founded ones.

Gorgias, therefore, is an exception to Aristophanes' thesis in his comedy the *Clouds* that the sophists are nourished by natural philosophy.[14] For Gorgias, natural philosophy is just another species of mutable opinion.

Gorgias continues with examples of how persuasion molds the mind:

> Second, compulsory debates with words where a single speech to a large crowd pleases and persuades because composed with art [*techne*] not spoken with truth.
>
> Third, contests of philosophical arguments where it is shown that speed of thought also makes it easy to change a conviction based on opinion.

Gorgias then illustrates the power of speech over the soul by comparing it to the power of drugs over the body, to say nothing of their power over the mind:

> The power of speech has the same effect on the disposition of the soul as the disposition of drugs on the nature of bodies. Just as different drugs draw forth different humors from the body—some putting a stop to disease, others to life—so too with words: some cause pain, others joy, some strike fear, some stir the audience to boldness, some benumb and bewitch the soul with evil persuasion.

Then Gorgias draws his conclusion: "The case has been made: if [Helen] was persuaded by speech her fortune was evil not her action."[15]

---

[14] See my chapter on Aristophanes' *Clouds* in *The Trial of Socrates*.
[15] *Encomium of Helen*, p. 193.

Finally, I want to look at a fragment from Gorgias that argues that deceptive speech can also produce wisdom, not just folly: "Tragedy produces a deception in which the one who deceives is more just than the one who does not, and the one who is deceived is wiser than the one who is not."[16]

The tragedian is a liar, but he improves us through his stories. He edifies our spirits and purges negative emotions. Thus he is more just than the person who doesn't write tragedies, who does not deign to deceive or benefit us. The tragedian is a better man for lying to us.

How is it that we are wiser for being deceived? Imagine watching *Hamlet*. You suspend disbelief and are swept up in the story. You are truly beguiled and deceived. Thus you can have a powerful experience and become wiser for it. Whereas the one who just can't get into it, who sits there thinking, "God, this is so long, so flowery, so implausible," is not deceived. Therefore, he does not really experience the story. Thus he remains in a state of folly. This is as powerful a defense of the "noble lie" as anything in Plato.

In sum, for Gorgias the power of speech over the human mind is truly awe-inspiring. Moreover, Gorgias' art of rhetoric gives us power over speech, both freeing our minds and giving us power over the minds of others. Thus you can forgive Gorgias for thinking that rhetoric is the king of all the arts, that it has the right to rule over everything, because in many societies it does.

Socrates doesn't deny that rhetoric rules. He just denies that it is the *rightful* ruler. Rhetoric is a mere pretender. Instead, Socrates argues that philosophy is the rightful ruler of all human affairs.

THE FIRST WORD (447a–447c)

The first word of the Gorgias is "*polemos*," war, and it is spoken by Callicles: "War and battle, this, they say, is how you

---

[16] Gorgias, fragment 10, in *Early Greek Political Thought from Homer to the Sophists*, p. 204.

should do your part in them, Socrates."[17] To this, Socrates replies: "Oh? Did we 'arrive when the feast was over,' as the saying goes? Are we late?"

What is being said here?

Socrates has arrived late, after an event is over. As we will soon learn, the event is one of Gorgias' display speeches, followed by a Q&A session. Callicles apparently greets Socrates with a saying to the effect that arriving *after* the battle is the best way to go to war. As we shall see, Callicles is a shameless advocate of 'might makes right.' But here he is sharing a coward's counsel, perhaps merely to mock Socrates, but he may also believe it. After all, we will learn that Callicles is a hedonist, which may mean that he has little taste for actual fighting and risk.

Plato could have started the *Gorgias* with any other word. So the fact that he chose "war" must be significant. First, it alludes to the setting of the dialogue, which spans almost the whole of the Peloponnesian War but is still set *within* the war. Second, it foreshadows the theme of the dialogue, which is power politics. Third, it foreshadows the mode of the dialogue, which is a battle of words and wits.

As we shall see, Socrates is not shirking battle. In fact, he is game for a fight. But merely listening to one of Gorgias' stunt speeches is not Socrates' idea of a real battle. Nor is watching him answer random questions from the audience. The real battle is yet to come.

This is why Socrates likens what he has missed not to a battle, which would be the vice of cowardice to shirk, but to a feast, which it would be the virtue of moderation to skip. (Even though if you are invited to a feast, the polite time to arrive is early, not late. Virtue is not always consistent with etiquette.) As we shall see, moderation is one of the central virtues that Socrates defends in his discussion with Callicles. As we have seen in the *Greater Alcibiades*, it is the primary virtue violated by tyrants.

Olympiodorus the Neoplatonist claims that the Athenians re-

---

[17] Here I will use (with my revisions) Plato, *Gorgias*, trans. Donald J. Zeyl, in Plato, *Collected Works*, ed. Cooper; henceforth cited as Zeyl.

ferred to Gorgias' stunt speeches as "feasts."[18] Donald Zeyl suggests that the two proverbs, about the right times to arrive at a battle and a speech, namely late and early, were perhaps conjoined, as in the English phrase "first at a feast, last at a fray," which does not describe a virtuous man either.[19]

Callicles responds by revealing what Socrates has missed: "Yes, and a very urbane one it was. Gorgias gave us an admirable, varied presentation just a short while ago." To this, Socrates says something odd: "But that's Chaerephon's fault, Callicles. He kept us loitering about in the marketplace [*agora*]."

Socrates, of course, is the one who was accused of always frittering his time away in the agora talking. Talking about what? Philosophy, of course! But here, he's blaming his friend Chaerephon for making him late to see a long speech by a sophist by frittering their time away in the agora, presumably conversing about philosophy. But, as becomes clear, Socrates doesn't think philosophical conversation is a waste of time. Moreover, he has no patience for sophistical speechifying.

Now, if Socrates *wanted* to see Gorgias, surely he would not have let Chaerephon stop him. Thus he didn't want to. So why does Socrates blame Chaerephon for his absence? I think he's telling a lie to be polite. He's saying that he didn't miss Gorgias' speech on purpose. He was detained by Chaerephon, whom he is making a scapegoat.

Chaerephon takes this accusation in stride and promises to make it up to Socrates: "That's no problem, Socrates. I'll make up for it, too. Gorgias is a friend of mine, so he'll give us a presentation—now if you see fit, or else some other time, if you like" (447b, Zeyl). Then Callicles chimes in: "What's this Chaerephon? Is Socrates eager to hear Gorgias?" (447b, Zeyl). Chaerephon says yes, at which point, Callias invites Socrates to his house, where Gorgias is staying, promising him a presentation any time he wants.

At this point, I imagine poor Socrates' heart is sinking. He may not have wriggled out of listening to a speech by Gorgias

---

[18] Olympiodorus, *Commentary on Plato's Gorgias*, p. 56.
[19] Plato, *Collected Works*, p. 792, n1.

after all. So Socrates finally just states his preference: "Very good, Callicles. But would he [Gorgias] be willing to have a dialogue with us? I'd like to find out from the man the power [*dunamis*] of his art [*techne*], and what he both makes claims about and teaches. As for the other thing, the presentation, let him put that on another time, as you suggest" (447c, Zeyl).

Callicles responds, "There is nothing like asking him, Socrates" (447c, Zeyl). Apparently after his speech, Gorgias invited the audience to ask him any questions they liked, so it seems likely he would entertain Socrates' questions too. At this point, Gorgias himself seems to have come out of the building. Thus Socrates replies, "An excellent idea."

THE BATTLE OF THE EPIGONES (447c–449a)

Socrates then turns to Chaerephon and says, "Ask him [Gorgias], Chaerephon." This is a very odd gesture. Why does Socrates not ask Gorgias directly? Does he really need Chaerephon as an intermediary? We have already seen Socrates use his friend as a shield. Now he is using him as a proxy to ask a question.

This brings to mind Plato's *Apology*, where Socrates tells the story of Chaerephon's question to the oracle of Delphi: "Is anyone wiser than Socrates?" (21a). There is every reason to think this event actually occurred, because even though Chaerephon was dead at the time of the trial, Socrates mentions that Chaerephon's brother could testify to its truth.

Did Socrates send Chaerephon to ask the oracle, as he sends him to ask Gorgias? Perhaps not, for Socrates had his own art of divination, based on knowledge of human nature.

Moreover, there is no reason to think that the Delphic oracle's response is *why* Socrates became a philosopher, because no one would have asked "Is anyone wiser than Socrates?" if Socrates didn't *already* have a reputation for wisdom. Thus the claim that Socrates philosophized because of the oracle is a fiction that allows Socrates to present his philosophical activity as pious. So again we have Socrates using his friend Chaerephon as a shield to deflect public disapproval.

CHAEREPHON: Ask him [Gorgias] what?

SOCRATES: What he is.
CHAEREPHON: What do you mean?
SOCRATES: Well, if he were a maker of shoes, he'd answer that he was a cobbler, wouldn't he? Or don't you see what I mean?
CHAEREPHON: I do. I'll ask him. [Turning to Gorgias:] Tell me, Gorgias, is Callicles right that you say that you will answer any question anyone might ask you?
GORGIAS: He is, Chaerephon. In fact, I just now made that very claim, and I say that no one has asked me anything new in many a year. [Gorgias, as we will see, is a boastful fellow. But with good right.]
CHAEREPHON: In that case I'm sure you'll answer this one quite easily, Gorgias.
GORGIAS: Here's your chance to ask me, Chaerephon.
(447c–448a, Zeyl)

Clearly, Socrates has taught Chaerephon the art of "Socratic" questioning. When Socrates says that the question is "who he is," Chaerephon is correct to ask for clarification, since there are many categories in which Gorgias could place himself: nationality, species, sex, profession, etc.

As in the *Greater Alcibiades*, here philosophy is deeply connected with *self-knowledge*. To be wise, we must be able to answer the question: Who are you? Here, however, Socrates specifically wants to know Gorgias' art and its power.

But before Chaerephon can actually *ask* the question, Polus — with his coltish enthusiasm — interrupts:

POLUS: By Zeus, Chaerephon! Ask me, if you like! For I think that Gorgias, who has been talking a long time, is quite tired.[20]
CHAEREPHON: Really Polus? Do you think that you can answer better than Gorgias?
POLUS: What does that matter, as long as it is good enough for you? [This is a prickly and arrogant answer. The

---

[20] Here I switch to the translation by Benjamin Jowett.

colt nips and kicks.]

CHAEREPHON: Not at all! Answer us then, if you like. [Chaerephon simply ignores the implied insult.]

POLUS: Ask.

CHAEREPHON: My question is this: If Gorgias had the art of his brother Herodicus, what should we call him? Isn't it by the same name as his brother?

POLUS: Certainly.

CHAEREPHON: Then we would be right to call him a doctor?

POLUS: Yes.

CHAEREPHON: And if he had the art of Aristophon the son of Aglaophon, or of his brother Polygnotus, what should we call him?

POLUS: Clearly, a painter.[21]

CHAEREPHON: But now what shall we call him [Gorgias] — what is the art in which he is skilled?

POLUS: O Chaerephon, there are many arts among mankind which are experimental, and have their origin in experience, for experience makes the days of men to proceed according to art, and inexperience according to chance, and different persons in different ways are proficient in different arts, and the best persons in the best arts. And our friend Gorgias is one of the best, and the art in which he is proficient is the finest [fine is *kalon*, also translatable as beautiful and noble]. (448a-c, Jowett)

First of all, why does Plato include the detail that Gorgias is tired? If Gorgias is tired, then he's less formidable as an opponent to Socrates. Wouldn't that make it easier for Socrates to

---

[21] According to Olympiodorus, Chaerephon's examples of a doctor and a painter anticipate Socrates' later distinction between true and false rhetoric, true rhetoric being likened to medicine and false rhetoric being likened to cosmetics, which is a form of painting, i.e., painting the surfaces of the body to give the appearances and health and youth (Olympiodorus, *Commentary on Plato's Gorgias*, p. 76).

defeat him? Couldn't someone then object that Socrates is, in effect, merely refuting "strawmen"? If so, wouldn't that undermine Socrates' victory? Isn't it an unfair fight? Maybe so, but as far as I know, I am the first commentator to raise this question.

Why would Plato include a detail that implies that Socrates doesn't fight fair? Perhaps he is trying to communicate that Socrates regards Gorgias and what he represents as so dangerous that he is willing to defeat them at all costs. Only a fool would allow a mortal enemy a fair chance to win.

Chaerephon is clearly well-versed in the art of Socratic questioning. But there's still something clumsy about his performance here. It brings to mind the painstaking and frankly tedious exchanges between Socrates and Alcibiades in the *Greater Alcibiades*. But Polus is not a beginner like Alcibiades. Thus Chaerephon should not deploy such elementary and finely-minced questions, which would just annoy Polus. He should get to the point.

When Chaerephon finally asks what Gorgias' art is, Polus begins speechifying. You can't really blame him. He's clearly annoyed by Chaerephon's style of questioning. Classicists speculate that Plato is actually parodying Polus' known oratory. This is certainly possible. I like Benjamin Jowett's translation here, because of its pretentious and bloviating style.

Socrates, however, has no tolerance for sophistical speech-making. Thus as soon as he realizes that a filibuster is about to spring forth, he cuts Polus off and for the first time speaks directly to Gorgias:

> **SOCRATES**: Polus has been taught how to make a fine speech, Gorgias; but he is not keeping the promise that he made to Chaerephon.
> **GORGIAS**: What do you mean, Socrates?
> **SOCRATES**: I mean that he has not exactly answered the question he was asked.
> **GORGIAS**: Then why not ask him yourself?
> **SOCRATES**: But I would much rather ask you, if you are willing to answer: for I see, from the few words that Polus has uttered, that he has attended more to the art

> which is called rhetoric than to dialectic.
> POLUS: What makes you say so, Socrates?
> SOCRATES: Because, Polus, when Chaerephon asked you which art Gorgias knows, you praised it as if you were answering someone who found fault with it, but you never said what the art was.
> POLUS: Why, did I not say that it was the finest of arts?
> SOCRATES: Yes, indeed, but that was no answer to the question: nobody asked what was the quality, but what was the nature, of the art, and by what name we were to describe Gorgias. (448d–449a, Jowett)

Socrates makes a good point here. Polus was asked what Gorgias' art is. Instead of naming the art itself, he simply describes one of its qualities, namely that it is the finest. But Socrates wants to know the art itself, not one of its qualities.

There is, however, a sense in which Polus has answered the question, but instead of talking *about* rhetoric, he simply displays an *example* of rhetoric. This, of course, is what Gorgias himself has just finished doing on a much grander scale with one of his famous display speeches. As we shall soon see, Gorgias too is unable to speak coherently *about* rhetoric. Thus Socrates rightly begins to suspect that Gorgias and his school don't really have an *art* of rhetoric. Instead, they have a mere *knack* for it. But although they are incapable of speaking coherently about rhetoric, they are able to teach rhetoric to others by offering them examples for emulation.

Socrates continues: "And I would still beg you [Polus] briefly and finely, as you answered Chaerephon when he asked you at first, to say what this art is, and what we should call Gorgias." But then Socrates turns to Gorgias himself and poses the question: "Or better, Gorgias, why don't you tell us yourself what we must call you based on the art that you know?" At this point, Socrates' conversation with Gorgias begins.

Why doesn't Socrates immediately begin speaking with Gorgias? Why does he send Chaerephon, a relative amateur, instead? Why does he send a boy to do a man's job? And why does Polus chime in, so we then have a conversation between two students, two epigones, rather than the masters who taught them? Plato obviously did this for a reason.

There are several possible reasons. First, Chaerephon is literally an intermediary, a middleman. Mediation is an alternative to a direct relationship, and it is an opportunity for errors to creep in. Second, Socrates is the original Socratic, and Chaerephon is a copy. Gorgias is the original, Polus a copy. For Plato, copying always involves falling away from the original.

The problems of mediation and copying illustrate the nature—and the dangers—of the teacher-student relationship. Students seldom excel their teachers, and when they do, it is not by imitating them. It is because they were always potentially more than their teachers. Usually, there's a decline in quality from teacher to student. We see this decline in the series of conversations to follow, first with Gorgias, then with his student Polus, then with Callicles, who is not a sophist but a wealthy consumer of the sophists' art.

This brings us to a moral and political question. If students do not represent their teachers well, then it is unjust to judge teachers by their students. But Socrates was not just judged by his students. He was tried, condemned, and executed because of such students as Alcibiades, the would-be tyrant, and Charmides and Critias, two actual tyrants. Thus the *Gorgias*, like most of Plato's dialogues, has an apologetic aspect. It seeks to acquit Socrates in the eyes of posterity by depicting the sophists as the true teachers of tyranny and Socrates as their greatest foe, who attacks tyranny at its roots.

Also, if Chaerephon and Polus are both intermediaries for their masters and inferior to them, this seems highly appropriate for the *Gorgias*, because the dialogue deals with rhetoric, and the two men are images of the power of rhetoric to bridge the gap between the few who know the truth and the many who at best hold only true opinions, as well as the dangers that attend such attempts.

PHILOSOPHY VS. RHETORIC

GORGIAS' ART (449a–c)

When Socrates finally speaks directly to Gorgias, he asks a simple, straightforward question: "What should we call you based on the art [*techne*] that you know?"[1] To which Gorgias gives a simple, straightforward answer: he knows "rhetoric" (*rhetorike*). Socrates continues: "Then is it best to call you a rhetorician [*rhetor*]?" Gorgias agrees and amplifies: "Yes, Socrates, and a good one too, if you want to call me what, as Homer puts it, 'I boast myself to be'" (449a, Zeyl).

Earlier Gorgias said nobody has asked him anything new in years. He's heard it all. Now he says that he is not just a rhetorician, he boasts of being a good one. Later, when Socrates asks him to confine himself to short answers, Gorgias says that long speeches are sometimes necessary—as Socrates clearly knows, since he uses them himself—but, still, Gorgias is better than anyone else at short answers. In short, Gorgias thinks very highly of himself. But he has every reason to. He is highly accomplished.

But is it right to brag about such things? The Greeks thought it was impolite to show off to one's inferiors. But they saw nothing wrong with frankness among friends.[2] Thus Gorgias may simply think that he is among peers, not inferiors.

RHETORIC & *LOGOS* (449c–452d)

Remember, however, that Socrates wants to know more than the name of Gorgias' art. He wants to know its power (*dunamis*). First, he asks if Gorgias is able to teach his art to others. Gorgias says yes. I will call the theorists and teachers of rhetoric "rhetoricians" and "sophists." I will call the students and practitioners of

---

[1] I am back to using the Zeyl translation, with some modifications.
[2] See Aristotle, *Nicomachean Ethics*, book IV, ch. 4, 1124b27ff; cf. book IV, chapter 7. Gorgias is not a braggart, because he is genuinely accomplished, and he is not ironic about his accomplishments, because that form of dishonesty is gracious and proper only when among inferiors.

rhetoric "orators."

Then Socrates asks, "What is rhetoric about?" Weavers make garments. Composers make music. What do rhetoricians make? Gorgias replies that rhetoric is about "speech" (*logos*).

But aren't speeches about something? Rhetoric may be about speeches, but what are those speeches about? Thus Socrates asks Gorgias to distinguish the speeches rhetoric deals with from the *logoi* of other arts like medicine and physical training.

At this point, Gorgias could introduce a distinction between the *form* and *content* of speeches. Rhetoric could deal with all kinds of speeches, but it could focus on their *common formal qualities* rather than their *particular contents*. Aristotle, for instance, takes this route, focusing on the formal properties of all persuasive *logoi*: logic, dialectic, and rhetoric. For Aristotle, rhetoric can be defined as the study of the techniques of persuasion about human affairs.[3]

Gorgias, however, does not take this route. Instead, he claims that rhetoric differs from other *technai* because it consists *entirely* of speeches, without any grubby hands-on work. Doctors deal with speeches, but they also deal with blood, phlegm, and pus. Physical trainers deal with speeches, but they also deal with strenuous, sweaty exercise regimens. Rhetoricians, however, deal only with speeches. Their hands are clean. Thus it is a perfect art for gentlemen.

At this point, Socrates introduces a distinction between two kinds of art. Socrates is assuming that all true arts are teachable. They are teachable by means of speeches (*logoi*). Thus all true arts involve *logoi*. But they involve them in different ways. For instance, such arts as sculpture and painting primarily involve physical actions. Yes, *logoi* are involved in teaching them. But

---

[3] In *Being and Time*, Heidegger describes Aristotle's *Rhetoric* as the "first systematic hermeneutic of the everydayness of [human] Being with one another," i.e., social life. Logic, dialectic, and natural science are modifications of this primordial human being with one another. See Martin Heidegger, *Being and Time*, trans. John Macquarrie and Edward Robinson (New York: Harper, 1962), p. 178, which corresponds to Heidegger, *Sein und Zeit*, 16th edition (Tübingen: Niemeyer, 1986), p. 138.

once taught, they can be carried on in silence. Gorgias agrees that these arts do not fall into the province of rhetoric.

However, other arts don't just have *logoi* annexed to them for teaching. They also take place entirely through the medium of *logoi*. This is how Gorgias describes rhetoric. But the problem with this account of rhetoric is that it does not distinguish it from other arts that take place entirely through the medium of *logoi*, such as mathematics. Beyond that, to say that rhetoric takes place entirely in the medium of *logoi* still does not make clear what the *logoi* are *about*. Finally, rhetoric does *not* take place entirely through the medium of language, since meaningful gestures and pauses are parts of rhetorical performances, and the image and implied character of the speaker plays a role in the total effect of his speech.

RHETORIC & THE GREATEST GOOD (452d–e)

Gorgias then says that rhetoric is about, "The greatest [*megista*] of human concerns, Socrates, and the best [*arista*]." But Socrates points out that experts in other arts—physicians, trainers, money makers—say that their arts pursue the greatest and best for man: health, fitness, money, etc. Besides, Gorgias doesn't actually say what the greatest and best is, so Socrates asks ". . . what is this greatest good [*megiston agathon*] for mankind of which you are the craftsman [*demiurge*]?" (452d, Zeyl).

Gorgias replies: "The thing that is in actual fact the greatest good . . . It is the cause [*aitia*] of personal freedom for oneself and at the same time the source of rule over others in one's own city" (452d, Zeyl). For Gorgias, the greatest good is the cause of freedom for oneself and power over others in one's city. Note that Gorgias limits power over others to power over *one's fellow citizens*. This seems arbitrary. Alcibiades, for instance, wanted more than to rule over Athens. He wanted an empire. Is Gorgias mindful that he is an outsider in Athens and thus wishes to reassure the Athenians that *he personally* has no ambitions to rule over them? Moreover, isn't the acme of freedom for yourself and power over others *tyranny*? Gorgias, of course, doesn't openly teach tyranny. That would be disreputable. But as we will see, some of his students draw precisely that conclusion.

Rhetoric is the greatest good, because it is the power to persuade the law courts and the legislative assemblies to give you power over other men.

What is greater than the speech that persuades the judges in the courts, or the senators in the council, or the citizens in the assembly, or at any other political meeting? — if you have the power of uttering this speech, you will have the physician as your slave, and the trainer as your slave, and the money-maker of whom you talk will be found to gather treasures, not for himself, but for you who are able to speak and to persuade the multitude. (452e, Zeyl)

The art of rhetoric gives one the power literally to enslave the practitioners of all the other arts, because rhetoric allows one to grasp the levers of political power, which allow one to regulate the whole of society.

One wonders, however, if rhetoric is the greatest good only in democracies, where the multitude is empowered. The greater the power of non-knowers, the greater the need for smooth-talking persuaders. For instance, in a polity where power is inherited, rhetoric would be useless for getting into power. The same is true of a society in which power is based on technical expertise.

But rhetoric would remain important even in societies where the masses are not empowered, simply because what makes rhetoric necessary is the gap between those who know and those who don't. Even in a regime in which power is based entirely on technical expertise, there will be multiple areas of expertise, and experts in one field will be laymen in another. Thus, to the extent that experts need to communicate with one another, rhetoric will still be necessary to bridge the gap.

THREE BASIC KINDS OF RHETORIC

At this point in the discussion, we have encountered the three basic kinds of rhetoric classified by Aristotle in *Rhetoric*, book I, chapter 3.

Epideictic rhetoric is what Socrates has just missed: a display speech. Two things are on display: the talent of the orator and the subject matter of the speech, which is usually the object of praise or blame. Epideictic rhetoric is thus by nature connected with values, primarily the noble and the base.

Epideictic rhetoric is generally contemplative, since its primary purpose is display, although it plays a practical role as an advertisement of the speechwriter's skill. Aristotle says that the audience of an epideictic speech is a "spectator" (*theoron*) which has the same root as "theorize,"[4] i.e., disinterested contemplation.

The other two forms of rhetoric are primarily practical. Their audience consists of decision-makers.

Forensic rhetoric is more past-oriented. Its audience is judges/jurors in the courts. Such speeches deal with the recent past (what the defendant did or did not do) in order to decide guilt or innocence in the present and take appropriate action in the immediate future (punishment, exoneration). According to Aristotle, such speeches are governed by considerations of justice and injustice.

Plato's *Apology of Socrates* is an example of forensic rhetoric. Gorgias' two surviving speeches, his defenses of Helen of Troy and Palamedes, partake of forensic rhetoric, for they concern guilt or innocence. But since the defendants are fictional or long dead, these speeches have no practical consequences, and their sole purpose is contemplation of the ideas and skill of the speaker.

Deliberative rhetoric is more future-oriented. Its audience is legislators weighing different courses of action for the immediate future, based of course on past and present circumstances. Thucydides relates many deliberative speeches in *The Peloponnesian War*. A good example is the Mytilenean debate between Cleon and Diodotus.[5] Aristotle points out that deliberative rhetoric is less concerned with justice and injustice than advantage or disadvantage.[6] Socrates and Plato, of course, have a problem

---

[4] Aristotle, *Rhetoric*, book I, ch. 3, 1358b1–10.
[5] Thucydides, *The Peloponnesian War*, 3.36–49.
[6] Aristotle, *Rhetoric*, book I, ch. 3, 1358b20–25.

with that. Both wish to subject politics to justice.

THE ART OF PERSUASION (452e–454b)

At this point, Socrates thinks that Gorgias has given an adequate account of rhetoric, namely that "rhetoric is the craftsman of persuasion; this is the whole of its business and its sole purpose" (452e, Zeyl). Gorgias agrees.

Then Socrates begins to butter up Gorgias, saying that he is obviously motivated purely by the love of truth. Gorgias, to his credit, reacts warily, wondering where this is leading.

Socrates then asks if rhetoric is the *only* art that persuades, or do others persuade as well. For instance, do teachers persuade? Gorgias agrees that they do. The same is true of mathematicians. The same is true of all arts, because all arts can be taught. Thus what distinguished rhetoric from all the other arts, if all of them produce persuasion? Clearly, what differentiates them would have to be *that about which* they persuade, the *object* of their persuasion. So *about what* does rhetoric persuade us?

Gorgias answers that "rhetoric is the art of persuasion in courts of law and other assemblies . . . and about the just [*dike*] and unjust [*adike*]" (454b, Zeyl). At the mention of justice and injustice, I imagine Socrates' ears pricking up like a dog's, for now we are entering the territory of philosophy.

KNOWLEDGE VS. BELIEF (454c–455a)

But before Socrates talks of justice and injustice, he introduces another philosophical distinction between knowledge (*mathesis*) and belief (*pistis*) (454c–d). You can have true or false beliefs, but you can't have true or false knowledge. If you know something, it is true. If your putative knowledge turns out to be false, it was only a belief. If you put forth a view as a belief, you are saying "I believe it, but I could be wrong." Gorgias accepts this distinction.

Then Socrates asks if there are two kinds of persuasion: one that yields belief (which may or may not be true) and the other that yields knowledge. Gorgias agrees. Then Socrates asks whether rhetorical persuasion produces knowledge or belief. Gorgias readily agrees that rhetoric produces only belief. Then

Socrates draws his conclusion: "Then rhetoric, it seems, crafts a persuasion that creates belief about the just and unjust but not knowledge about them" (454e, Zeyl). Gorgias agrees.

Then Socrates makes an important concession to Gorgias. He argues that rhetoricians are forced to impart beliefs—rather than knowledge—about justice to law courts and legislative assemblies, because it is impossible to teach deep ideas to large numbers of people in a short time. Gorgias agrees emphatically (455a). But if rhetoricians don't have the option of imparting *knowledge* of justice to the many, then they can't be *blamed* for merely imparting belief. Again, this underscores that Gorgias' idea of the greatest good for mankind is very much the creature of a particular regime: democracy.

Moreover, the same limits would apply to philosophers when they address law courts and legislative assemblies. This implies, for one thing, that when Socrates addressed the jury in his trial, he was trying to invoke belief rather than impart knowledge. He was acting as a rhetorician not a philosopher.

By introducing the distinction between belief and knowledge, Socrates is laying the groundwork for a new conception of rhetoric. Epideictic, forensic, and deliberative rhetoric are defined in terms of their audiences (spectators and decision-makers) and their goals (contemplation of the noble and base, taking action based on considerations of justice or advantage).

Socrates, however, is introducing a distinction between the speaker and the audience, as well as distinctions within the audience. If the speaker knows something—for instance, the art of ship-building—and needs to communicate this before the assembly so they can make decisions about equipping a fleet, his audience consists primarily of people who do not share his knowledge.

How do experts who know communicate with laymen who don't? To answer this, we must be mindful that the audience contains two kinds of non-knowers: non-knowers who can become knowers and non-knowers who can't.

First, there are people who can learn the art of ship-building and thus make a fully-informed decision on the expert's testimony. But who has time for that? People who are smart enough to learn new arts probably have plenty of other things to do with their time. The whole point of calling in an expert to testify is so that we don't have to become experts ourselves. Legislators must make decisions about many things. They can't become experts in all of them. Second, there are people who simply don't have the capacity to learn a particular art.

If experts must convince laymen but cannot do so by transferring their knowledge, then they need something else to bridge the gap. Socrates suggests that rhetoric does so by communicating belief in place of knowledge.

RHETORICIANS VS. EXPERTS (455b–d)

Then Socrates poses an objection to Gorgias. When the legislative assembly meets to choose a physician or a shipbuilder or any other artisan, do they really consult rhetoricians, or do they consult experts on medicine, shipbuilding, etc.? When walls, harbors, and docks are constructed, the assembly consults with expert builders, not rhetoricians. When generals are chosen, military experts are consulted, not rhetoricians. What does Gorgias have to say to this?

But before Gorgias can answer, Socrates puts him on the spot. He reminds Gorgias that they have an audience. Many of the people who attended Gorgias' speech followed him outdoors and stayed to watch his conversation with Socrates. Socrates points out that many of these young men are potential students of Gorgias. Of course they are also potential students of Socrates. Which one they choose depends on the outcome of the present conversation. Socrates suggests that these young men are too shy to challenge Gorgias themselves, so he will speak for them. "'What good is it to come to you, Gorgias?' they will say – 'What will you teach us to advise the city about? Only the just and unjust, or about these other things that Socrates has just mentioned?' How will you answer them?"

Gorgias is game for this challenge, pointing out that the walls, docks, and harbors of Athens were built because of the oratory of Themistocles and Pericles, not because of the expert testimony of the builders. Socrates accepts this. Indeed, he saw Pericles speak about the middle wall of Athens. Gorgias also points out that when decisions are being made on such issues, those who have rhetoricians advising them usually win.

THE *DAIMONIC* POWER OF RHETORIC (455d–456a)

Socrates agrees, saying he finds the "power" (*dunamis*) of rhetoric "wondrous" (*thaumazon*). For Plato, "wonder" (*thaumazein*) is the experience that gives rise to philosophy. Socrates also characterizes the power of rhetoric as nothing short of *daimonic*.

Gorgias says, "Yes, Socrates, if only you knew the whole of it, that it [rhetoric] encompasses and subordinates to itself just about all powers" (456a, Zeyl). Beyond that, Gorgias claims that rhetoric makes all the other arts *effective*. Without rhetoric, none of the other arts can achieve their ends.

Gorgias then gives a striking example of this. On certain occasions, he accompanied his brother Herodicus, a physician, to see his patients. Sometimes, when a patient refused the treatment Herodicus prescribed, Gorgias would use rhetoric to persuade the patient to comply. He adds that if a rhetorician or a doctor were to speak to the assembly about medicine, the people would more readily believe the rhetorician than the doctor. For rhetoric allows people to speak persuasively to the public on any subject, regardless of expertise. Such is the power of rhetoric.

This throws light on Gorgias' willingness to answer questions on any subject and his claim that he has heard nothing novel in many years. Gorgias is something of a polymath if he can speak on any subject. But he is an expert only in rhetoric. However, because of his expertise in rhetoric, he can persuade non-experts that he knows more than he actually does. In short, he's a master of fraud, specifically giving the fraudulent impression of having the authority that comes with genuine knowledge.

PHILOSOPHY'S EVIL TWIN

At this point it becomes clear why Socrates regards the sophists as rivals. Gorgias has basically defined rhetoric as 'the art that allows one to make use of all things.' Rhetoric comprehends all other arts, subordinates all other arts to it, and makes them effective, i.e., persuades people to accept their fruits.

The sophists are the teachers of rhetoric; thus, they possess what can be called the master art: the *techne* that rules over all other *technai*. Because this master art rules over all other arts, it is the *political* art. This is why the sophists were also understood as teachers of what one could call "political science." We have a word for rule by *techne*: "technocracy." Sophistry is technocracy.

The Socratic philosopher pursues wisdom, which I define as 'the ability to make *right* use of all things.' Like rhetoric, wisdom is practical. It is about *using* things, making them effective. Like rhetoric, wisdom is comprehensive. It is about using *all* things.

But there is a crucial difference. Rhetoric is simply concerned with *effective* use, whereas wisdom is concerned with *right* use. The Greeks thought that every *techne* is morally neutral. The same techniques can be used for good or evil ends. For instance, the same medicine can be used to cure or to kill. The poison is in the dose. Thus every *techne* needs something else—something outside or above it—to direct it toward good ends and away from bad ends: this is wisdom, which can make *right* use of all things because it has knowledge of the good.

The problem with technocracy is that it makes the use of *techne* into another technical problem. All arts are problematic, because they can be misused. The technocrat mistakes this for another technical problem, to be solved by a higher-order art, until one arrives at a master art, which holds supreme power over society. How can we be assured that this supreme art itself is not misused? The short answer is: we can't. For the master art, because it is an art, is also morally neutral as well.

Every art is a form of power (*dunamis*) to do things. But no power is *unconditionally good*, because arts can be used for good or evil ends. Only the good is unconditionally good. Thus, for the arts to be good, they must borrow their goodness from outside them. Wisdom is based on knowledge of the good, which gives it the ability to direct all things to good ends. The standard of right use is: human well-being.

The only solution to the problem of *techne* is to step outside of *techne* altogether. One must bring in practical wisdom, which uses its knowledge of the good to ensure that all arts are used rightly.

Technocracy is dangerous, because the technocratic mind

thinks that the accumulation of more power is the solution for the problems of lesser forms of power. But the wider the empire of technique, the greater the concentration of power, the greater the danger of its misuse, for power is never unconditionally good.

Because both philosophy and sophistry are concerned with the use of all things, they are easily confused. Only the moral factor separates them. Because sophistry focuses on power, regardless of right and wrong, Socrates regards it as a dangerous rival, philosophy's evil twin.

ETHICS AS AN AFTERTHOUGHT (456d–457c)

Is Socrates right that sophistry is essentially amoral and technocratic? After all, the sophists were widely seen as not just teachers of rhetoric but also as teachers of morals. However, as we shall see, both Polus and Callicles strongly embrace the amoral and technocratic idea of sophistry. Moreover, in the *Meno*—which is set in 402 BCE, after the Peloponnesian War and the latest possible date of the *Gorgias*—Meno tells Socrates: "I admire this most in Gorgias, Socrates, that you would never hear him promising this [to teach virtue]. Indeed, he ridicules the others [other sophists] when he hears them making this claim. He thinks one [the sophists] should [only] make people better speakers" (95c).[7]

The evidence, however, is contradictory. Recall that Gorgias' dedication in Olympia claimed that he trained men for the "contests of virtue." And, as we shall see, in this very conversation with Socrates, Gorgias shows that he is aware of the question of right use.

But the question is not: Did the sophists *take note* of morals? The real question is: Did the sophists believe that rhetoric or moral philosophy had *the right to rule*? Gorgias presents rhetoric as the ruling art: the art that encompasses, subordinates, and makes all other arts effective. But if rhetoric cannot assure that it will be used rightly, then it cannot be the highest authority. It must look to moral philosophy for guidance.

---

[7] Plato, *Meno*, trans. G.M.A. Grube, Plato, *Complete Works*, p. 893.

After lauding the *daimonic* power of rhetoric, Gorgias hastens to add that this power should be used rightly like any other power (456d). Specifically, he says that rhetoricians should use their powers against their enemies, not their friends. (This is the idea that justice is helping one's friends and harming one's enemies, which Socrates criticizes in *Republic*, book 1.[8])

Gorgias gives the example of a man trained in boxing who "strikes his father or mother or one of his familiars or friends" (456d, Zeyl). This is an allusion to Aristophanes' *Clouds*, in which the young man Pheidippides ends up beating his father after being corrupted by Socrates' (and Chaerephon's) sophistical teachings. In Plato's *Apology*, Socrates says that the *Clouds* is the origin of the accusation that Socrates corrupts the youth. But was the *Clouds* based on real events? Where there's smoke, there's fire. (Socrates's defense in the *Apology* is essentially: the *Clouds* was the fire, not the smoke; it was the source of Socrates' bad reputation, not merely a sign of it.)

Gorgias argues that, as an art, rhetoric is morally neutral. Whether an art is used well or badly is up to the practitioner. The teacher is entirely innocent. Thus it is unjust to punish teachers for the misdeeds of their students. This would be Gorgias' *Apology* if he were indicted for corrupting the youth.

It is noteworthy that it is not Socrates' apology. Indeed, in Plato's *Euthyphro*, Socrates agrees in principle that society should not tolerate the corrupters of the youth.[9] But Socrates thinks that he is *not* one of the corrupters. Unfortunately, the public can't tell the difference between Socrates and the sophists.

LOVE OF TRUTH VS. LOVE OF VICTORY (457c–458d)

At this point, Socrates thinks that Gorgias has contradicted himself. But before he points out the contradiction, Socrates introduces a distinction between two kinds of men. One kind of man primarily wants to win an argument. The other kind of man primarily wants to get to the truth. Of course we all want both: to win and to know the truth. But if we are forced to

---

[8] Plato, *Republic*, 331e–336a.
[9] See my lecture on the *Euthyphro* in *The Trial of Socrates*.

choose, one type prefers truth to winning; the other prefers winning to truth.

The kind of man who is primarily concerned with winning will never allow himself to be refuted, even if he's wrong. He'll be stubborn. He'll filibuster. He'll commit every sophistry in the book. He'll grandstand to the audience, of course, because if he's wrong, the only way to "win" is to make other people *think* he's won. Because he is so concerned with maintaining the *image* of being correct, he will never discover his errors and actually *be* correct.

By contrast, the man who is primarily interested in the truth is happy to be refuted if he's wrong, because by getting rid of his false beliefs he gets closer to having true beliefs.

Then Socrates puts Gorgias on the spot by asking what kind of man he is: Is he primarily concerned with truth or victory?

Of course Gorgias says he is primarily concerned with truth. But when put on the spot like that in front of an audience, wouldn't everyone say that?

But since Socrates has brought the audience into it, Gorgias says that although he is willing to continue the conversation, perhaps they should think of their audience. After all, they have already heard Gorgias' speech and Q&A session. Perhaps they are tired. Perhaps they wish to leave and are lingering merely to be polite. Chaerephon, Callicles, and the crowd enthusiastically press Gorgias to continue. To this, Gorgias replies that it would be "shameful" for him to back out now, especially after declaring that he would answer any question.

This little episode is very rich. First, it shows that Socrates is a rather cagey operator, boxing Gorgias into answering lest he make the embarrassing admission that he is not the kind of man who prefers truth to victory. Second, it shows that Gorgias is equally cagey, by putting the decision in the hands of the audience out of politeness. Was Gorgias hoping that the crowd would get him out of a tight spot? If so, the *demos* had other ideas. Gorgias abides by the decision of the majority and keeps his promise to answer any question. Plato includes these dramatic details to show that Gorgias has a sense of shame, which means that he has a sense of honor, which means he's a gentleman. As we shall see, Gorgias' sense of shame makes it possible for Socrates to catch him in a contradiction.

Gorgias' Contradiction (458d–461b)

To show Gorgias that he is contradicting himself, Socrates first secures his assent to the following statements. Gorgias claims he can teach men to be orators. An orator can speak to the many on any subject and gain their assent by evoking belief, not by imparting knowledge. An orator can be more persuasive than a doctor, even on matters of health. But this works only among the many who are ignorant of medicine, not among the few who are knowledgeable of it. An orator who is not a doctor is ignorant of medicine. Socrates then concludes that when an orator is more persuasive than a doctor, this is a case of an ignorant man being more persuasive to the ignorant than a knowledgeable man. Gorgias agrees.

Then Socrates generalizes to the other arts: a successful orator need not know the truth about any of the arts, as long as he can persuade the ignorant that he knows more than the experts. Gorgias agrees. He thinks that it is wonderful to be able to beat experts in any art in the eyes of the many by becoming proficient solely in one art, namely rhetoric.

Socrates then asks: Are orators as ignorant of "the just and unjust, noble and shameful, good and evil" as they are of medicine and the other arts? If students are ignorant of good and evil, will Gorgias simply teach them to fake such knowledge before the ignorant? Or must students know about good and evil before they study rhetoric?

Gorgias replies that if students come to him ignorant of good and evil, they will learn these from him alongside rhetoric. Socrates then concludes that whoever learns rhetoric "must either know the nature of the just and unjust already, or he must be taught by you [Gorgias]" (460a, Zeyl). Gorgias agrees.

Socrates then argues that, just as a man who learns carpentry is a carpenter, and a man who learns medicine is a doctor, a man who learns justice would be a just man. Here Socrates is assuming a thesis that he argues for in the *Meno* and the *Protagoras*, namely, that virtue is a kind of knowledge, thus if one *knows* what is virtuous, one will *be* virtuous.[10] Thus if a man knows justice, he will be a just man. A just man always desires to do justice. He always performs just deeds. And he never does injustice. Gorgias agrees on all points.

At this point, Socrates reveals Gorgias' contradiction. On the one hand, Gorgias maintains that rhetoric is a morally neutral *techne*. Thus when students of rhetoric misuse this *techne*, it is their fault, not the fault of rhetoric or their teachers. On the other hand, Gorgias holds that every student either knows about justice before studying rhetoric or he picks up knowledge along the way. But, if to *know* justice is to *be* just, then no orator would misuse rhetoric.

Gorgias can resolve the contradiction by dropping his claim that orators necessarily learn what is just. Or he can challenge the premise that those who *know* the just will *act* justly.

But the deeper problem is his insistence that rhetoric is the master art. The *polemos* of the *Gorgias* is a struggle between rhetoric and philosophy for supremacy. If rhetoric must look outside itself to moral philosophy to ensure right use, then it is not the highest form of knowledge. Philosophy is. If moral knowledge is intrinsic to rhetoric—which seems to be what Gorgias is driving at with the idea that all orators will know the good—then rhetoric is no longer a *techne*. In effect, it becomes philosophy, so philosophy still rules.

Socrates says that it will take a great deal more discussion for them to untangle this contradiction. He swears an oath "by the dog" (461b, Zeyl) to indicate his seriousness about pursuing the truth. Later in the *Gorgias*, we learn that the dog is an Egyptian god, probably Anubis (482b).

POLUS INTERRUPTS (461b)

But before Socrates can continue to question Gorgias, Polus interrupts again, and this time he maintains control of the conversation.

The substance of Polus' objection is that Gorgias was defeated by his own sense of shame. When Socrates asked whether

---

[10] Plato, *Meno*, 87b–89a; *Protagoras*, 358d–361b.

students of rhetoric need to know the just, Gorgias was too ashamed to say "no" and maintain that rhetoric is a value-neutral *techne*.

Prudence might also have played a role. According to Meno, Gorgias mocked the idea that sophists should teach morals in addition to rhetoric. Here, he defends that idea.

One explanation for the contradiction is that the former view was Gorgias' private conviction, which he related to his students and peers. The latter view, however, is for public consumption, to ward off the charge of being a corrupter of the youth. However, whether from shame or prudence or a mixture of the two, Gorgias' claim that every student of rhetoric knows justice is definitely playing to the crowd.

A KNACK FOR PANDERING

SETTING THE STAGE (461b–462b)

Socrates' conversation with Polus deals with four important philosophical issues. First, Socrates explains the true nature of rhetoric, which requires that he contrast it with philosophy. This discussion requires four important distinctions: soul vs. body, art vs. quackery, edification vs. corruption, and friendship vs. flattery. Second, Socrates explains the true nature of freedom. Freedom is not doing what you *think* you want. It is doing what you *really* want, which is to lead a good life. This generates a powerful argument against liberalism and for paternalism. Third, Socrates makes a very powerful argument that, if forced to choose one or the other, it is better to suffer wrong than to do it. Fourth, this is connected to a theory of punishment as rehabilitation, basically as medicine for the soul.

An important theme running through this discussion, and the whole dialogue, is power politics. Gorgias claims that rhetoric is the greatest of human goods because it secures freedom for oneself and power over others. Rhetoric is the master art that encompasses and subordinates all other arts and the whole of society. Thus rhetoric is the art of taking and keeping comprehensive political power. As we shall see, Polus argues that orators and tyrants have the same power, the greatest power, which allows them to kill or exile their enemies and expropriate their property. When we get to Callicles, he basically argues that might makes right and defends tyranny as the best life.

So all of Socrates' interlocutors believe in power politics to one extent or another. Gorgias believes that power needs to be justly governed, but Polus and Callicles chafe against such strictures. Thus throughout the *Gorgias*, Socrates is trying to argue the case of right against might. This is the true *polemos* of the dialogue. What separates Socrates from the sophists is his conviction that morality must rule over political power.

Another important theme is shame. Polus is a rude and disagreeable man. He twice interrupts conversations with his teacher, Gorgias. The second time he interrupts, Polus manages to hijack the conversation from Gorgias completely and hold the floor longer than Gorgias did (although there is a brief interlude when Socrates speaks again to Gorgias, who expresses annoyance at Polus).

Polus begins by questioning the sincerity of Socrates' views about rhetoric. Then he claims that Gorgias agreed merely out of shame that students of rhetoric must know justice. He was afraid of looking bad in front of his audience.

Polus also says it is bad manners for Socrates to exploit Gorgias' natural reluctance to admit that, no, it is not his responsibility to teach his students about justice. Polus has a cynical, 'We're all men of the world here' attitude. Asking Gorgias before an audience if he cares about justice is as boorish as asking him if he's ever been drunk. Everybody has been drunk, thus asking about it in public is to demand that everyone act the hypocrite out of politeness. Similarly, everyone cuts corners about morals, so it is just bad manners to ask everyone to pay lip service to justice. But Polus is proud to be shameless enough to declare the truth: rhetoric is a value-neutral art.

Was Gorgias genuinely and sincerely concerned with justice, or did he merely want to *seem* that way, because that's the socially appropriate and politically prudent thing to do? As we will see, for Socrates, all men are always-already concerned with justice, no matter what their motives for speaking about it. Polus, however, immediately assumes that both Socrates and Gorgias are acting in bad faith. That's a very cynical assumption, and gentlemen aren't cynical.

But Polus isn't entirely cynical. He has some sense of right and wrong. Even accusing people of arguing in bad faith assumes a standard of right conduct and a willingness to uphold it. So does accusing Socrates of bad manners.

It is noteworthy that Socrates refutes Polus based on the latter's belief that certain actions are "fine" or "noble" (*kalon*) and others are "shameful" (*aischron*). Socrates peppers his conversation with Polus with these terms. The Greek concept of the gentleman is the *kalos k'agathos*, literally the noble and good man. A susceptibility to such concepts means there's something slightly gentlemanly about Polus as well, which allows Socrates to defeat him in the end.

Then Callicles jumps in. Callicles realizes that to defend rhetoric and tyranny, one must overthrow justice and argue that might makes right. But, as we will see, Socrates discovers that Callicles' concept of might is not mere physical force or mere force of numbers. It is an elitist notion of what is fine or noble which makes even Callicles susceptible to feelings of shame.

Both Polus and Callicles interpret shame to be merely a "social" feeling. Shame is how society enforces conformity to mutable human conventions. Socrates, however, seems to believe that shame is natural, based ultimately on our innate knowledge of the good.[1]

Socrates receives Polus' interruption and outburst in good humor, responding with the words "O finest [*kalliste*] Polus," working in the superlative form of "*kalon*" at the very start. Socrates notes that Polus is younger than himself and Gorgias, but he generously allows that this may not be mere bad manners on Polus' part. This may be a genuine opportunity for the young to school the old. Socrates invites Polus to expose his errors so that he may correct himself.

But on one condition: he must keep his answers brief, meaning no speechifying. Socrates also insisted on this with Gorgias. Why? To keep control. In a dialogue, he can intervene at every step in the argument to guide it to his desired conclusions. In a speech, he won't be able to get a word in edgewise. Instead, he and his audience will be drowned in superficially impressive but ultimately empty and stultifying clichés.

Polus bristles at this condition, but Socrates tartly remarks that if Polus wishes to avail himself of Athenian freedom of speech at too great a length, Socrates will invoke his Athenian freedom to ignore him. This points to a major weakness of all forms of argument: words alone can't force people to listen. Moreover, if Polus claims to know what Gorgias knows, surely

---

[1] See Richard McKim, "Shame and Truth in Plato's *Gorgias*," *Platonic Writings, Platonic Readings*, ed. Charles L. Griswold, Jr. (New York: Routledge, 1988).

he can answer questions just as well as his teacher. To sweeten the deal, Socrates invites Polus to ask the first question.

ART VS. QUACKERY (462b–465e)

Polus asks Socrates, "What is rhetoric?" Socrates asks if he wants to know what sort of "art" (*techne*) rhetoric is. Polus says yes. Socrates then claims that rhetoric is not an art at all. Citing Polus' own book, Socrates thinks that rhetoric is a "knack." The Greek word is "*empeiria*," from which we get the word "empirical." An *empeiria* is a skill based on experience.

Every art has a practical dimension, because arts change reality. No art is pure theory. Even arts that consist entirely of speeches require practice. To learn rhetoric, you can't just *talk about* speeches, you've got to *make* them.

But a true art is not just practice. The true master of an art has taken a step back from the practices, reflected on them, and articulated some general principles: rules of thumb as well as explanatory theories. These are *logoi*, which you can translate as "verbal accounts." A true art can give a rational account of itself. A true *techne* is thus *empeiria* plus *logoi*.

Because true artists have *logoi*, they are good at teaching their arts to others. Those who have mere knacks tend to be poor teachers. The best they can do is to urge others to imitate them and practice, practice, practice.

The main reason why philosophy is not, ultimately, an art for Socrates is that philosophy can't be taught. That's not because philosophy lacks *logoi*. Philosophy isn't a knack. Philosophy isn't teachable because *we already know it*. Therefore, philosophical education for Plato is primarily a matter of articulating what we already know.

In eighteenth-century English, the word "empiric" referred to a quack doctor, a charlatan, a bumbler. Quacks practiced medicine based solely on knacks: experience refined merely by trial and error. Thus Socrates is drawing a contrast between true arts and quackery, and rhetoricians are quacks.

Socrates' contrasts are best summed up in a table, generated by two distinctions: the body vs. the soul and true well-being vs. the mere appearance of well-being, which is feeling good.

	Well-being = real health **Produced by:** work (self-discipline, friendship, edification, education, building up) **Aided by:** True art (*techne*) = (knack + *logos*) **Guided by:** the good	Merely Feeling/Looking Good = apparent health **Produced by:** flattery (*kolakeia*), pandering, stooping down, self-indulgence, corruption **Aided by:** knack (*empeiria* = skill without *logos*) + guesswork, schmoozing, puffery, bravado **Guided by:** The pleasurable
Care of the Body	**Health Production & Restoration** (produces physical well-being) 1. **gymnastics** (health production = diet, exercise, healthy living) 2. **medicine** (restores good health, purges bad health)	**Counterfeit Health** (produces the appearance of physical well-being) 1. **cosmetics** (creates the appearance of good health) 2. **confectionery** (creates the feeling of good health while creating bad health)
Care of the Soul	**Politics** (produces spiritual well-being) 1. **legislation** (builds up spiritual health) 2. **justice** (punishment, purges spiritual sickness)	**Counterfeit Politics** (produces spiritual corruption) 1. **sophistry** (in legislatures, produces unjust legislation) 2. **oratory** (in law courts, produces unjust punishments)

Socrates is talking about caring for the body and caring for the soul. Such care can produce true and false forms of well-being for both body and soul.

Why is well-being different from merely feeling good? Because sometimes pains are good for us and pleasures are bad. It is always easier to take children to the candy store than the dentist, because candy tastes good and dentistry feels bad. But dentistry is good for our physical well-being and candy is bad.

Let's begin with the first column, well-being, both of body and soul. Well-being basically means genuine physical and mental health. For Socrates, we all naturally seek well-being. But we don't always achieve it, for several reasons. First, well-being requires external conditions that aren't always available. Second, well-being requires efforts that don't always work. Third, well-being requires knowledge that isn't always available. Fourth, well-being has counterfeits that are often highly tempting, even addictive.

Counterfeit well-being brings us to the second column. When you have genuine well-being, you feel good and look good. Well-being is the cause. Feeling and looking good are the effects. Thus it is natural to try to reverse the causal relationship: by looking and feeling good, we hope to achieve well-being. But it doesn't always work that way.

First, any good thing in excess becomes bad. Second, some pleasures are so destructive that they can't be enjoyed even in moderation. For instance, highly addictive drugs and behaviors destroy your ability to moderate them. Third, merely looking good can secure some of the external rewards of well-being, but this simply makes one less likely to achieve *actual* well-being.

Well-being is produced by work, specifically edifying work, work that builds up both body and soul. These include a good diet, exercise, and education, both of character and mind. All of these require self-discipline, principally the virtue of moderation, as well as a willingness to defer gratification to the future and a refusal to settle for counterfeits and shortcuts.

Edification is impossible, however, if one feels one is "good enough." Thus to raise people up, we need to put them down, i.e., to purge them of smugness, complacency, and laziness. This often requires some tough talk, which is why friendship is one of the things that produces well-being. True friends tell you what you need to know to live well, regardless of whether you want to hear it.

Socrates also adds that producing well-being is aided by genuine arts. But to be successful, the whole process must be guided by an understanding of the good, namely the well-being we are all pursuing.

Merely apparent well-being is appealing, because it requires less work, less self-discipline, less delayed gratification, and less discernment. The purveyors of fake well-being don't try to break down your laziness and complacency to build you up. Instead, they flatter you by saying you are good enough the way you are.

Socrates uses the Greek word "*kolakeia*" here, which can be translated as "flattery." A better translation might be "pandering." Pandering caters to, exploits, and confirms people in ignorance and vice. It is the opposite of edification. Pandering offers shortcuts and easy solutions.

Pandering is the realm of quacks who have some genuine skills but paper over their weak points with bold guesswork and fraudulent fast talk. Because quacks produce apparent rather than real well-being, they are highly attuned to people's psychology and opinions, which they manipulate. They are consummate puffers, flatterers, and schmoozers. But of course they will resort to bullying and gaslighting when cornered.

Just as edification is guided by the good, corruption is guided by a fake good: pleasure.

Let's look more carefully at the care and corruption of the body.

The care of the body involves both the production and the restoration of health. Socrates calls the production of health "gymnastic," which refers broadly to any health regimen, principally exercise and diet. Socrates calls the restoration of health "medicine."

The fake care of the body also has two modes: production and restoration. Socrates calls the production of the appearance of health "cosmetics," which would include every means of faking youth, health, and beauty: makeup, hair coloring, sun tanning, even plastic surgery.

Socrates calls the fake restoration of health/removal of illness "confectionery," which basically means anything that makes you feel good while ruining your health, whether it be food, drink, or drugs. On this account, Dr. Feelgood prescribing uppers and downers would be a confectioner as well. Think of a doctor who prescribes morphine to a dying patient. The morphine suppresses pain and even produces a feeling of bliss, but it does not restore health. It is merely a temporary simulacrum of health.

Now let's turn to the care and corruption of the soul. In the *Gorgias*, Socrates assigns the care of the soul not to philosophy but to politics. Statecraft is soulcraft. As with the care of the body, the care of the soul has two modes: the production of health and the removal of disease.

Socrates calls the production of spiritual health "legislation" (*nomothetes*), literally laying down the law. The word for law here is *nomos*, which has a wider meaning than mere statutory law. It encompasses all social norms. Laying down the law basically means upholding standards and creating institutions and practices that morally and intellectually edify the people. Socrates calls the removal of spiritual sickness "justice." By this he means rehabilitative punishment. As he explains later to Polus, Socrates sees punishment as spiritual medicine, as opposed to retribution or deterrence.

The fake care of the soul is counterfeit politics. It too has two modes: imparting fake health and appearing to remove illness. Socrates calls counterfeit legislation "sophistry," which is somewhat confusing, because it does not necessarily require the services of the sophists. I am sure that Socrates is primarily thinking of the role of sophistry in the rise to power of men who look good but act bad. But if real legislation produces spiritual health for the city as a whole, then sophistry as fake legislation would produce fake spiritual health for the city as a whole. Some examples of this would be economic prosperity, military power, and impressive buildings and monuments—

basically, everything that characterized Athens at its peak.

Socrates calls the false version of punishment "oratory," which is again confusing, since it need not involve the use of oratory. The primary example Socrates is thinking of is the use of oratory in the courts to produce unjust outcomes. Think, for example, of Gorgias' show speech the *Encomium of Helen*, which argues that Helen of Troy is not responsible for her actions. The same arguments, of course, could be used to exculpate any criminal. Fake justice can include false and ineffective forms of punishment. Furthermore, oratory could encompass the whole realm of propaganda, including the art of "spin-doctoring." Moreover, the flip side of false exculpation is also false blame, which is a staple of political corruption as well.

Perhaps the best example of the fake restoration of health to the body politic is the scapegoat, who is first magically burdened with the guilt of the whole community and then punished in its place. Socrates, of course, was made a scapegoat for the crimes of Alcibiades and the Thirty Tyrants, although in truth no Athenian citizen was entirely innocent.

Once we lay out this scheme, we can generate a set of wonderful analogies:

1. **Gymnastics is to Cosmetics as Medicine is to Confectionary**. Meaning that gymnastics produces real health whereas cosmetics produces apparent health, just as medicine restores real health and confectionery restores apparent health.
2. **Gymnastics is to Medicine as Cosmetics is to Confectionary**. Meaning that gymnastics produces real health whereas medicine restores real health, just as cosmetics produces apparent health and confectionery restores apparent health.
3. **Legislation is to Sophistry as Justice is to Oratory**. Meaning that legislation makes society genuinely flourish whereas sophistry makes society apparently flourish, just as justice restores society's health while oratory only apparently restores society's health.
4. **Legislation is to Justice as Sophistry is to Oratory**.

Meaning that legislation and justice either produce or restore genuine social health, whereas sophistry and oratory only produce or restore apparent social health.

5. **Gymnastics is to Cosmetics as Legislation is to Sophistry**. Meaning that gymnastics produces real physical health whereas cosmetics produces only apparent physical health, just as legislation produces real spiritual health and sophistry only apparent spiritual health.
6. **Medicine is to Confectionery as Justice is to Oratory**. Meaning that medicine restores real health, whereas confectionery only restores the feeling of health, just as justice restores real spiritual health whereas oratory only apparently restores spiritual health.
7. **Gymnastics is to Legislation as Medicine is to Justice**. Meaning that both gymnastics and legislation produce real health, the first in the body, the second in the spirit, whereas medicine and justice restore real health in the body and spirit respectively.
8. **Cosmetics is to Sophistry as Confectionery is to Oratory**. Cosmetics and sophistry both produce apparent health in the body and soul respectively, whereas confectionery and oratory both restore apparent health in the body and soul respectively.

We can also generate some pithy metaphors:

1. Legislation is the gymnastics of the soul.
2. Gymnastics is the legislation of the body.
3. Medicine is the justice of the body.
4. Justice is the medicine of the soul.
5. Confectionery is the oratory of the body.
6. Oratory is the confectionery of the soul.
7. Cosmetics is the sophistry of the body.
8. Sophistry is the cosmetics of the soul.

The proper care of both the body and the soul is guided by knowledge of the good. This means, ultimately, that the soul rules itself and the body. Flattery in the care of both the body and the soul is guided by pleasure, which means rule by desire. This, Socrates argues, can only lead to chaos:

> ... if the body presided over itself, and were not under the guidance of the soul, and the soul did not discern and discriminate between confectionery and medicine, but the body was made the judge of them, and the rule of judgment was the bodily pleasure each produces, then the word of Anaxagoras—that word with which you, friend Polus, are so well acquainted—would prevail far and wide: "chaos" would come again, and confectionery, health, and medicine would mingle in an indiscriminate mass. (465d, Zeyl)

For the Greeks, the opposite of "chaos" is "cosmos," order. Later in his conversation with Callicles, Socrates sets forth a model of the cosmos that can bring order to the soul.

It is significant that Socrates asserts that Polus is familiar with the natural philosophy of Anaxagoras. In his *Clouds*, Aristophanes claims that sophistry is nourished by natural philosophy, which undermines belief in the gods and teaches that traditional morals are mere conventions which lack the dignity of nature.[2]

It is noteworthy that in the *Gorgias*, Socrates operates simply with a distinction between the soul and the body, whereas in the *Republic*, he makes a distinction between the body and three parts of the soul, from highest to lowest: reason, *thumos*, and desire. Thus, in terms of the *Republic*, the proper care of body and soul, since it is guided by knowledge of the good, would be the rule of *reason* over both body and the lower parts of the soul. Whereas flattery, because it caters to desire, is the rule of *desire*, which is the lowest part of the soul, over the body and the

---

[2] For an extensive discussion of the relationship of natural philosophy and sophistry, see the Introduction and the following two chapters of *The Trial of Socrates*.

higher parts of the soul.

This is a very long answer to the short question "What kind of art is rhetoric?" The answer is: rhetoric is not the master art, as Gorgias claimed. The true master art is politics, which, because it encompasses all things and thus all human affairs and looks to the good, is identical with philosophy. Furthermore, rhetoric isn't even an art at all. It is quackery. It is, moreover, quackery of the most dangerous kind, because it corrupts all of society from the top down, promoting every false standard of health and impeding every attempt to remove sickness and vice, thereby ruining the souls of all the citizens.

But it is worth asking: Is there a good form of rhetoric? Socrates would have to say there is. Socrates gives us no reason to think that rhetoric is intrinsically or necessarily evil. At worst, it is a value-neutral art. But if it is value-neutral, it can also be used for good as well as for ill.

SOCRATES THE PUGILIST (465e–466b)

After Socrates outlines why he thinks that rhetoric is not an art but rather merely a "knack" for pandering and corrupting, he apologizes for lapsing into speech-making, but he explains that it was necessary, because Polus was incapable of answering short questions. He also grants that it would be only fair for Polus to resort to speech-making if Socrates is unable to answer Polus' short questions.

Socrates is being a bit patronizing and nasty with Polus. When Polus replies with the question, "Do you think that rhetoric is flattery?" Socrates responds, "No, I said a *part* of flattery. If at your age, Polus, you cannot remember, what will you do when you get older?" (465a, Zeyl). When Polus asks if rhetoricians are held in low esteem in cities as flatterers, Socrates does not take the question in good faith but instead badgers Polus, asking "Is that a question or the beginning of a speech?" (466b, Zeyl). Socrates is not merely trying to refute Polus' positions, he is trying to impeach him as a man in the eyes of the audience and undermine his own self-confidence.

Why does Plato include such details? Why does he depict Socrates resorting to the lowest forms of rhetorical thuggery?

Socrates is merely responding to Polus' provocations in kind. But it raises a question: Is there a philosophical rhetoric—a good rhetoric—since Socrates is surely a user of rhetoric?

Polus interrupts. Polus impugns the sincerity of both Gorgias and Socrates. Polus filibusters. Polus asks rhetorical rather than real questions. Polus cites the authority of the people and grandstands to the audience. Polus at one point simply laughs at Socrates. Socrates is, of course, primarily concerned with the truth. But he is also committed to winning the argument by hook or by crook.

Plato repeatedly insists that philosophers are very different from sophists in their first principles and ultimate goals. But he also shows that, to the naïve observer, philosophers and sophists look pretty much the same in their techniques, which is why Socrates ended up being convicted as a teacher of tyrants and a corrupter of the youth. Plato believes it was a case of mistaken identity. But he also shows that it is an easy mistake to make.

Socrates responds to Polus that rhetoricians are not held in high regard at all. Socrates surely knew that if one were to conduct a poll of the Athenian public, they would hold rhetoricians in high regard. So what is the meaning of his claim?

Socrates holds that neither Polus nor the public at large really respect rhetoricians. But they don't know their own minds. In other words, Socrates is assuming a distinction between what we *really* believe and what we merely *think* we believe.

For Socrates, all of us always-already know the truth about the most important things: what constitutes a good life, what it entails, and how to attain it. These are truths about human flourishing, and we are human.

The difference between Socrates and Polus is that Socrates *knows what he knows*, and Polus *doesn't fully know what he knows*. Thus Socrates' approach to Polus is first to find whatever moral truths he is aware of. Then, working from that foundation, he will lead Polus step by step into agreement with Socrates. But Polus will really be agreeing with himself.

This is not, however, a purely *ad hominem* approach, for although each man has a *different*, more-or-less inadequate grasp of moral truth, we all know the *same* truth.

TWO CONCEPTS OF FREEDOM (466b–468e)

Polus' objection is quite natural. "Don't rhetoricians have great power in cities?" (466b, Zeyl). The answer is clearly yes. So how could they enjoy great power yet be held in low esteem? Socrates' answer is: just as the esteem rhetoricians are held in is merely apparent, so is the power they enjoy.

Socrates begins with the premise that "Power is a good to its possessor" (466e, Zeyl). Polus agrees. From that premise, however, Socrates will argue that rhetoricians "have the least power of all the citizens" (466d-e, Zeyl). Recall that in the *Gorgias* power is identified with freedom. Thus rhetoricians would have the least freedom as well. Polus is incredulous: "What! Are they [rhetoricians] not like tyrants? They kill and rob and exile any one whom they please" (466c, Zeyl).

After a bit more bullying and badgering, Socrates replies: "rhetoricians and tyrants have the *least* possible power in cities, as I was just now saying; for they do literally *nothing that they want*, but only *what they think best*" (466d-e, Zeyl). This is not power, however, because, as Polus has already agreed, true power is good for its possessor. Thus when a fool is mistaken about what really is best and acts accordingly, he does not have real power.

Let's explore Socrates' distinction between "doing what we want" and "doing what we think best." This distinction should be sharpened by contrasting "doing what we *really* want" to "doing what we *think* we want." The main issue is truth versus opinion, fact vs. fancy. We are not free if we pursue false goals.

So what do we really want? We want what is actually good for us.

Socrates divides things into three categories: goods, evils, and things that, in themselves, are neither good nor evil, but they can be used for both good and evil ends. Socrates offers "Wisdom [*sophia*] and health and wealth" as examples of goods, "their opposites evils" (467e).[3]

---

[3] Polus agrees, but in other contexts, Socrates would classify wealth not as a good, but as something that could be good or bad depending on its use.

Another helpful distinction is between intrinsic goods, which are things that we pursue as ends in themselves, and instrumental goods, which we would never pursue as ends in themselves but only as means to intrinsic goods. For instance, we pursue health as an end in itself. We take medicines and submit to surgeries not as intrinsic goods, but only as means to the end of health.

Socrates offers as a universal truth that, "If a man does something for the sake of something else, he wills not that which he does, but that for the sake of which he does it" (468b, Zeyl). If we do something that is not good or bad in itself, we do so only as a means to something that is good. As Socrates puts it:

> When we walk, we walk for the sake of the good, and with the idea that it is better to walk, and when we stand we stand equally for the sake of the good. . . . When we kill a man, we kill him or exile him or despoil him of his goods, because, as we think, it will conduce to our good. (468b, Zeyl)

If, however, we do not think these acts are good, we will not do them. Polus accepts all this.

Then Socrates drives home his conclusion. If all action aims at what is really good for us, then *real* freedom and *real* power are best defined as getting what is *really* good for us. If, however, we don't know what is good for us, then we don't have real freedom or real power. Thus, if a tyrant or an orator kills a man, or seizes his property, or exiles him, "under the idea that the act is for his own interests when really not for his own interests" (468c, Zeyl), then we can say that he did what he *thought* best. But he didn't do what he *really* wanted. Therefore, he is neither powerful nor free, even though he seems that way to the naïve observer.

But isn't everyone capable of making mistakes about what is best for him? Is there any reason to think, then, that tyrants and orators are worse off than other men? Yes. We can appreciate how by using the distinction between friendship and flattery.

In the *Greater Alcibiades*, Socrates points out that tyrants are surrounded by people who fear to tell them the truth, which allows them to ruin themselves, both physically and spiritually. For Socrates, friends tell us the truth, even painful truths, even truths we don't want to hear. Flatterers, however, only tell us what we want to hear.

For tyrants and rhetoricians, however, flattery is the coin of the realm. They rise by flattering the public. They exploit the people's vices rather than helping the people overcome them. Then, when tyrants and rhetoricians attain power, they bask in the flattery of their inferiors. Such men are far more likely to be ignorant of what is truly good for them than humble and honest men who surround themselves with frank and honest friends.

Thus, for all their power and freedom to do what they *think* they want, tyrants and orators are less likely to have the power and freedom to do what they *really* want.

The *Gorgias* is the origin of a debate in political philosophy that continues to the present day. It is the debate between advocates of *positive* vs. *negative* freedom or liberty, which is also a debate between *paternalism* and *libertarianism*. Defenders of positive freedom define freedom as Socrates does: getting what we *really* want, which is well-being. Defenders of negative freedom define freedom as being able to do what one *thinks* one wants, even if one is mistaken about what constitutes well-being.

The critique of negative liberty is that it allows people to choose forms of slavery under the guise of freedom: addictive habits, junk culture, junk food, ignorance, sloth, ugliness, obesity, degradation—all the forms of physical and spiritual flattery that Socrates outlines. If real freedom is getting what we really want, namely well-being, then negative liberty is not freedom. It is simply a form of slavery to our own lowest desires. We are miserable because we are free, in the libertarian sense of freedom.

Thus, if we were *forced* to lead healthier lives—if we were prevented from buying addictive drugs and unhealthy foods, if we were forced to exercise and diet, if we were barred from empty and degrading pastimes—we would actually be *freer*, because we would be more likely to attain well-being, which is what freedom truly aims at. Thus, as Jean-Jacques Rousseau put it most pointedly and paradoxically, we can be "forced to be free."

DOING INJUSTICE VS. SUFFERING IT (468e–469c)

Polus grudgingly accepts Socrates' argument, yet he doesn't really believe it. Nor does he think that Socrates believes it either. Polus says that Socrates surely envies the power to rob, imprison, or kill anyone he pleases, whether justly or unjustly. Socrates replies that no, he does not envy unjust men. He pities them because they are wretched (*athlios*). Polus is incredulous. How can tyrants or powerful orators be wretched and pitiful?

Polus asks if Socrates pities those who kill justly. Socrates says no, because they are not wretched. But still, he does not envy the hangman his job.

Polus asks if those who are killed unjustly are wretched. No, says Socrates, they are to be pitied, but they are not made wretched just by being killed unjustly. Their killers, however, are made wretched by injustice.

Socrates explains that "doing injustice is the greatest of evils." Polus asks, "Is not suffering injustice a greater evil?" Socrates replies "Certainly not" (469b, Zeyl).

When Polus asks Socrates "Would you rather suffer than do injustice?," Socrates replies, "I would not like either, but if I must choose between them, I would rather suffer than do" (469c, Zeyl).

Let's pause here to take stock. To make sense of what Socrates is saying, let's create another table.

To understand this table, we must keep six sets of distinctions in mind.

1. Body vs. soul. Both bodies and souls may be harmed or helped by justice and injustice.
2. Things we do vs. things that happen to us, or, to put them more economically, deeds vs. fortune. We do deeds. Fortune happens to us.
3. Deeds can be just or unjust.
4. Fortune can be good or bad.
5. Deeds can be praiseworthy or blameworthy: good deeds are praiseworthy; bad deeds are blameworthy.

6. Fortune can be enviable or unenviable. We envy good fortune. We do not envy bad fortune. We can also envy good deeds and not envy bad deeds. But we don't praise and blame people for their good or bad fortune, because humans are not responsible for fortune.

	Doing (deeds)	Suffering (fortune)
Justly	❖ Good deeds ❖ Improve the soul but may harm the body (courage in battle) ❖ Praiseworthy and enviable	❖ Good fortune ❖ Improves the soul but may harm the body (for instance, just punishment) ❖ Enviable
Unjustly	❖ Bad deeds ❖ Harm the soul but may help the body (for instance, cowardice in battle) ❖ Blameworthy and not enviable	❖ Misfortune ❖ Does not harm the soul but may harm the body (for instance, unjust punishment) ❖ Not enviable or blameworthy

Deeds done justly are good deeds. Good deeds may harm the body. For instance, behaving courageously in battle exposes us to wounds or death. But good deeds improve the soul, which is why they are praiseworthy. We also think good character is enviable.

Deeds done unjustly are bad deeds. Bad deeds may benefit the body. For instance, cowardice in battle may save one's skin. But bad deeds harm the soul, which is why they are blameworthy and not enviable.

If something is done to you justly, that is good fortune. Good fortune may harm your body. For instance, just punishment for a crime. There is some question whether punishment will actually *improve* one's soul, expiate one's crimes, make one no longer worthy of blame, and even lead to happiness. None of that may be possible. But Socrates at least affirms that not being punished will make one more miserable than if one is caught. At best, punishment may only halt one's further degradation and deepening misery. But even that may be enviable.

If something is done to you unjustly, that is bad fortune. Bad fortune may harm your body. For instance, unjust punishment for a crime. But bad fortune cannot harm your soul. Or, to put it more precisely: it cannot harm your soul *unless you let it*. In other words, our souls can be harmed only by our own deeds, not by misfortune. People can make you physically miserable, but they can't make you into a monster unless you cooperate with them. (We must leave aside the case of extreme abuse in childhood, which destroys people before they attain moral agency. Aristotle would classify such people as "bestial" [*theriodes*], i.e., submoral and subhuman.[4]) Thus a victim of unjust punishment is not enviable because of his physical state. But neither is he spiritually corrupted and blameworthy.

Thus when Socrates says he would prefer neither to do nor to suffer injustice, he is saying that he wishes to act justly and be acted upon justly. But if he had to choose between suffering and doing injustice, he would prefer to suffer it. Why? Because the soul is more important than the body. Doing injustice always corrupts the soul. But merely suffering injustice does not corrupt the soul.

---

[4] Aristotle, *Nicomachean Ethics*, book VII, ch. 1 (1145a15–35) and ch. 5 (1148b15–1149a20).

Crime & Punishment

The Case of Tyrants (469c–474b)

When Socrates declares that, if forced to choose between suffering and doing injustice, he would prefer to suffer it, Polus' response is telling: "Then you would not wish to be a tyrant?" To which Socrates replies, "Not if you mean by tyranny what I mean," which would be doing injustice. Polus makes clear that tyranny is "the power of doing whatever seems good to you in a city, killing, banishing, doing all things as you like" (469c, Zeyl).

Socrates points out that anyone could take a knife to the agora and stab anyone he pleases. Which implies the question: What makes tyrants so special? To which Polus replies: because if you stabbed a person at random, you "would be certain to be punished" (470a, Zeyl). In other words, what sets tyrants apart is that they can *get away* with their crimes. Polus is assuming that "punishment is an evil."

At this point, Socrates has gotten Polus to accept that true freedom and power is doing what is good for oneself. But he has not yet explained the connection between benefitting oneself and justice. Socrates says that deeds "are good when they are just, and evil when they are unjust" (470c, Zeyl).

Polus scoffs that Socrates is usually hard to refute, but even a child could refute that claim. Socrates says he would be in the child's debt if he could be relieved of his error, and in Polus' debt as well.

Polus offers an example from current events: Archelaus, the son of Perdiccas, had just become the king of Macedonia (470d). This would place the dialogue in 413 BCE Polus thinks that we can know that Archelaus is happy simply because he is now a king and can do whatever he pleases. Socrates says he cannot determine if the man is happy or wretched without getting to know him, meaning getting to know his character (470d).

Polus, however, scoffs at this. He thinks one can make such a judgment from afar, based simply on Archelaus' position in life. Polus says, "Then clearly, Socrates, you would say that you did not even know whether the Great King is happy" (470d, Zeyl), as if this were a *reductio ad absurdum* of his position. The Great King is how the Greeks referred to the Persian Emperor, by far the richest and most powerful man in their time. As far as Polus is concerned, if any man is happy, it would have to be the Great King.

To this Socrates makes a surprising response: "And I should speak the truth; for I do not know how he stands in the matter of education [*paideia*] and justice [*dike*]" (470e, Zeyl). Polus is incredulous, asking "Does happiness consist entirely of these?" Socrates replies flatly, "Yes, indeed, Polus, that is my doctrine; men and women who are noble and good [*kalon kagathon*] are also happy, as I maintain, and the unjust and evil are wretched" (470e, Zeyl). These are very straightforward knowledge claims from the philosopher who allegedly claimed that he knew only his own ignorance.

Socrates' principle implies that Archelaus is wretched if he is wicked. Polus then lists the wicked acts by which Archelaus seized the Macedonian throne, after which Socrates chides him for presenting a speech, not an argument, much less a refutation of his views. But Polus is certain that Socrates already agrees with him. Why wouldn't he, since everyone else apparently believes what Polus believes?

Socrates then launches into a speech on proof in which he contrasts how rhetoricians persuade in the court of law with how philosophers persuade in dialogue (471e–472d). In the law courts, the more witnesses of good repute who support an unjust cause, the more likely it is to triumph, whereas men with justice on their side may fail without witnesses on their side as well. Polus can cite all the great men of Athens in favor of his views, but that does not matter, for it cannot convince Socrates that he is wrong. Only a better argument can do that.

If argument is all that matters, then Socrates wins if he can convince Polus, and Polus wins if he can convince Socrates. The rest of society does not matter at all.

The distinction between these two forms of argument is important, because they are arguing about moral questions. Moral knowledge is honorable. Moral ignorance is shameful. Beyond that, the chief moral questions are the nature of happiness and misery, which are not matters of idle speculation. They are of vital practical importance to all men, because we care about *our happiness* and *our wretchedness*.

Socrates then asks Polus if he believes that an "unjust" man can be "happy." Polus says "certainly" (472d, Zeyl). Then Socrates asks if an unjust man will still be happy if he is punished. Polus says "No, in that case he will be most wretched" (472d, Zeyl). Socrates, however, holds the precise opposite view. An unjust man cannot be happy under any circumstances, but he will be most wretched if he is unlucky enough not to be caught and properly punished.

Polus scoffs at this, launching into another speech:

What do you mean? If a man is detected in an unjust attempt to make himself a tyrant, and when detected is racked, castrated, has his eyes burned out, and — after having had all sorts of great injuries inflicted on him, and having seen his wife and children suffer the like — is at last impaled or tarred and burned alive, will he be happier than if he escapes, becomes a tyrant, and continues his whole life doing what he likes and holding the reins of government, the envy and admiration both of citizens and strangers? Is that the paradox which, as you say, cannot be refuted? (473c–d, Zeyl)

Socrates just brushes this off as more rhetoric: "Now, well-born Polus, you are just trying to raise goosebumps instead of refuting me. Just before you were calling witnesses. But please refresh my memory a little. Did you say, 'in an *unjust* attempt to make himself a tyrant'?" (473d, Zeyl).

Polus says, "yes." To which Socrates responds that neither will be happy, the successful tyrant or the unsuccessful one, but the successful tyrant will be the more wretched. Even though the unsuccessful tyrant meets a terrible end, at least it will be brief, and it will halt a long decline even deeper into infamy.

Polus simply laughs. When Socrates chides him that laughter is not an argument, Polus turns to the crowd and states that nobody would agree with Socrates. Socrates replies, "O Polus, I am not one of your politicians" (473e, Zeyl). Then he recounts his incompetence in taking a vote the previous year (which would set this dialogue in 405 BCE). Now, as then, Socrates is not cut out for counting votes.

But if Polus has a better argument, Socrates is all ears. But if not, Socrates wants to take over, for he believes that he can win the argument by producing only one witness: Polus himself. He is confident, because "I believe that you and I and every man really believe that doing injustice is worse than suffering it, and not to be punished is worse than being punished" (474b, Zeyl). Polus, of course, is skeptical. But he agrees to be questioned.

POLUS REFUTED (474b–475e)

Before Socrates begins his refutation of Polus, he establishes that Polus believes the following claims.

1. Suffering injustice is worse for a victim than doing injustice is for a perpetrator.
2. Doing injustice is more shameful (*aischron*) for a perpetrator than suffering injustice is for a victim.
3. The more shameful is not the greater evil (*kakon*).
4. In sum: "The noble [*kalon*] is not the same as the good [*agathon*], or the disgraceful [*aischron*] as the evil [*kakon*]."

On the contrary, Socrates believes that doing injustice is both evil (*kakon*) and shameful (*aischron*). He also believes that, deep down, Polus believes the same thing but doesn't know it yet. Socrates' argument aims to get Polus in touch with his real beliefs.

Socrates begins his refutation by establishing the principle that things (bodies, colors, figures, sounds, institutions) are *kalon* (noble, fine, beautiful) *either* because they are *useful* (*chresimon, ophelimon*) *or* because they give us *pleasure* (*hedone*). Polus agrees with this heartily. Socrates also establishes that something is *aischron* (shameful, the opposite of *kalon*) because it is *either* painful (*luperon*) *or* useless/evil (*kakon*). Again, Polus agrees.

From this, Socrates argues that if one thing is nobler than another, it is because it is either more useful, pleasurable, or both. Likewise, if one thing is more shameful than another, it is because it is either more useless/evil, more painful, or both. Polus assents to both claims.

Then Socrates analyzes Polus' claim that doing injustice is more shameful than suffering it. If doing injustice is more shameful than suffering injustice, then it must be either (1) more useless/evil or (2) more painful or (3) both.

Doing injustice is not more painful than suffering it. For instance, the man who commits an assault feels less pain than the victim. *Thus doing injustice must be more shameful by being more useless/evil.* (If doing injustice is not more painful than suffering it, then it cannot be shameful in virtue of being *both* more useless/evil *and* more painful.)

Socrates now confronts Polus with a contradiction in his own beliefs. Before Socrates began his argument, Polus assented to the claim that the more shameful (doing injustice) is not more evil (*kakon*) than suffering it. But now Polus has come around to the admission that doing injustice increases one's level of evil. How then can Polus really believe that it is better to do injustice than to suffer it? Socrates asks Polus to level with him, to speak honestly from his heart. "Would you prefer a greater evil or a greater shame to a lesser one? Answer, Polus, and fear not; for you will come to no harm if you nobly resign yourself into the healing hand of the argument as to a physician without shrinking, and either say 'yes' or 'no' to me."

> POLUS: I should say "no."
> SOCRATES: Would any other man prefer a greater to a lesser evil?
> POLUS: No, not according to this way of putting the case, Socrates.
> SOCRATES: Then I said truly, Polus, that neither you, nor I, nor any man, would rather do injustice than suffer it; for to do injustice is the greater evil of the two.
> POLUS: That is the conclusion. (475e, Zeyl)

Socrates has tamed the colt, sometimes with harsh words,

sometimes with gentle ones. But simply by speaking.

IS IT BETTER FOR THE GUILTY TO ESCAPE JUST PUNISHMENT? (475e–479e)

Socrates then turns to the question of whether it is better for the guilty to escape punishment. Earlier, Polus said yes. Now, Socrates will change his mind.

Before beginning his argument, Socrates first establishes that suffering punishment means being justly corrected when one does wrong. Then he establishes that just things are *kalon* (noble, fine, beautiful).

Socrates' argument begins with the premise: where there is an agent, there must be a patient. Meaning, whenever there is action, there is also the acted upon. If someone strikes, there must be something struck. If someone burns, there will be something burnt. If someone cuts, there will be something cut. These examples are clearly chosen to bring punishment to mind.

Socrates' second premise is that the agent communicates its qualities to the patient. For instance, if someone strikes violently and quickly, that which is struck will be struck violently and quickly. If a cut is deep and painful, the one cut will experience it as deep and painful.

Socrates' third premise is that a punisher is an agent, and the punished party is a patient.

If a punisher punishes justly, then he communicates that quality to the punished party. If this is true, then one becomes more just by being punished. And, as has been established, justice is *kalon*. Thus just punishment makes one better than escaping just punishment. Socrates specifies that being justly punished means improving the soul: "He who is punished is delivered from the evil of his soul" (477a, Zeyl).

Socrates then argues that the evil of the soul is the greatest evil. The greatest evil of one's possessions is poverty. The greatest evil of one's body is sickness. The greatest evil of the soul consists of things like "injustice and ignorance and cowardice," in other words, vices (477b, Zeyl).

Polus readily admits that vice is more shameful than the other evils. Now Socrates offers an argument that vice is more evil than poverty and sickness. Recall that if something is worse, it is worse either because it is more painful, more useless/evil, or both. Neither Polus nor Socrates thinks that vice is necessarily more painful than poverty or sickness. Thus vice must be bad in virtue of its uselessness/evil. Indeed, vice is characterized by "monstrously great harm" and "astonishing evil." Thus, "injustice and intemperance, and in general the depravity of the soul, are the greatest of evils" (477e, Zeyl).

If the art of money-making delivers us from poverty, and if the art of medicine delivers us from sickness, Socrates suggests that the art of the judge would deliver us from the sicknesses of the soul by means of just punishment. Since the soul is more important than property and the body, justice is the most important of the arts.

If the art of justice is more important than money-making and medicine, it is more important in terms of pleasure or usefulness or both. Since punishment is not pleasurable, justice must be more important in terms of its usefulness, specifically for restoring the health of the most important thing: the soul.

In terms of physical health, the happiest is the man who never gets sick. The next happiest is the man who gets sick but is then healed. The worst off is the man who gets sick and is never healed because he refuses to undergo the necessary pains.

In terms of spiritual health, the happiest is the virtuous man who never does wrong. The next happiest is the man who commits injustice but receives just punishment. The worst off is the man who commits injustice and gets away with it. He is never stopped from doing bad things. Nor does he have the opportunity to purge his soul of the effects of past injustices. He just sinks deeper and deeper into vice. The greater the crimes, the greater the suffering. Thus, "he lives worst who commits the greatest crimes, and who, being the most unjust of men, succeeds in escaping rebuke or correction or punishment; and this, as you say, has been accomplished by Archelaus and other tyrants and rhetoricians and potentates" (479d–e, Zeyl).

Socrates' argument raises three issues: Is this an adequate theory of punishment? Is justice rightly seen as an art? What is the use of rhetoric?

Is This an Adequate Theory of Punishment?

There are four basic theories of punishment: deterrence, retribution, restoration (of the victim), and rehabilitation (of the offender). None of them are adequate on their own, but all of them can be elements of a criminal justice system.

If our goal is deterring future crimes, then we really need only one punishment: death, death for murder, death for double parking, death for lying about the check being in the mail. Nothing deters like death. But we all recognize that there's something a bit excessive, perhaps even *unjust*, about death for double parking. So deterrence can't be all there is to punishment. The punishment must "fit" the crime. Socrates seems entirely indifferent to punishment as deterrence.

Retribution seems more in keeping with the idea of a fitting and balanced punishment. Serious crimes merit serious punishments; less serious crimes merit less serious punishments.

But what is the purpose of punishment? Is it to restore what was damaged or lost? In cases of property crimes, that would be best. If someone burns your house down, shouldn't the criminal buy you a new house, rather than you, the victim, contribute to housing and feeding him for years in prison? Socrates' theory of punishment, however, makes no reference whatsoever to making the victim better off, only the criminal.

Of course, with the most terrible crimes, restoration is simply impossible. Is the purpose of punishment, then, to make other people feel better, as a catharsis for feelings of injury? I see no reason why vengeance should not play a role in punishing particularly heinous crimes. Why shouldn't the guilty suffer? Why shouldn't the aggrieved take pleasure in that? Socrates seems entirely indifferent to these motives as well.

Socrates is positing a very narrow conception of just punishment here: rehabilitation. Rehabilitative justice is entirely about *improving the criminal*. It is about doctoring his soul. This approach to punishment might make sense when talking about childrearing and education, since the characters of young people are still relatively fluid. Beyond that, we love the little "criminals" and want them to do better because we envision them becoming adult members of society. Rehabilitative punishment might also work with adults who commit minor crimes and who can be made into good citizens.

But how would spiritual rehabilitation work with hardened criminals? How would it work for people who commit monstrous crimes? How would it work with Archelaus or any other tyrant? Since Socrates' goal seems to be the restoration of the criminal's soul to health, that would presumably exclude the death penalty entirely.

Socrates' views here seem entirely too naïve and optimistic. The best we might be able to do for most criminals is simply stop them from committing more crimes. The closest thing to rehabilitation, then, may simply be *arresting* them. Restoring their souls to a state of justice may be impossible. Moreover, if a criminal is incarcerated, he generally becomes worse, because prisons are vast schools and playgrounds for crime and depravity. Thus usually the only people who are benefitted by arresting a criminal are his potential innocent victims.

Moreover, isn't there something obscene about society taking the role of stern and loving father with dictators, serial killers, and cannibals? Do we really envision a world in which they will be restored to society? Aristotle recognized that it is possible for human beings to fall below the level of moral agency and become "bestial" (*theriodes*). When dealing with the bestial, the only possible medicine for the soul may be euthanasia. They might be better off dead. There's little question that the rest of us would be better off if they were dead as well. But the public interest is never mentioned by Socrates here.

One final note. If you, dear reader, have gotten away with a crime and now feel in need of healing, I hope that you will not be so naïve as to turn yourself over to the local authorities, wherever you are, in the hope that they will restore your soul to health. That's not their goal. If anyone is spiritually improved by our criminal justice system, it is only by accident. You are better off talking to a priest or a psychotherapist.

So is it really better to be punished than to escape punishment? Yes, if punishment can actually improve your soul. If your soul is irredeemable, then you are still better off if your crimes are stopped. There's at least a chance that will prevent you from sinking deeper into vice (to say nothing of the interest of the rest of society in stopping you). But that can be accomplished simply by arrest. Punishment may produce no improvement whatsoever. Indeed, given most criminal justice systems today, incarceration will probably make you worse.

Socrates is committed to arguing that justice is always in our self-interest. This is commendable, for it gives us reasons to do the right thing of our own free will. But where self-interest fails to produce justice, we can always fall back on arguments from the common good. And where arguments fail, we can always resort to force; the rest of society can *make* justice in our interest.

IS JUSTICE AN ART?

There is a deeper problem with Plato's account of justice in the *Gorgias*. He treats it as an art (*techne*). But is justice really an art like medicine? In such dialogues as the *Meno*, *Charmides*, and *Euthydemus*, Plato explores the problems of treating moral wisdom as a *techne*. This is the error of the sophists.

In the *Gorgias*, however, Socrates does not challenge the idea that moral knowledge is a form of *techne*. Instead, he assumes that *techne* is the ultimate horizon. Within that horizon, he is fighting to establish philosophy, not sophistry, as the master art. Thus we should be watchful, for the whole argument of the *Gorgias* is premised on an idea treated as problematic elsewhere in Plato.

How does moral wisdom—virtues like courage, temperance, and justice—resemble *techne*, and how does it differ? The main resemblance is that both moral wisdom and *techne* are practical. They are all related to action. They change the world. Even what we think of as theoretical *technai*, like arithmetic and geometry, arise from practical problems and are applied back to them. So it is natural to model moral wisdom on *techne*.

Remember also that alongside the *technai* there are nontechnical knacks that also relate to action and production. They differ from *technai* insofar as they lack *logoi*, but they resemble them insofar as they are all practical.

But the analogy between *technai* and knacks on the one hand and moral wisdom on the other soon breaks down when we get more specific.

Such practical arts as shipbuilding, horse-training, and medicine all deal with delimited subject matters. Shipbuilders build ships. But they don't build houses; that is the job of housebuilders. Horse trainers train horses. But they don't train dogs or children. Medicine heals sickness. But it doesn't produce health. That is the job of the dietician and the physical trainer. We can also say that the various knacks have delimited subject matters. Cooking, for instance, existed as a knack long before it became a *techne*.

So if courage is an art, what is its delimited subject matter? What does it produce? The same questions can be asked about all virtues: temperance, prudence, justice. These virtues don't really have delimited fields of activity or products. Instead, one can do virtually anything *with* courage, temperance, prudence, or justice. Virtue isn't a particular product or action. Rather, it is a *manner of performing any act whatsoever*, including producing virtually anything.

Thus moral wisdom, unlike *techne*, doesn't have a particular subject matter. If *technai* and knacks have divided up and parceled out all realms of human affairs, then moral wisdom cannot find its place among them. It must stake out a higher-order realm of its own. Thus moral wisdom steps back from all realms of action and production and surveys them. If *technai* and knacks encompass all first-order activities, moral wisdom is a second-order activity. If *technai* and knacks are specialized, moral wisdom is comprehensive. If *technai* and knacks have their own activities and ends, those activities can still be performed in different manners, producing good or evil results. Thus, once moral wisdom steps back from all *technai* and knacks and surveys them from a higher vantage point, it directs them all in a particular manner: namely, toward the good.

This brings us to another important difference between *techne*/knack and moral wisdom. *Technai* and knacks are morally neutral. The same skills can produce radically different results. A pharmacist can cure or kill. The poison is in the dose. The skills of a surgeon also make him an effective torturer. Thus all arts and knacks need to be supplemented by moral wisdom to ensure they are used rightly. What is the standard of right? Producing human well-being.

If, however, *techne* is morally neutral, then it is unlike moral wisdom in an absolutely crucial way. Moral wisdom is obviously not morally neutral. Thus, returning to the scheme of the *Gorgias*, if legislation and justice are both concerned with the well-being of the soul (the first producing it, the second restoring it), then they are both forms of moral wisdom. Thus can we really speak of them as *technai*? If they were *technai*, wouldn't they need to look elsewhere for moral wisdom? Is the *techne* of justice, then, a contradiction in terms?

Am I just getting hung up on words here? No. For instance, I have no objection to describing moral wisdom as a very special kind of *techne*, as long as one does not lose sight of how distinct it is from all first-order *technai*.

But when two things are different in fundamental ways — and what difference is more fundamental than the difference between the moral and the amoral — perhaps we should find different words for them. For instance, I would like to argue that moral wisdom is better likened to a knack than a *techne*.

There's another difference between moral wisdom and *techne* proper. Both *technai* and knacks are bodies of practice. They differ in that *technai* articulate their practices into principles and rules. *Technai*, in short, have *logoi*. Because *technai* have *logoi*, they can be explained and taught verbally, whereas knacks can only be learned by mute imitation and practice. Socrates claims that moral wisdom, unlike *techne*, is not teachable. Indeed, Socrates noted that even conspicuously virtuous people who spare no expense in educating their children somehow fail to pass on their virtues.

However, such dialogues as the *Symposium* and *Theages* testify that even though Socrates did not teach virtue, young men who hung around him and imitated him still became more virtuous.[1] So if virtue is not a *techne*, teachable through *logoi*, it may still be a knack, which can be learned by imitation and practice. This is why I characterize Socratic/Platonic wisdom as "The

---

[1] Plato, *Theages*, 128c; *Symposium*, 221c–d.

ability to make right use of all things." Wisdom is not an art. It is not a theory. It exists first and foremost as a knack. It is a kind of moral know-how.

But if moral wisdom is a kind of knack, then couldn't it be turned into a *techne* simply by articulating its implicit *logoi*? Socrates might simply reply that if it were possible, it would have happened by then. After all, given the crucial importance of morality, surely we have a strong motive to make it into a *techne*. So if a moral *techne* were possible, surely it would have happened in the nearly two-and-half millennia since the time of Socrates?

Beyond that, there is a real question as to whether any knacks can be *fully* and *meaningfully* articulated in the form of *logoi*. We always know more than we can say. That goes for know-how as well. Therefore, any articulation of tacit know-how is inevitably an abridgement, a reduction, in a crucial sense a *falsification* of the richness of practice. Such rules may be useful for teaching. But they are merely adjuncts to the primary way that we learn any practice: imitation and repetition of the practice itself.

If philosophy is a knack, not a *techne*, this would explain why Plato claimed that he never wrote his philosophy down, i.e., sought to fully articulate it into *logoi*. Instead, he philosophized in dialogue with others. Plato also chose to write dialogues, not philosophical treatises. The Platonic dialogues of course contain *logoi*. But they are also works of art which *imitate* Socrates and other philosophers in the *practice* of philosophizing. Thus reading Plato makes it possible not just to learn *logoi* but also—and more importantly—to imitate Socrates and learn his knack.

It may be depressing to think that something as important as moral wisdom is less teachable than carpentry. Fortunately, according to Socrates, we don't need to be taught virtue, since we are all *born* with moral knowledge. Thus moral education is less about putting articulated knowledge into us than awakening us to something far richer: a practical wisdom that we have known all along.

If we always-already possess moral wisdom, that brings us to another strong disanalogy with *techne*. *Techne* is a form of specialized expert knowledge. When we want to build a house, train a dog, or lance a boil, we go to the experts, because they know more than the rest of us. But if we all possess moral wisdom, in what sense can there be moral experts?

Of course, just because we all possess moral wisdom, that doesn't imply that we are all equally morally accomplished. Obviously, some people are more virtuous than others. But they are not more virtuous in terms of knowledge. Instead, they are more virtuous in terms of putting their knowledge into practice. Let's call these moral exemplars "heroes." How do we learn from moral exemplars? We imitate them. Thus, when we face moral questions, one way to get an answer is to ask ourselves what a hero would do in the same situation.

Beyond that, just because we all possess the same moral wisdom, that doesn't imply that we are all equally good at dispensing moral advice. Setting aside differences in intelligence, some people are better at articulating their tacit moral wisdom than others. Thus we can turn to such people for moral advice. Let's call these people "philosophers."

Finally, if we all have innate moral wisdom, the first way such wisdom is articulated is in the form of moral opinions. Longstanding and widespread moral opinions are what we call "traditions." There is a moral wisdom embodied in traditions, especially those that are the most ancient and widespread. Thus such traditions should be treated with deference and authority, not simply brushed aside impatiently by those who claim technical expertise.

There can be higher-order arts that dispose of the products of other arts. Generals, architects, theater directors, and rhetoricians all make use of first-order arts. Is there, then, a ruling art that stands above, surveys, and employs all first-order arts? Would this not be the master art, the ruling art, the kingly art?

Yes, such an all-encompassing *techne* is conceivable. But it can't really rule, for insofar as it is a *techne*, it is morally neutral. Thus to rule rightly, it must look to a higher authority than *techne*: moral wisdom.

Wisdom makes right use possible because it knows the morally good. Wisdom itself, however, does not need to be used rightly. It *just is* the right use of all things. You can never be too wise for your own good. Wisdom is unconditionally good, whereas everything else is good only on the condition that it is used rightly. Wisdom, therefore, has the right to rule—over everything.

But how does wisdom rule if it cannot be modeled on *techne*? The wisely-ordered society is not a technocracy, ruled by moral experts, *because there is no moral techne. Thus there are no moral experts.* But wisdom can rule if the state follows heroes, philosophers, and moral traditions. Nor should it disdain the participation of the masses, whose moral intuitions are often superior to the deliverances of experts. Whatever form such a regime takes, it will not be a technocracy.

WHAT USE IS RHETORIC? (480a–481b)

Having established that it is better to suffer injustice than to do it, and better to be punished for one's crimes than to get away with them, Socrates returns to the question of rhetoric, specifically forensic rhetoric, which is practiced in the law courts. Recall that Socrates has argued that rhetoric in the law courts is a sham of justice. The purpose of justice is to restore health to the soul. The purpose of rhetoric is to avoid justice by giving the false appearance of being just. But if there is no advantage in merely *appearing* to be just, as opposed to actually *being* just, then what use is rhetoric? If Socrates is right, we don't *want* to get away with our crimes.

Of course, rhetoric is not merely used to make the guilty look innocent. It is also used to make the innocent look guilty. And this suggests a use for rhetoric: What if an innocent man is accused of a crime? What if, moreover, the innocent man *looks guilty* to the untutored eyes of the public? Wouldn't rhetoric be helpful in convincing the public of the truth, in getting opinion to match reality? For example, wouldn't rhetoric have helped Socrates?[2] We will return to this question, for this precise objection is raised by Callicles.

Socrates has established that the happiest men do no wrong. But if a man should err, Socrates says, "He ought of his own

---

[2] Plato depicts Socrates as a masterful rhetorician in the *Apology of Socrates*. See my commentary on the *Apology* in *The Trial of Socrates*.

accord to go where he will be immediately punished; he will run to the judge, as he would to the physician, in order that the disease of injustice may not be rendered chronic and become the incurable cancer of the soul" (480a–b, Zeyl).

This, of course, would only make sense if judges actually possess a reliable *techne* of diagnosing and healing spiritual illness. That was certainly not the case in ancient Athens. Nor is it the case today. Thus even if one were guilty of a crime in ancient Athens, the last place one could expect healing would be from the law courts. Indeed, if you are serious about restoring your spiritual health, you would want to be acquitted, precisely so you can work on overcoming your guilt. And that would require rhetoric. The Catholic confessional is far more likely to restore the soul than any criminal justice system.

Moreover, running to a judge for punishment would only work if all spiritual diseases can be healed. If Socrates wishes to lean on the medical analogy, what about the spiritual equivalents of incurable diseases? What about spiritual diseases that are not only incurable but highly infectious?

If we should be the first to accuse ourselves of our crimes, Socrates suggests that this might be a use for rhetoric after all. Of course, in this case, rhetoric would be used to make reality apparent, not cover it up. This is a legitimate use of rhetoric and should be taken seriously. But it becomes hard to do so, because at this point in the dialogue, it becomes clear that Socrates is being intentionally paradoxical and provocative:

> So, if oratory is used to defend injustice, Polus, one's own or that of one's relatives, companions, or children, or that of one's country when it acts unjustly, it is of no use to us at all, unless one takes it to be useful for the opposite purpose: that he should accuse himself first and foremost, and then too his family and anyone else dear to him who happens to behave unjustly at any time; and that he should not keep his wrongdoing hidden but bring it out into the open so that he may pay his due and get well; and compel himself and the others not to play the coward, but to grit his teeth and present himself with grace and courage as to

a doctor for cauterization and surgery, pursuing what's good and admirable without taking any account of the pain. And if his unjust behavior merits flogging, he should present himself to be whipped; if it merits imprisonment, to be imprisoned; if a fine, to pay it; if exile, to be exiled; and if execution, to be executed. He should be his own chief accuser, and the accuser of other members of his family, and use his oratory for the purpose of getting rid of the worst thing there is, injustice, as the unjust acts are being exposed. Are we to affirm or deny this, Polus? (480b–d, Zeyl)

Polus is skeptical:

POLUS: I think these statements are absurd, Socrates, though no doubt you think they agree with those expressed earlier.
SOCRATES: Then either we should abandon those, or else these necessarily follow?
POLUS: Yes, that's how it is. (480e, Zeyl)

Polus is obviously uncomfortable with Socrates' line of argument, and with good reason. Accusing one's own family of crimes contradicts a widespread and deeply held Greek conviction that families should stick together, not accuse one another of crimes before the civil authorities. Even today the principle that spouses cannot be compelled to testify against each other is a matter of law.

Accusing one's family brings to mind the behavior of Euthyphro in the dialogue of the same name, who scandalized his family by accusing his father of murder. Euthyphro's act verges on father-beating, which is the outrage produced by Socrates' youth-corrupting arguments in Aristophanes' *Clouds*.[3] In the *Euthyphro*, however, Socrates works to dissuade Euthyphro from accusing his father. Thus we should be on guard. There may be something dangerously simplistic about Socrates' position here.

---

[3] See my commentary on the *Euthyphro* in *The Trial of Socrates*.

Socrates, moreover, is giving us an engraved invitation to question his premises. What premises does Socrates in the *Gorgias* share with Euthyphro?

First, in both cases, they are talking about justice. Euthyphro claims to be accusing his father out of piety, but piety is understood to be part of justice.

Second, in both cases, the accusers believe that traditional beliefs about family members sticking together don't matter in the face of *expert knowledge* about justice. Expert knowledge is supposedly more true than moral traditions. In Euthyphro's case, he claims to be an expert on piety due to divine inspiration, thus he has license to ignore the opinions of non-experts on family solidarity. In the *Gorgias*, Socrates claims that justice is a *techne*, meaning that expert knowledge of justice exists, such that we can ignore the opinions of non-experts as well.

There are, however, good reasons to be skeptical of expert moral knowledge and to respect widespread moral opinions.

First, if there is moral expertise, especially moral *techne*, then virtue should be as teachable as any other *techne*. Yet it isn't. Again, Socrates noted that virtuous people routinely fail to make their own children virtuous. And nothing has changed since then. A *techne* of virtue would be a wonderful thing. Moral and religious thinkers have worked unstintingly for millennia to develop one. Yet none exists. At this point, the most plausible explanation for this failure is that a moral *techne* is impossible.

Second, for Socrates the unteachability of virtue is not a problem because all of us *already know* the truth about the good life. But it is largely tacit knowledge. The first articulation of tacit moral knowledge is in the form of widespread moral opinions, the very opinions that the moral experts wish to brush aside.

Socrates concludes his discussion with Polus with more paradox and provocation. If it is better for the guilty to be punished than to get away with their crimes, then the cruelest revenge upon our enemies would be to help them to go unpunished. This, Socrates thinks, would be another way to make rhetoric useful.

> . . . suppose a man had to harm someone, . . . if the enemy did something unjust against another person, then our

man should see to it in every way, both in what he does and what he says, that his enemy does not go to the judge and pay his due.... And if his crimes merit the death penalty, he should scheme to keep him from being executed, preferably never to die at all but to live forever in corruption, but failing that, to have him live as long as possible in that condition. Yes, this is the sort of thing I think oratory is useful for, Polus, since for the person who has no intention of behaving unjustly it doesn't seem to me to have much use — if in fact it has any use at all — since its usefulness hasn't in any way become apparent so far. (480e–481b, Zeyl)

Note, however, that Socrates hinges this whole argument on a conditional statement: "suppose a man had to harm someone." We know from the *Republic*, however, that Socrates rejects the definition of justice as helping one's friends and harming one's enemies.[4]

According to Socrates, one can justly use forensic rhetoric for oneself and for others. One can also use it in cases of innocence and guilt. These possibilities yield the following table:

JUST USES OF FORENSIC RHETORIC

	If Guilty	If Innocent
For Oneself	Self-accusation, i.e., confessing one's crimes	Self-defense, i.e., proving one's innocence
For Others	Prosecuting wrongdoers	Defending the innocent

---

[4] Plato, *Republic*, book I, 335e–36a.

Socrates only deals with the first column: forensic rhetoric used on oneself and others in case of guilt. The two possibilities Socrates discusses are highly questionable: accusing oneself of crimes and exculpating one's enemies so they are denied punishment and thus suffer more than they otherwise would. The first option would make sense only if one had a criminal justice system that actually worked to improve one's soul. The second option is based on a definition of justice that Socrates rejects.

Socrates has won his argument with Polus. So why does he continue to beat Polus over the head with such provocative and problematic arguments? Is this just arrogance, as we saw in the *Greater Alcibiades*, where Socrates was also not content with winning the argument but instead provoked Alcibiades by attacking the great statesmen of Athens? Was Socrates trying to prolong the discussion with Polus out of sheer contentiousness?

Now let's return to the table and discuss the highly significant possibilities Socrates declined to mention. First of all, exculpating the guilty is not a *good* use of forensic rhetoric, but prosecuting the guilty definitely is.

Socrates' own categories also imply that it is a legitimate use of forensic rhetoric to defend one's own innocence and the innocence of others. If forensic rhetoric can be used for the good, then one would be foolish to disdain it. And Socrates was no fool.

Taking Stock

Before we turn to Socrates' long debate with Callicles, let's summarize the different forms of rhetoric that we have been introduced to thus far, to map out holes in Socrates' arguments, and perhaps to project what is to come.

First, there are three forms of rhetoric in the *Gorgias*: epideictic rhetoric or display speeches (the speeches themselves are displays, but things are also displayed in the speeches; for Socrates, the latter is most important); deliberative rhetoric, which is used in legislative assemblies; and forensic rhetoric, which is used in law courts.

Second, each form of rhetoric can be good or bad, which yields the following table of possibilities.

FORMS OF RHETORIC, GOOD & BAD

	Good	Bad
Epideictic	Edifying speeches	Corrupting speeches
Deliberative	Legislative rhetoric	Sophistry
Forensic	Judicial rhetoric	Oratory

Deliberative and forensic rhetoric are explicitly discussed in the *Gorgias*. But epideictic rhetoric is referred to only in its absence. Socrates contrived to miss Gorgias' stunt speech. But epideictic rhetoric is also *displayed* in the *Gorgias*, most notably at the very end, when Socrates takes Callicles by the hand and leads him into the underworld for judgment.

If the myth of the *Gorgias* is a public display speech designed to edify its listeners, what would be an example of a corrupting display speech? One example could be Gorgias' *Encomium of Helen*, a dazzling technical display to exculpate a guilty woman. Perhaps Socrates skipped just this speech, or one like it.

When Socrates developed the distinction between pandering knacks and edifying arts, he defined sophistry as a pandering counterfeit of legislation, for legislation imparts spiritual health to the city while sophistry corrupts the city by imparting gratifying counterfeits of health. Likewise, Socrates defined oratory as a pandering counterfeit of justice. Justice restores the health of the city by removing injustice, whereas oratory corrupts the city by merely imparting gratifying simulacra of justice.

Legislation and justice are not forms of rhetoric. They are specialized arts (*technai*). But, as was made clear in the discussion with Gorgias, rhetoric is necessary to explain expert knowledge to laymen. Therefore, every art needs a rhetoric of its own. Moreover, since legislation and justice are guided by the good, their rhetorics are as well. Thus they will be genuinely edifying.

Thus far, Socrates only discusses public and collective forms of the care of the soul, namely legislation as a way to impart spiritual health and criminal justice as a way to restore it. But this leaves out private and individual forms of caring for *one's own* soul. Given that Athens has a terrible regime that is almost indifferent to imparting or restoring spiritual health, surely private and personal care of the soul are paramount. This absence will be underscored in Socrates' debate with Callicles, which is structured around the distinction between the private life and the public life.

The care of the soul can be public and private, and it takes the form of imparting and restoring health. These options can be summarized as follows:

THE CARE OF THE SOUL, PUBLIC & PRIVATE

	Public Care of the Soul	**Private Care of the Soul**
Imparting Health	Legislation	Philosophical "gymnastic" [?]
Restoring Health	Justice	Philosophical "medicine" [?]

There is no question that the private care of the soul is philosophy. The only question is: What are the names of the two forms of private care of the soul? As a place-holder, I will deem them philosophical gymnastic and medicine, on the analogy with the care of the body.

MIGHT & RIGHT

HARMONY WITH SELF VS. HARMONY WITH OTHERS (481b–482c)

After beating Polus, Socrates continued to badger him with intentionally provocative and paradoxical arguments until Callicles cut in. The conversation between Socrates and Callicles takes up the rest of the *Gorgias*.

At first, Callicles does not speak directly to Socrates. Instead, he turns to Socrates' friend Chaerephon and says, "Tell me, Chaerephon, is Socrates serious about this, or is he joking?" To which Chaerephon says, "I think he's dead serious about this, Callicles. There's nothing like asking him though" (481b, Zeyl). Again, the dramatic detail of turning to Socrates' student before Socrates himself underscores the problem of the teacher-student relationship, which is a version of the deeper metaphysical issue of the relationship of the original to the copy.

Callicles is a vivid, well-drawn character. He could have been a real person. There is no evidence for his existence outside of Plato's *Gorgias*, but that doesn't necessarily prove anything, given that very few ancient historical records have survived.

Callicles presents himself as thoroughly shameless and unscrupulous. But in fact, he has a number of intellectual virtues. Indeed, he's the most philosophical of Socrates' three interlocutors.

First, Callicles is tough-minded. He realizes that in order to defend the idea that might is right, one has to overturn all conventional notions of right and wrong. Gorgias doesn't see this. He thinks he is teaching people how to get ahead while leaving the received moral order intact. Polus thinks he is free of traditional morals, but he is mistaken. He will not say that doing injustice is bad. But he still thinks it is shameful, which is how Socrates defeats him.

Second, Callicles is a daring thinker. He's not bound by convention. That's a prerequisite for being truly philosophical. No matter how much lip service one might feel it prudent to pay to reigning conventions, one can't let them inside. One can't let them impede one's thinking. Callicles has liberated his mind from purely conventional notions of justice to a greater degree than Gorgias and Polus.

One sign of Callicles' emancipation from convention is his outspokenness, which Socrates praises. Callicles will say things that he thinks are true, even if they might damage his reputation. Despite his wealth and polish, there is something ungentlemanly about Callicles which verges on Socrates' own philosophical boorishness.

Third, the flipside of Callicles' emancipation from convention is his concern about nature, specifically what's right by nature. The first known usage of the phrase "law of nature" or "right by nature" ("*nomon . . . physeos*") appears in the *Gorgias* in the mouth of Callicles (483e). Thus Callicles isn't a completely amoral person. He is only amoral by conventional standards. But he upholds nature as a standard. On this basis, he argues for the admirability of the life the sophists teach: the public life of pursuing freedom for oneself through power over others, the paradigm of which is the tyrant.

Socrates has no quarrel with Callicles' tough-mindedness, unconventionality, outspokenness, and appeal to nature. But Socrates argues that the idea of natural right leads to a very different life than the one Callicles defends. It is the life of the philosopher, not the tyrant.

Callicles turns to Socrates and says:

> Tell me, Socrates, are we to take you as being serious now or joking? For if you are serious, and these things you're saying are really true [namely that it is better to suffer injustice than to do it], won't this human life of ours be turned upside down, and won't everything we do evidently be the opposite of what we should do? (481c, Zeyl)

Socrates replies:

> Well Callicles, if human beings didn't share common experiences, some sharing one, others sharing another, but one of us had some unique experience not shared by oth-

ers, it wouldn't be easy for him to communicate what he experienced to the other. I say this because I realize that you and I are both now actually sharing a common experience. Each of us is a lover of two objects, I of Alcibiades, Cleinias' son, and of philosophy. And you of the *demos* [the Greek word for the people of Athens] and the Demos who's the son of Pyrilampes. [Pyrilampes was Plato's stepfather, and so Demos was Plato's stepbrother. Demos might very well be present in the audience.] I notice that in each case you're unable to contradict your beloved . . . (481c–e, Zeyl)

We're getting a sense of who Callicles is. He's in love with the people, which means that he wants to rule the people. To rule the people, he flatters them. This goes back to the distinction between rhetoric as flattery, which panders and corrupts by telling people what they want to hear, as opposed to the true political art, which builds the people up, which sometimes means telling them things that they need to hear but don't want to hear. If the people change their mind, Callicles must change his mind to please them. Thus Callicles not only corrupts the people, he corrupts himself in the bargain. Moreover, he has the same sort of mutually corrupting relationship with his boyfriend.

This is not a very flattering picture of Callicles. He's a people pleaser, who puts the good opinion of others over pursuing and holding fast to the truth. Most politicians and public figures are people pleasers, which means they are willing to overthrow solid principles or affirm absolutely deadly ones because it pleases the person they're speaking to in the moment.

Because Callicles is a panderer, he thinks that Socrates is the same way. But he couldn't be more mistaken. For Socrates loves philosophy, and philosophy, unlike the people of Athens, is not fickle. The public is the realm of opinion, and opinion is always shifting and changing. Philosophy is the pursuit of truth, which is unchanging. Philosophy says the same things over and over, whereas the public is constantly changing its mind. The love of truth makes Socrates grounded and internally consistent. The love of the public makes Callicles internally contradictory.

The same dynamic is present in the personal relationships of Callicles and Socrates. Callicles is in love with Demos, the son of Pyrilampes, whom he pursues through flattery. This flattery means adopting Demos' shifting opinions as slavishly as Callicles adopts the opinions of the Athenian *demos*. Thus Callicles corrupts both Demos and himself.

The fact that Demos was the stepbrother of Plato, combined with the vividness of his depiction of Callicles, inclines me to think that the Platonic character of Callicles is based on a real person. It strikes me as unlikely that Plato would invent a fictional paramour for a real member of his family.

Socrates, however, has a very different relationship with Alcibiades, as we have seen in the *Greater Alcibiades*. There is no question that Socrates flatters Alcibiades at first, appealing to his grandiose self-image and aspirations. But once Socrates has Alcibiades' attention, he systematically tries to lead him away from tyranny toward philosophy. This is edification, not flattery—friendship, not corruption. It is essentially the same path that Socrates tries to lead Callicles down, which is why the two dialogues go together so well.

The claim that "It is better to suffer injustice than to do it" is not a Socratic *opinion*. It is a philosophical *truth*. Socrates then challenges Callicles to refute, not Socrates, but philosophy herself:

> . . . either refute her and show that doing what's unjust without paying what is due for it is not the ultimate of all bad things, as I just now was saying it is. Or else, if you leave this unrefuted, then by the dog the god of the Egyptians, Callicles, Callicles will not agree with you Callicles, but will be dissonant with you all your life long. And yet for my part, my good man, I think it's better to have my lyre or a chorus that I might lead out of tune and dissonant, and to have the vast majority of men disagree with me and contradict me, than to be out of harmony with myself, though I'm only one person. (482a–c, Zeyl)

Note that Socrates is making a speech, a wonderful speech at that. When he was talking to Gorgias and Polus, he insisted on short answers to his questions. Now he is giving speeches, and Callicles matches him in kind. Later, the dialogue form returns. But then it breaks down again when Callicles lapses into sullen silence. Then we are treated to the farce of Socrates having a dialogue with himself. Finally, the *Gorgias* ends with Socrates spinning a myth about the underworld.

As in the beginning of the conversation with Polus, Plato is underscoring the limits of speech, both rhetoric and philosophical reasoning. In the conversation with Gorgias, it became clear that people need to be informed and intelligent to talk about philosophy. With the uninformed and unintelligent, rhetoric has the advantage. In the conversation with Polus, Socrates made it clear that speeches are ineffective if nobody will listen to them. The same, however, is true of philosophy. Now Callicles will demonstrate that dialogue is ineffective if nobody will answer. Where reason is ineffective, rhetoric and myth take their place.

The myth at the end of the *Gorgias* is foreshadowed by Socrates' oath. Earlier, he has sworn an oath "by the dog." One might take this as a profane oath or a euphemism, somewhat analogous to "doggone it," as opposed to "Goddammit." So now Socrates makes it clear that he is swearing "by the dog, the god of the Egyptians." This is probably a reference to Anubis, the jackal-headed god who leads souls into the underworld for judgment, which is the topic of the closing myth.

Now we come to the idea of harmony. There are two senses of harmony here.

On the surface, it simply means having non-contradictory beliefs. If you follow the crowd and adopt opinions because they please the people around you, your mind is going to be a junk heap of contradictory opinions, because the people are contradictory. They contradict one another. They contradict themselves from one minute to the next. And if you're trying to pursue their good opinion, rather than pursue the truth, you're going to be full of contradictions as well.

You can call consistency of belief "harmony of the mind." But the deeper harmony is the harmony of the soul, which has to do with virtue, which is spiritual health. There is more to the soul than just the mind, although in the *Gorgias*, Socrates doesn't introduce the tripartite division of the soul that appears in the *Republic*, he does distinguish between the soul and the body and also between reason and desire.

To pursue inner harmony of the mind, and harmony within the soul as a whole, often requires disharmony with the people around you, because most people, most of the time, are intellectually sloppy and morally lax. So if you harmonize with them, you're going to be out of harmony with yourself, both intellectually and morally.

And that's really the choice. Do you pursue internal integrity, harmony with yourself, at all costs, in which case you must have the courage to be out of touch, out of harmony, out of tune with the people around you? Or do you pursue harmony with others at the cost of always being out of harmony with yourself? Because there's a conflict there. Just how often do you think that the conventions and the opinions of the people around you will be in total harmony with what you need to be a moral human being? And even if that happened, how long do you think it would last, given how fickle and changeable public opinion is?

If you're going to slavishly harmonize yourself with public opinion, you'll always be out of harmony with yourself. This is why people who pursue power are slavish: they must pander to the ever-changing opinions of others. Thus they cannot be true to themselves. Whereas the person who puts caring for his own soul first needs to deal with the fact that he will often be out of harmony with public opinion. Socrates poses this as an absolute, stark choice, and he's right. I think he puts it magnificently using the language of harmony and discord.

RIGHT BY CONVENTION VS. RIGHT BY NATURE (482c–484b)

Socrates has delivered a scathing indictment of Callicles as a man who wishes to lead the people but in fact slavishly follows them by pandering to their shifting whims. But Callicles is not cowed. In fact, he responds with an indictment of his own, in the form of a brilliant speech, which falls into two parts.

Callicles begins by turning the tables on Socrates. He accuses Socrates of grandstanding to the crowd. Socrates, not Callicles, is the real people pleaser.

When Socrates questioned Gorgias, he caught him in a contradiction. On the one hand, Gorgias maintained that rhetoric was a morally neutral *techne*, thus Gorgias and other teachers of rhetoric cannot be blamed if their students misuse rhetoric. On the other hand, when Socrates asked Gorgias if his students all knew justice, Gorgias agreed, saying that if a student came to him ignorant of justice, Gorgias would teach it alongside rhetoric. But, on the premise that to know justice is to do justice, this would imply that no rhetoricians would do injustice. Polus claimed that Callicles erred by allowing himself to be shamed into claiming that he would teach justice alongside rhetoric.

When Socrates questioned Polus, the latter claimed that doing injustice is not wrong, but it is shameful. This premise allowed Socrates to defeat Polus. Thus Polus fell victim to the very same sense of shame for which he criticized Gorgias. Thus, although Socrates claims to be pursuing the truth, he's in fact depending upon merely conventional and popular ideas of the fine and shameful. These ideas are:

> . . . fine [*kalon*] only by convention [*nomos*], not by nature [*physis*]. These, nature and convention, are for the most part opposed to each other. So if someone out of embarrassment shrinks from saying what he thinks, he is bound to contradict himself. You've spotted this little trick too, and are very unscrupulous about using it in argument. If people talk about the way things are by convention, you question them about the way things are in nature. If they talk about how things are in nature, you ask them about how things are by convention. (482e–483a, Griffith)

The Greek word *nomos* means law or convention. *Nomos* is opposed to *physis* or nature. This distinction is absolutely central to early Greek natural philosophers and many of the sophists. Nature is distinguished from convention because nature is everywhere the same, whereas convention varies from place to place. Nature also remains the same over time, whereas conventions change. The Greeks had a deep, core conviction that the universal and unchanging are good. Permanence is good; change is bad. Universality is good; particularism is bad. Therefore, nature is good, and convention is bad.

If moral conventions are contemptible, how should we live? For the sophists, the answer is to look out for number one, i.e., to pursue wealth and power for oneself, liberated from all moral scruples. But if you no longer follow conventional norms, what do you follow? You follow nature, in the sense that nature furnishes you with desires, and the satisfaction of these desires brings pleasure. But if this is the case, then nature and norms are no longer necessarily opposed. Norms are not all conventional. Nature can serve as a norm as well. Hence Callicles offers the idea of what is "right by nature."

But what does Callicles think is right by nature?

> In my view ... nature itself shows clearly what is just—for the better man to have more than the worse, and the more powerful more than the less powerful. It is evident in many areas that this is how things are, both in the animal world and among humans, in whole cities and races—that justice has been adjudged to be precisely this—the stronger ruling over, and getting the better of, the weaker. By what right, after all, did Xerxes lead his expedition against Greece—or his father [Darius I] against the Scythians? (483c–d, Griffith)

Interestingly enough, Xerxes was defeated by the Greeks. And Darius I, his father, was defeated by the Scythians. Every Greek knew that. So Plato is putting words in Callicles' mouth that undermine his case. But let's leave that aside. Callicles continues:

> You could give any number of similar examples. These people, I take it, act as they do in accordance with nature—the nature of the just. Yes, by Zeus, and in accordance with the law of nature/the right by nature, though possibly not with this law which we put in place. (483e, Griffith)

For Callicles, the right by nature is that the strong rule the weak. The strong also should have a greater share of the world's goods.

Callicles rejects the distinction that Polus makes between the good and the shameful (doing injustice is good but also shameful). Instead, he holds that the bad and the shameful are the same thing:

> In nature, anything that is worse is also more shameful: being treated unjustly, for example, though by convention acting unjustly is more shameful. And that's because a real man doesn't have this happen to him, this being treated unjustly. It only happens to some slave for whom death is preferable to life, who, when he is treated unjustly and downtrodden, is incapable of defending himself or anyone else he cares for. (483a-b, Griffith)

Callicles believes that what is "right by convention" is laid down by the weak, not the strong:

> If you ask me, the people who put laws—conventions—in place are the weak, the many. It is with an eye to themselves and their own advantage that they put the laws in place, praise the things they praise, and blame the things they blame. They intimidate the more forceful among mankind, the ones capable of getting the better of others, and to stop them getting the better of them, they say that getting the better of others is shameful and unjust, and that this is what injustice is: trying to get the better of everyone else. (483b-c, Griffith)

Conventional laws aim to secure the equality of the weak and the strong, in terms of power and goods: "For themselves, I imagine they are well pleased if they can have an equal share, given their inferiority" (483c, Griffith). "We take the best and most forceful among us—catching them young, like lions—mold them with spells and bewitchments, and enslave them. We tell them they should have what is equal, and that this is what is fine and just" (483e–484a, Griffith).

However, some men see through conventional ideas of justice, throw them off, and follow what is right by nature. What makes this possible is strength of nature:

> ... if a man is born with a strong enough nature, he shakes all this [i.e., convention] off, breaks through it, makes his escape from it. He tramples on our prescriptions, our charms, our spells, our laws which all run counter to nature, and rising up, he stands revealed as our master ..., and there what is just in nature shines forth. (484a, Griffith)

This ends the first part of Callicles' speech, so let's pause here to take stock. Not only does this speech contain the first known occurrence of the idea of the right by nature, it also anticipates Nietzsche by more than two millennia. Indeed, this may be the source of Nietzsche's ideas of master and slave morality. For Callicles, the law of nature is the struggle for power. Nature is red in tooth and claw. What is right by nature is that the strong rule the weak and have more. This is what Nietzsche called master morality. According to Callicles, conventional right is instituted by the weak to protect themselves from the strong. This is what Nietzsche called slave morality. Whereas the masters insist on inequality, the slaves desire equality. But in certain men, nature is stronger than convention, so they burst the trammels of conventional morals and seek to set themselves up as masters.

Socrates agrees that there is a right by nature. This is the core of the moral revolution of Socratic philosophy.[1]

Callicles, moreover, believes that Socrates agrees with him about natural right. Thus he is accusing Socrates of acting in bad faith by exploiting what Callicles thinks are purely conventional morals and the shame that attaches to them. Socrates defeated Gorgias and Polus by their attachment to conventional morals and their sense of shame. But Callicles sees himself as entirely

---

[1] In *The Trial of Socrates*, I argue that this idea emerges first in Aristophanes' *Clouds*. See the chapter on Aristophanes' *Clouds*.

free of conventional morals and conventional shame. Thus he is willing to speak the truth, regardless of public opinion, and he believes that this will make him invincible in argument with Socrates. (Socrates, by contrast, thinks that shame is natural and helps us discover what is right by nature.)

Why does Callicles call out Socrates for exploiting conventional morals and grandstanding to the public? If Callicles is a real sophist, shouldn't he be admiring Socrates for exploiting people's attachment to conventional norms? That's how you win in law court. That's how you win in politics. You don't stand before the public and tell them frankly that all their ideals are bunk. No, you speak about "traditional moral values" or "freedom" or "fairness": whatever nonsense the people you're manipulating believe in. Callicles is indignant that Socrates is exploiting people's residual attachment to what he thinks are fake norms in order to win an argument. From a sophist, this is surprising.

But then there's something more philosophical than sophistical about Callicles. First, Callicles stands for truth, not opinion — nature, not convention. Indeed, he holds the revolutionary philosophical idea that nature can provide norms of conduct. Second, Callicles has a sense of intellectual probity that makes him indignant when he sees Socrates apparently exploiting convention and playing to the crowd to win an argument. Third, Callicles believes in frank speech, which is pretty much the opposite of what we can call "politic" speech. Callicles is not just mentally liberated from convention, he also publicly challenges and flouts it.

Although Callicles is indeed more philosophical than Gorgias or Polus, Socrates still disagrees with Callicles about what norms are sanctioned by nature. Moreover, as we shall see in the second half of his speech, Callicles may have a philosophical education or temperament, but he does not think that philosophy is an honorable way of life. Instead, he has embarked upon a life of pursuing power. Socrates, however, will try to build upon Callicles' philosophical temperament to convert him from the love of power to the love of wisdom.

Two Ways of Life

Power vs. Wisdom (484c–485e)

Callicles is more philosophical than Gorgias or Polus. So it comes as some surprise that the second part of Callicles' speech is a critique of philosophy. As we shall see, this critique is based on mistaken assumptions about Socrates and philosophy in general.

Callicles holds that philosophy is part of a liberal education. But it becomes a liability if carried on into adulthood: ". . . philosophy is a charming thing for anyone who gets a modest dose of it at the right age" (484c, Allen).

> Philosophy is no doubt pleasant enough, Socrates, taken moderately and in youth, but it is the ruination of a man if he stays in it too long. However well-endowed his nature, if he dwells in philosophy much past youth he necessarily becomes a stranger to affairs in which he ought to be experienced, if he is to be well regarded and a gentleman, noble and good. Philosophers in fact are inexperienced in the laws [*nomoi*] of their city, inexperienced in the language to be used in business contracts, public and private, inexperienced in human pleasures and desires, utterly inexperienced, in a word, in human character. So when they come to action, public or private, they make fools of themselves, just as, I think, politicians do when they turn to your discussions and disputes. Euripides drew the proper conclusion: "Each man is drawn to the thing in which he shines, allotting the greatest part of his day where he is at his best." He avoids and decries what he is weak at, and praises the other out of kind regard for his own, thinking that in that way he praises himself. But the most proper way I think is to get a share of both. It is a fine thing to partake of philosophy for the sake of education, and it is not shameful to pursue philosophy while young. But when a man is old and still at it, the thing becomes

ridiculous, Socrates, and I feel very much the same toward people who engage in philosophy as I do toward grown men who act childishly and lisp. When I see a little child doing that at an age when it is still proper, playing and lisping, I rejoice; it appears pleasing and freeborn and befitting his childish years, and when I hear a little child speaking distinctly, it seems distasteful and hurts my ears, and seems like something slavish. But when one sees a grown man act childishly and hears him lisp, he appears ridiculous and effeminate and worthy of a whipping. That's just how I feel about philosophers. I'd like to see philosophy in a lad; it seems fitting, and I believe there is even a certain free born liberality in the young man, and that if he doesn't engage in philosophy he is unfree, someone who will never think himself worthy of any noble or beautiful thing. But when I see an older man still engaged in philosophy and not turning from it, I think the fellow at that point deserves a whipping, Socrates. (484c–485d, Allen)

If one employs the Socratic idea of philosophy as the ability to make right use of all things, then Callicles is not actually discussing philosophy, for any activity or study that needs to be managed cannot be philosophy. For Socrates, only wisdom is unconditionally good. All other things are good only if they are rightly used, which is the function of wisdom. Therefore, if one can raise the question of right use about something called "philosophy," as Callicles does here, we are not talking about genuine philosophy. Indeed, Callicles' standpoint from which he criticizes "philosophy" is closer to genuine philosophy. And indeed, he later characterizes it as a form of worldly and practical wisdom.

The reference to beating adult men brings to mind the theme of father beating from Aristophanes' *Clouds*, and this clue helps us to understand Callicles' indictment of philosophy. Callicles sees philosophy pretty much as it is depicted in Aristophanes' *Clouds*: a theory-centered, unworldly, impractical activity. For instance, according to Callicles, the philosopher,

> ... Even if well-endowed by nature, is bound to become unmanly, fleeing the center of the city and its marketplace [*agora*] where, as the poet said "men grow distinguished."[1] He is sunk and hidden from sight, spending the rest of his life whispering with three or four adolescents in a corner, never uttering anything free, important, or sufficient. (485d, Allen)

This is true of Socrates in the *Clouds*, who retires from the world to his "Thinkery," where he discusses semantics, cosmology, and zoology with spindly youths. Note, however, that Callicles omits the other side of Aristophanes' critique, namely that Socrates also teaches rhetoric, specifically sophistry, i.e., how to make the speech that is weaker in truth and justice beat the speech that is stronger in truth and justice.

Callicles says that philosophy is unsuitable for adults because it does not equip you to be a gentleman taking part in public affairs. Philosophy leaves us ignorant of human character and the ways of the world. But aren't the ways of the world a kind of wisdom too? Isn't Callicles talking about practical wisdom here?

What are the consequences for philosophers who lack practical wisdom? Basically, they become laughingstocks. This is another allusion to the *Clouds*, which depicts Socrates as an unworldly buffoon. But, as in the *Clouds*, there are far more serious consequences than laughter:

> ... if someone were to take you or anyone like you and drag you off to jail, accusing you of guilt when you had done no wrong, you would know perfectly well you wouldn't know what to do. You'd gape with dizziness and wouldn't have a word to say. And once brought to court, even though your accuser was a completely contemptible knave, if he chose to exact the death penalty you would die. (486a–b, Allen)

This is obviously a reference to Socrates' eventual trial and

---

[1] Homer, *Iliad*, 9.441.

death, which Socrates in the *Apology* claims was the result of his first accuser, Aristophanes in the *Clouds*. Callicles is saying that philosophy is all well and good as part of a liberal education. But when you grow up and become a man, you don't just need practical wisdom, you also need rhetoric. For what? For self-defense.

Callicles even questions whether the sort of philosophy depicted in the *Clouds* is really wisdom at all:

> How is this wise, Socrates? What sort of art is it which "takes folk well-endowed and makes them worse,"[2] unable to help or save themselves or anyone else from the greatest dangers, but stripped of their whole estate by their enemies, they live on in their city utterly without rights. To put it perhaps crudely, on can punch a man like that on the chin and pay no penalty. (486b–c, Allen)

This is a pertinent question. For if anything can be criticized as unwise, it cannot be philosophy, whereas if you are in the position to criticize something as unwise, you are already practicing philosophy.

In sum, Callicles depicts Socrates as Aristophanes does in the *Clouds*: off whispering in his little Thinkery with a few emaciated youths, ignorant of human nature and society, the sort of nebbish who can't defend himself.

This isn't, however, a very good description of Socrates in Plato's dialogues, because our Socrates is almost always out in public talking. In fact, they're talking in public that very moment. Socrates is also masterful at judging people's characters and accommodating his speeches to his audience. Socrates, in short, was a master of rhetoric in his own way.

However, Callicles seems dead right when he says that Socrates is the kind of guy you could do injustice to. Just think of his trial and execution. However, even that's not really true, because Socrates had the political connections and wherewithal to prevent the trial from ever taking place. Moreover, once he

---

[2] Dodds thinks this is a quote from Zethus in Euripides' *Antiope* (p. 278). See the next section, below.

was on trial, he had the rhetorical skills to save himself. But he chose not to.

TWO WAYS OF LIFE (485e–486d)

Another strand of Callicles' speech is the contrast he draws between two kinds of life: the philosophical life and the political life. Callicles illustrates this distinction by quoting *Antiope*, a lost tragedy by Euripides. In the play, the two sons of Zeus and Antiope, Zethus and Amphion, debate about which life is the best. Zethus, a hunter, takes the side of the active life, which would include politics. Amphion, a musician, defends the creation of culture and the cultivation of the self, which would include philosophy. Each brother naturally defends what he is good at and denigrates what he is bad at. Callicles takes the side of Zethus:

> Now, Socrates, I feel somewhat friendly to you. I feel very much as Zethus, whom I just mentioned, felt toward Amphion in Euripides. In fact, it occurred to me to say the same sort of thing to you that he said to his brother: "Socrates, you neglect what you ought to care for. The nature of your soul is noble, and yet you bend it out of shape into something very like that of a schoolboy. You could not make a proper speech in the councils of justice, you cannot be plausible or persuasive, and you advise no bold plan on behalf of others." And yet, my dear Socrates — and please don't be angry at me, for I speak with kind regard — why don't you think it's shameful to be in the state I think you are in, along with the rest who keep pressing ever farther with philosophy? (485e–486a, Allen)

> Stop refuting people and practice the music of affairs. Practice that which will make you seem wise. Leave these bits of cleverness to others, whether they should be called nonsense or folly, "from which you'll dwell in empty houses."[3] Do not emulate men who practice refutation in these petty matters, but rather those who possess life and glory and many other goods. (486c–d, Allen)

---

[3] Probably another quote from Zethus in *Antiope*.

Socrates and Plato would find Callicles' approach here laudable, because they understand philosophy as a way of life and formulate the great moral and political questions as the choice of which life to lead. Philosophy is the life of pursuing wisdom. Politics is the life of pursuing power.

But as Callicles draws it, the distinction between the two is not airtight. For, following Aristophanes, Callicles depicts philosophy as lacking in practical wisdom, whereas the political life possesses a genuine store of practical, worldly wisdom.

The Socratic revolution in philosophy called philosophy "down from the heavens," as Cicero put it, where philosophy was focused on theoretical questions, and directed it toward the affairs of men.[4] Thus Socratic philosophy is first and foremost practical wisdom.

But in the *Clouds*, Socrates was also depicted as a practitioner of rhetoric. If there was truth in this, we can ask: How did the Socratic moral revolution affect rhetoric? The most plausible answer is that it subordinated rhetoric, like all other *technai*, to knowledge of the good.

SOCRATES' REACTION TO CALLICLES' SPEECH (486d–488a)

Callicles has made a fairly long speech, as sophists are wont to do. Note that Socrates doesn't cut him off and say, 'Callicles, I'm going to leave unless you confine yourself to short answers.' Plato includes this little deed for a reason, and it says a lot. Socrates listens! Why? Obviously, because he thinks Callicles is saying something worth listening to.

Nonetheless, despite Callicles' professions of friendship, his speech is extremely arrogant and condescending. Socrates is smart enough to see this. He's also a normally constituted man. He has *thumos*. So he is bound to have been offended. Thus his reaction is surprisingly gentle and diplomatic, a sterling example of moderation (*sophrosyne*), the virtue he lauds throughout the conversation to come:

> If my soul were made of gold, Callicles, don't you think

---

[4] Cicero, *Tusculan Disputations*, book V, section 10.

> I'd be delighted to find one of those stones, and the very best, they use for testing gold? I could apply my soul to it, to see if the stone agreed that my soul had been well cared for; that way I could finally be sure that I was in satisfactory shape and that I had no need of any further test. (486d, Griffith)

Socrates is referring to a "touchstone." To test the purity of a golden object, one rubs it on the touchstone and compares the color of the gold left on the surface to samples of known purity.

The idea of a golden soul brings to mind the *Republic*, where Socrates proposes a noble lie, known as the myth of the metals, to justify social inequality.[5] In creating men, the gods compound gold, silver, or bronze into their souls. Golden souls are suited to rule. Silver souls are suitable as guardians. Bronze souls are suited to do manual labor. In the *Republic*, the rulers are ultimately philosophers. If this carries over to the *Gorgias*, then Socrates' well-cared for golden soul is the soul of a philosopher.

But how is Callicles a touchstone? Socrates specifically likens *philosophical conversation* with Callicles to a touchstone. Socrates' soul forms opinions, which he then tests against Callicles in dialogue. If Callicles agrees, then Socrates thinks this is good evidence that his views are true. But what makes Callicles an ideal interlocutor? Socrates explains:

> I'm quite sure that if you agree with me about the opinions my soul is forming, then these are finally the real truth. It strikes me that the person who is going to be an adequate touchstone for the soul, to see whether or not it lives rightly, must in fact possess three things, all of which you have: knowledge [*episteme*], goodwill [*eunoia*], and frankness [*parrhesia*]. I meet many people who can't test me because they're not wise [*sophoi*] like you. Others are wise, but refuse to tell me the truth because they don't care about me like you do. As for our two friends here, Gorgias and Polus, they are both wise, and both my friends; but they lack frankness, and are rather more ashamed than they

---

[5] Plato, *Republic*, 414b–415d.

should be. That must be it. They've both taken concern for what people will think to the point where, out of embarrassment, each of them resolutely contradicts himself, before a large number of people, and about things of greatest importance at that. Whereas you have all these qualities which other people do not have. You have had a good enough education, in the opinion of many Athenians, and you are well disposed towards me. (486e–487b, Griffith)

Socrates praises Callicles as an ideal interlocutor because he is knowledgeable, wise, well-meaning, and frank. He agrees with Callicles' statement that Gorgias and Polus ended up contradicting themselves because they put shame before frankness. Callicles, however, is frank, which means that he is willing to say things that some might regard as shameful. (I think that Socrates may be flattering Callicles here, since shame may not be merely social. It might be one manifestation of our innate knowledge of the good.)

Socrates is willing to overlook Callicles' arrogance and take his professions of goodwill at face value. One reason he gives for this is Callicles' behavior toward his friends:

What evidence do I have for [Callicles' good will]? I'll tell you. I know there are four of you, Callicles, who are associates in wisdom with you, Tisander of Aphidnae, Andron son of Androtion, and Nausicydes of Cholarges. I overheard you once discussing how far the practice of wisdom should be taken, and I know that the opinion which prevailed upon you was something like this: you shouldn't throw yourselves into the philosophizing that sets store by extreme precision; rather you are urging one another to be careful not to acquire more wisdom than was called for, and so come to grief without realizing it. When I hear you giving me the same advice you give your own closest friends, that's evidence enough for me that you really are well disposed towards me. (487c–d, Griffith)

This is a reasonable inference. If Callicles gives Socrates the same advice he gives his closest friends, that is a sign of good will.

Tisander, Andron, and Nausicydes are all historical figures, which increases the likelihood that Callicles was one as well. E.R. Dodds assembles the surviving historical fragments and testimonia and concludes, "The general picture which the evidence suggests is that of a group of ambitious young men, drawn from the *jeunesse dorée* of Athens, who have acquired just enough of the 'new learning' to rid them of inconvenient moral scruples."[6]

Socrates also agrees with and underscores Callicles' contrast between the philosophical and the political ways of life:

> Of all possible enterprises this inquiry is the finest, Callicles, though you criticized me for it. It's about the kind of person a man should be, be he older or younger, what he should pursue, and up to what point. For my part, if there is some way in which I am not doing the right thing in my own life, then believe me, I am not doing wrong on purpose, but as a result of my own stupidity. So it's up to you. You've started taking me to task, so don't give up, but make it absolutely clear to me what this thing is I should be pursuing, and in what way I might be able to acquire it. And if you catch me agreeing with you now, but at some later time not doing the things I have agreed to, then you can regard me as a complete numbskull, and never take me to task again, since I'll not be worth bothering with. (487e–488a, Griffith)

Socrates' claim that if he is living the wrong way, it is out if ignorance not ill-intent, is a statement of his principle that nobody does wrong intentionally but only out of ignorance. If Socrates is ignorant of the most important things, however, he is anxious to learn the truth and will be grateful to Callicles or anyone else who manages to teach it to him. This is why Socrates describes finding an ideal interlocutor like Callicles as "a stroke of luck." This is high praise, but by praising Callicles, Socrates is urging him to be on his best behavior. He'll need it, for Socrates is about to deliver a stinging refutation.

---

[6] Dodds, p. 282.

THE BEST SHOULD RULE

WHO IS THE STRONGEST? (488b–489c)

Callicles argues that might makes right. The strongest should rule and have more of anything they want. Thus they are primarily talking about *political* inequality. Inequality of wealth derives from political inequality. Socrates agrees with Callicles that superior men have superior rights and deserve superior rewards. Socrates believes equals should be treated equally. But he does not believe in equal treatment for unequal people. Where Socrates disagrees with Callicles is about the question: *What sort of superiority is relevant to politics?* Is political superiority merely a matter of might, or is it something different?

Socrates asks Callicles to reprise his argument from the beginning. He asks if Callicles holds that:

> What's just in nature . . . [is] that he who is more powerful should carry off by force the things that belong to those who are less powerful, that he who is better should rule over those who are worse, and that the superior should have more than the inferior? (488b, Griffith)

Callicles agrees that this is his position.

Then Socrates establishes that Callicles calls "more powerful, stronger, and better . . . the same thing" (488b, Griffith), i.e., power = strength = goodness. Thus it is not possible to be "better but less powerful and weaker" or "more powerful but more wicked."

Then Socrates asks Callicles: "What you must define clearly for me is this: are 'more powerful,' 'better,' and 'stronger' the same thing? Or are they different things?" Callicles states flatly, "They are the same thing" (488d, Griffith).

Then Socrates points out that according to Callicles, "the many," who are average and below average, pass laws to control superior individuals and make them their equals. This assumes that "in nature . . . the many [are] more powerful than the single individual." Callicles agrees: "Of course they're more powerful." Socrates points out that this implies that "the rules prescribed by the many are the rules of the more powerful." Callicles agrees, "Absolutely" (488d-e, Griffith).

Then Socrates springs his trap. Callicles holds that the many use force to impose equality on their superiors. But Callicles also holds that "the more powerful are the better." The obvious implication is that the many are the better because they are the more powerful. Socrates gives Callicles the chance to back out, but he affirms the premise that the more powerful are the better. Socrates then asks, "And in the nature of things are the rules of these people, since they are more powerful, fine [*kalon*]?" (488e, Griffith). Fineness is a characteristic of superior men. Again, Callicles is given the option to change his position, but he agrees. Callicles seems oblivious of the conclusion Socrates is driving at, which at this point indicates that he's a bit thick.

Socrates presses forward and spells out his conclusion, asking if the many establish by convention the principle of equality and the principle that it is "more shameful to act unjustly than to be treated unjustly" (489a, Griffith). (As far as we know, Socrates was the first to defend this thesis, so it is interesting that he is ascribing it to the many here.) Apparently, at this point Callicles sees where Socrates' argument is driving and lapses into sullen silence. Thus Socrates prods him, "Please don't refuse me this answer out of pique, Callicles. If you agree with me, then I'll be getting full corroboration from you, since it will be a man of discernment who has agreed." So Callicles agrees, "Yes, if it's the many you're talking about, they do regard that as a general rule" (489a, Griffith).

Then Socrates states his final conclusion: "In which case, it's not only by convention that acting unjustly is more disgraceful than being treated unjustly, or that having what is equal is just. It is so in nature as well" (489a, Griffith). If by nature strength is the same thing as goodness, and if the many (the average and below average) together have the strength to impose equality on superior men, then equality is not merely right by convention, it is also right by nature. For behind convention is the *power* to establish and enforce convention. If power is right by nature, then power makes conventions right by nature, even if the convention is equality. The many also use power to establish the convention that it is more shameful to act unjustly than to be treated unjustly, and since power makes things right by nature, this convention is right by nature as well.

At this point, Callicles explodes: "Honestly! Will the man never stop babbling?" (489b, Griffith). Here, Callicles is clearly addressing the audience. Then he turns to Socrates:

> Tell me, Socrates, aren't you ashamed at your age to be catching at words, and thinking it's a real stroke of luck if someone slips up in a statement? I mean, do you think I'm saying that for people to be more powerful is anything other than for them to be better? Haven't I been telling you for some time that I maintain the better and the more powerful are the same thing? Or do you think I'm saying that if a rabble of slaves gathers, or some ill-sorted collection of humanity good for nothing except perhaps the exercise of physical strength, and if these people make some claim, that is what is lawful? (489b–c, Griffith)

Callicles isn't taking this well. He claimed that might makes right. This means that whoever wields power is *ipso facto* right, because whatever norms they establish are right by nature, because they are backed by superior power. When confronted with the fact that this means that the mediocre many are more powerful than the excellent few, thus the norms they establish are right, Callicles in effect says, 'I didn't mean it that way.'

Power is not actually Callicles' standard of the best. Instead, he thinks that the best are in some way noble or virtuous, whereas the worst are ignoble and base. Sometimes the noble lack power. But that does not deprive them of their excellence. Moreover, when base men have power, that does not make them noble. Thus Callicles doesn't believe that might makes right. Instead, he believes that nobility and baseness are defined independent of power. As for power, he believes that those who are noble *ought* to rule, and those who are base *ought not* to rule. Stated at this level of generality, Socrates would completely agree with Callicles. They differ only in their concrete ideas of what is excellent.

THE BEST MEN ARE THE PRUDENT (489d–490a)

Callicles has made it clear that by the best men, he does not mean the physically strongest. But it is not yet clear what he does mean by the best. So Socrates continues to question him.

> ... I've been guessing for some time that by the stronger you meant something like that, my fortunate friend, and I repeated my question out of greedy desire to know plainly just what you do mean. You surely don't mean you believe two men are better than one, or that your slaves are better than you because they're physically stronger than you. But tell me again from the beginning: Just who do you mean are better, if not the physically stronger? And do please teach me my lessons more gently, dear friend, lest I stop attending your class. (489d, Allen)

To this, Callicles responds with the charge that Socrates is being "ironic" (489e). This is an instance in which the Greek *eironeia* is best translated as "condescending." Socrates is pretending to be Callicles' student, when he obviously believes himself to be Callicles' teacher. Irony is a form of dissimulation practiced by Greek gentlemen around their inferiors. In order to spare the feelings of their inferiors, Greek gentlemen would pretend to be less than they really are. They would feign equality or even inferiority. If, however, your irony is seen through, then not only does it fail to hide your superiority, it is seen as an expression of superiority. Hence you are guilty of being condescending. This is self-defeating, because it inflames rather than spares the feelings of your inferiors. Callicles is clearly becoming increasingly annoyed.

Socrates parries the charge of irony by swearing an oath not by Zeus, the god of friendship, but "by Zethus," the son of Zeus in Euripides' *Antiope*. Socrates then accuses Callicles of being condescending to him. This is obviously true, particularly when Callicles was speaking as Zethus to Socrates. But Socrates is better at maintaining a cool head than Callicles, so he had not revealed his feelings until now. Having brushed aside this accusation, Socrates presses on: "Come and tell me: whom do you mean by the better?" (489e, Allen).

To this Callicles responds, "I mean the superior" (489e, Allen). But to say the better are the superior is not an answer. Superior in what, exactly? Thus Socrates suggests a more concrete answer: "Won't you say whether by the better and stronger you mean the more prudent [Socrates refers here to *phronesis*, i.e., practical wisdom], or somebody else?" Callicles responds, "Well of course I mean them. Emphatically so" (489e, Allen).

Stated at this level of generality, Socrates is in full agreement with Callicles that it is right by nature that the prudent rule. So now Socrates zeroes in on where they differ, which has to do with the idea that it is right by nature for the prudent to "have more." Socrates again sums up Callicles' position:

> So by your account, one wise man is often stronger than thousands of fools, and he should rule and they be ruled, and the ruler should have a greater share than the ruled. This is what you seem to wish to say, and surely I am not catching at phrases, if one man is to be stronger than thousands. (490a, Allen)

Callicles agrees entirely with this summary: ". . . that's just what I mean. I think that the just by nature consists in the better and more prudent ruling and having a greater share than their inferiors" (490a, Allen).

Again, at this level of generality, Socrates is in complete agreement with Callicles. The basic principle that the better should have more than the worse is not indefensible. Better athletes deserve to have more ribbons than worse athletes, and generally it's in proportion to how good they are. Better golfers win more money than worse golfers, and it's generally proportionate to differences in their quality. It would be a crazy and unjust system if great golfers got the exact same amount of prize money as mediocre golfers—indeed, if anybody who enters a golf tournament gets an equal portion of the prize.

TWO CONCEPTS OF EQUALITY (490a–491d)

Where Socrates differs from Callicles is his understanding of the nature of "equal" and "more." Callicles understands these terms "numerically" whereas Socrates understands them "proportionally." Let's explore this difference. Numerical equality is simply sameness in number. If Jack and Jill have the exact same incomes, they are numerically equal. If Jack gets one more dollar than Jill, then they are numerically unequal.

If Jack and Jill are equal, then it is unjust for Jack to get one dollar more. But what if they are unequal? Then paying them the same amount would be unjust. For Callicles, the height of injustice is to impose numerical equality on unequal people. Socrates would agree with this.

From this, Callicles draws the conclusion that justice requires numerical inequality, i.e., the better deserve to have more stuff than their inferiors. How much more? As much as they can get. The number series goes on forever. There is no limit. You can always add more.

But Socrates does not agree with this. If numerical equality leads to injustice, then the answer is not necessarily numerical inequality. The answer is to reject the numerical model altogether for another model: the *proportional*, which combines both equality and inequality.

If Jack is better than Jill, surely he deserves more. But how much more? Callicles believes as much as he can get. But if Jack is only twice as good as Jill, shouldn't he get twice as much? The inequality of rewards should be *proportionate* to the inequality of merit. Thus if Jack gets a dollar more or a dollar less than twice Jill's reward, that would be an injustice. If Jack gets a dollar less than twice, it is an injustice to Jack. If Jack gets a dollar more than twice, it is an injustice to Jill. The key to the idea of "proportional" justice is that unequal rewards should be *proportionate* to unequal merits. This gives equality its due, for justice also requires equal rewards for equal merits. Proportional justice can be expressed as an *analogy*:

Jack's merit is to Jack's reward as Jill's merit is to Jill's reward.

Or:

Jack's merit : Jack's reward :: Jill's merit : Jill's reward

The idea of proportional justice is spelled out in Plato's *Laws* (book VI), and in Aristotle's *Nicomachean Ethics* (book V). In the *Gorgias*, however, Socrates is clearly driving at this model of justice. As we have seen in Socrates' discussion with Polus, analogies are central to explaining the difference between true politics and sophistry. All of the analogies in the *Gorgias* depend on the key Socratic analogy:

Virtue : the soul :: health : the body

Which implies:

Philosophy : the soul :: medicine/nutrition : the body

Later in the *Gorgias*, Socrates will claim that one can introduce harmony into one's soul by imitating the *kosmos* as a proportional harmony of four terms: earth, heaven, gods, and mortals. (This may well be the source of Heidegger's idea of "the Fourfold," which is also a harmony of earth and heaven, gods and mortals.[1]) At this point in the dialogue, however, Socrates is simply concerned to establish that all questions of more or less stuff must be proportionate to the objective natures of the people who possess things. The idea of acquisition without measure, which the Greeks called *pleonexia*, is thus contrary to nature. Nature is finite. Thus all natural excellences are finite. Thus all natural rewards should be finite as well.

Socrates bids Callicles to imagine a group of men, like the ones gathered around them, forming a political community. As

---

[1] Martin Heidegger, "The Thing," in *Poetry, Language, Thought*, trans. Albert Hofstadter (New York: Harper and Row, 1971).

in every community, the members are unequal in countless ways. Imagine, also, that they take counsel from the wise. In matters of diet, they would take advice from a doctor. He would thus be the ruler in matters of diet. Callicles accepts this picture.

Then Socrates asks: If the doctor rules in matters of food, does that mean that it is right by nature for the doctor to have more food than the rest, regardless of his physical needs? What if the doctor is the smallest and weakest of the lot? If medical wisdom ruled, wouldn't the doctor get the least amount of food, not the most? Or, to use my own example: In the hospital where the doctor rules, would justice require that the doctor take more pills than the patients?

Callicles is indignant. This is not the sense in which he thinks that the better should have more. Socrates, however, continues to pester him with his typical *techne* analogies. A cloak-maker is the wisest man about cloaks. Does that imply that he should have the biggest cloaks, the most cloaks, or the prettiest cloaks? The shoemaker is wisest about shoes. Does that imply he should wear the biggest shoes or have the most shoes? The farmer is wisest about seeds. Does that mean that he should have the most seeds? All these examples have the idea of numerical inequality at their root, and the number line goes on without limit.

Obviously, in each case, the size and amount of stuff each artisan should have should be proportional to something objective. If the cloak-maker is small, he should not have the biggest cloak. Obviously, the size of the shoemaker's shoes should be proportional to his feet. Obviously, the amount of seed a farmer should plant should be proportional to his land. In all of these cases, the amount of stuff is finite because it is made proportional to something finite.

Like two millennia of Plato's readers, Callicles finds Socrates' *techne* analogies tedious and irritating.[2] But they serve a purpose, for they force Callicles to think in more concrete

---

[2] Xenophon drolly recounts Critias the tyrant's annoyance with Socrates' *techne* analogies in *Memorabilia*, II.2.37.

terms. Thus Socrates sweeps aside Callicles' annoyance and presses further: ". . . please say what things the stronger and wiser has more of, when he justly overreaches and gets more than his share? Or do you intend to reject my suggestions while offering none of your own?" (491a, Allen).

Callicles' response is that the stronger and better are: "people who are prudent in the affairs of the city, and courageous [the Greek for courage is "*andreia,*" which means "manliness"]. Those are the persons who should rule their cities, and the just lies here, that they should have more than the others, the rulers more than the ruled" (491c–d, Allen). Thus Callicles adds another virtue to his list. The men best suited to rule are not just *prudent* in the affairs of the city but *courageous* as well. Thus they are entitled to more stuff than their fellows.

PLEASURE & GOODNESS

MODERATION & SELF-RULE (491d–495a)

Socrates is pleased that Callicles has added courage to prudence. The *Gorgias* is slowly assembling the four so-called "cardinal virtues": first justice (*dikaion, dikaiosyne*), then wisdom (*sophia, phronesis*), then courage (*andreia*). The only one left out is moderation (*sophrosyne*), which Socrates immediately brings into play.

Moderation, of course, is uniquely relevant to the question of having more stuff. Moderation can also be understood as self-control. Self-control, moreover, presupposes self-knowledge. To control your intake of drink, for instance, you must know your limits.

Moderation can also be understood as ruling oneself, thus when Callicles says that superior men are entitled to rule others by virtue of their prudence and courage, and have more stuff than other people, Socrates asks, "Really? More than themselves, my friend?" (491d, Allen). In other words: If the ruler is to have more than the ruled, then doesn't that mean that the ruler will have more than himself?

The underlying assumption here is that, *within each man*, we can find the distinction between ruler and ruled, i.e., it is possible to rule oneself. Specifically, it is possible for one part of the self to rule over other parts.

When Callicles asks Socrates what he means, Socrates replies: "I mean that each of us is his own ruler. Or is there no need to rule oneself, but only others?" (491d, Allen). Here Plato is anticipating the central teaching of the *Republic*: the soul has parts (reason, spirit, and desire), the different parts of the soul can rule over each other, and different types of men are distinguished by what part of the soul rules.

When Callicles asks Socrates what he means by ruling oneself, the reply is, "Nothing fancy, just what most people mean: being moderate and controlling oneself, ruling the pleasures and the desires in oneself" (491d, Allen). This is relevant to Callicles' claim that the superior man should have unlimited stuff, for if the superior man should also rule himself, that entails putting limits on unlimited acquisition.

Callicles is scornful of the idea of ruling one's appetites, speaking to Socrates as if he were a naïve child: "How sweet you are. By the moderate you mean the stupid" (491e, Allen). Socrates rejects this indignantly, saying that everyone would know that's not what he means. But Callicles insists on identifying moderation with stupidity, offering a splendid speech in praise of immoderation:

> How can a man be happy [*eudaimon*] if he's enslaved by anyone at all? I tell you now quite frankly that by nature the fine and just [*to kata physin kalon kai dikaion*] is this, that he who would live rightly should allow his desires [*epithumia*] to become as great as possible and not restrain them, and when they have waxed great, he must be adequate to minister to them with courage [*andreia*] and prudence [*phronesis*], satisfying whatever desire he may chance to have. But this I think is impossible for most men, whence it is that out of shame they find fault with such people, hiding their own powerlessness and claiming that lack of restraint is shameful. This is why men of a better nature are enslaved, as I said before, and those who cannot provide for their pleasures to the full praised moderation and justice due to their own cowardice [*anandreia* = unmanliness]. If they started out as sons of kings, or were adequate in nature to achieve some kind of absolute rule, sole or oligarchic, what could in truth be more shameful and evil than moderation and justice for these men to whom it is given to enjoy good things without impediment? Would they then introduce a master over themselves, namely the law [*nomos*], the speech [*logos*], and the censure [*psogos*] of the multitude? How would they not become wretched through the fineness of justice and moderation, distributing no greater shares to their friends than to their enemies, even though they rule in their own cities? The truth Socrates, which you claim to pursue, is this:

luxury, license, and liberty, if adequately abetted, are virtue and happiness [*arete kai eudaimonia*], and these other embellishments, these agreements of men contrary to nature [*para physin synthemata anthropon*], are worthless nonsense. (491e–492c, Allen)

Here Callicles makes clear that he is operating within the broad opposition between nature (*physis*) and conventions (*nomoi, synthemata*). The earlier sophists held that matters of right and wrong are wholly conventional, and that one should take one's bearings from nature instead. But Callicles holds that there is a form of right and wrong by nature, which allows one to criticize all conventional norms. This is a step beyond the sophists and puts Callicles in the camp of Socratic philosophy.

Callicles identifies the right by nature as the satisfaction of unlimited desire. He defines the virtues of prudence and courage as *instruments* for the satisfaction of such desire.[1] Although Callicles claims this is freedom, his own speech hints that it is a form of slavery, speaking of desire as if it were a great beast whose appetites must be constantly catered to. How free is a man if he must minister to "whatever desire he may chance to have"?

It all depends on which part of the soul one identifies with. One is free if one identifies with unfettered desire. One is a slave if one identifies with the other parts of one's soul that must cater to desire. In terms of the *Republic*, Callicles makes desire sovereign in the soul. Desire rules over reason (one aspect of which is prudence) and spirit (one aspect of which is courage).

In the *Republic*, the sovereignty of desire is associated with three regimes: democracy, oligarchy, and tyranny. Naturally, Callicles has no truck with democracy, which is animated by the spirit of equality. Instead, he aims for oligarchy or tyranny, which allow maximum inequality of stuff.

Then Callicles offers a proto-Nietzschean argument for why

---

[1] As Thomas Hobbes puts it in *Leviathan*: "For the thoughts are to the desires, as scouts, and spies, to range abroad, and find the way to the things desired" (*Leviathan*, chapter 8).

moderation and justice were created and propagated as virtues: most men are weak and unable to satisfy infinite desires, so they preach moderation and justice as virtues to keep down those rare men who are capable of it. Preaching moderation and justice as virtues both protects inferior men from superior ones and also makes the inferior feel unashamed of their weakness while shaming the superior for their strength.

Socrates praises Callicles for his frankness, for saying what other men think but are unwilling to say. He does not mention whether or not he thinks Callicles' frankness is foolhardy or that other men are perhaps prudent in being more circumspect. Nor does he mention whether he himself belongs to the frank or the prudent camp.

Socrates urges Callicles not to shrink back from his views under examination, on the grounds that Socrates wishes to learn the right way to live from Callicles. Socrates then sums up Callicles' position as follows: "You say that the desires are not to be restrained, if one is to become the sort of person he should; he is to let them wax as great as possible, prepare to satisfy them in any way, and this is virtue?" Callicles responds, "I say exactly that" (492d, Allen).

The idea that the happy life is the endless satisfaction of endless desires sounds a bit like the proverbial "rat race."[2] Wouldn't

---

[2] Compare Hobbes:

> For there is no such *finis ultimus* (utmost aim) nor *summum bonum* (greatest good) as is spoken of in the books of the old moral philosophers. Nor can a man any more live whose desires are at an end than he whose senses and imaginations are at a stand. Felicity is a continual progress of the desire from one object to another, the attaining of the former being still but the way to the latter. The cause whereof is that the object of man's desire is not to enjoy once only, and for one instant of time, but to assure forever the way of his future desire....
>
> So that in the first place, I put for a general inclination of all mankind a perpetual and restless desire of power after power, that ceaseth only in death. And the cause of this is not always that a man hopes for a more intensive delight than he has al-

happiness be easier to secure if one had more limited desires? Socrates asks, "Is it therefore mistaken to say that those who need nothing are happy?" (492e, Allen). I take "those who need nothing" to mean: those who have limited desires and have managed to secure what they desire. This becomes clear later, when Socrates introduces a metaphor of men with leaky and tight jars (494a–c).

Callicles parodies needing nothing as being like a stone or a corpse. Stones and corpses don't need anything because they are dead. Rather than pushing back at this parody, Socrates for some reason runs with it, quoting Euripides: "Who knows whether to live is to be dead, and being dead is to live?" (492e–493a, Allen).[3] Then Socrates refers to a number of mystical and ascetic teachings, including those of the Pythagoreans, whom he refers to as Sicilians or Italians. Socrates grants that these stories are "a bit absurd" if taken literally. Yet they provide useful images.

One Pythagorean claimed that in Hades, the uninitiated will be "most wretched," condemned to fill a leaky jar by carrying water in a sieve. Leaky jars and sieves are, of course, "incontinent," insofar as they cannot contain something. Immoderate men who cannot rule their passions can also be called "incontinent," meaning that they cannot contain themselves. In Aristotle's *Nicomachean Ethics*, the Greek word "*akrasia*," which refers to the inability to resist shameful temptations, is commonly translated as "weakness of the will" but is also translated as "incontinence," which has the unfortunate connotation of bedwetting. (The opposite of *akrasia* is *enkrateia*, which is translated as continence, strength of will, or self-control.)

Socrates then offers another Pythagorean analogy about

---

ready attained to, or that he cannot be content with a moderate power, but because he cannot assure the power and means to live well, which he hath present, without the acquisition of more. (*Leviathan*, chapter 11)

[3] According to Dodds (p. 300), the quote is from one of Euripides' lost plays, either the *Phrixus* or the *Polyidos*, and was taken to express Orphic or Pythagorean ideas.

continence and incontinence:

> Consider whether you are not saying something of this sort about the life of moderate and immoderate men. Picture two men, each with many jars. One has sound jars, some full of wine, some full of milk, and some of honey, and many more are full of many other things, the sources of each scarce and hard to come by, procured only with much labor and difficulty. Well, the one man, when his jars are full, gives no thought to piping more into them; his mind is at rest about it. But the other man, though he can provide sources like the first, though with difficulty, has leaky, cracked vessels, and so he is ever compelled to keep filling them day and night or else suffer the extremities of pain. Suppose then that each life is of this sort. Do you still say the life of the immoderate man is happier than that of the well-ordered? Do I at all persuade you in saying this to agree that the well-ordered life [*kosmion bion*] is better than the immoderate one, or do I fail? (493d–494a, Allen)

Callicles is not persuaded: "That fellow with the full jars no longer has any pleasure, and as I just said, that is to live like a stone. Once he is satisfied, he neither rejoices nor feels pain. The life of pleasure consists in just this: maximum flow" (494a–b, Allen). Socrates' response is rather droll: "Then necessarily if the inflow is large, won't the outflow be large too, with big holes to flow out of?" (494b, Allen).

There's something distasteful about reducing a human being to a tube, especially when you think about the nether end. But Callicles agrees with this description without flinching. To which Socrates replies that Callicles is describing the life of a stone curlew, a bird that apparently excreted as fast as it ate. A more pointed avian analogy would be the goose: if you have the proverbial "gut like a goose," your food goes straight through. If Callicles thinks men are tubes, through which the things we desire pass, then the greatest men are the biggest tubes. Only the biggest tubes enjoy maximum flow.

Callicles has not flinched from this distasteful description, so Socrates tries to bring it home to him. Socrates ascertains from Callicles that we live well by satisfying hunger through eating, thirst through drinking. Then Callicles brusquely cuts to the final conclusion: "Yes, and having all the other desires and being able to satisfy them, and enjoying a happy life" (494c, Allen). Socrates says "fine," but cautions Callicles that as they continue in this vein, he will need to fight against feeling ashamed. Socrates, for his part, will also steel himself against shame and continue.

Then Socrates asks Callicles if scratching an itch is part of the happy life (*eudaimonia*). An itch is a petty bodily annoyance, but if the happy life is all about satisfying one's desires, then scratching an itch is part of the happy life. Callicles, however, is offended: "You're absurd, Socrates, an outright demagogue" (494d, Allen). Actually, it is not Socrates who is absurd, but rather Callicles, since his position entails that even a mean activity like scratching an itch is part of the happy life. But Callicles is ashamed to admit it, apparently because he thinks such mean pleasures are beneath him. But if Callicles thinks that some pleasures are *better* than others, doesn't this imply that he has a standard of the good over and above pleasure?

It is ironic that Callicles feels shame, for recall that he argued that shame was the fatal weakness of both Gorgias and Polus. They failed to defend their views because they were too ashamed to embrace immoral principles. Socrates now chides Callicles by reminding him of this fact: "That's precisely how I upset Polus and Gorgias, Callicles, and made them ashamed. But you must not be upset or ashamed, for you are manly and courageous. So just please answer the question" (494d, Allen). At this point, Callicles agrees that a man experiences pleasure by scratching himself, and to experience pleasure is the happy life.

At this point, Socrates says that he could inquire about all the other petty pleasures that can be won by stimulating the surface of the body, or he could just sum up the life of physical stimulation with a single figure: a catamite, meaning a boy who was on the receiving end of homosexual intercourse, something far more shameful than scratching an itch. How could something so "awful and shameful and wretched" [*deinos kai aischros kai athlios*] be part of the happy life? Does Callicles claim that such people enjoy *eudaimonia* "as long as they have a generous supply of what they need"? (494e, Allen).

Callicles tries to shame Socrates for using such an example, but Socrates stands his ground: the shame belongs to Callicles, for his premises lead to this conclusion. Callicles is a hedonist, because he "claims without reservation that those thus delighted, however they are delighted, are happy, and does not distinguish what kinds of pleasures are good and bad." At this point, Socrates demands that Callicles make his commitments clear: "Do you claim that the pleasant and good are the same, or are there some pleasures which are not good?" Callicles' answer is: "I say they are the same" (495a, Allen).

FOUR ARGUMENTS AGAINST HEDONISM (495a–499c)

Hedonism is the view that happiness (*eudaimonia*) is pleasure. In other words, pleasure is the good that all men seek. If pleasure is the good, that means that the distinction between good and bad things boils down to the presence or absence of pleasure. This implies that there are no bad pleasures, for pleasure is what makes things good. Thus if pleasure is present, so is goodness, whereas evil is the absence of pleasure.

Socrates' critique of Callicles gets very involved, with a lot of back and forth between them, so it is easy to lose the thread. To make the discussion easier to follow, I have distilled out four arguments.

But before we go into the arguments, we need to deal with some preliminaries. Socrates claims that Callicles is contradicting his earlier positions by upholding hedonism. Which positions, though? Is Socrates simply referring to Callicles' express distaste for certain low sorts of pleasures? If so, then Callicles can and will defeat Socrates simply by accepting that low forms of pleasure are also part of the good life.

After Callicles states that he thinks that pleasure and the good are the same and will not shrink (like Gorgias and Polus) from the shameful consequences, Socrates asks Callicles if he believes that knowledge (*episteme*) exists. Callicles says yes. Socrates then asks Callicles if courage (*andreia*) exists. Callicles says yes again.

Socrates then asks if courage and knowledge are different things. Callicles agrees that they are. Socrates then asks if knowledge and pleasure are different. Callicles agrees they are. Finally, Socrates asks and Callicles affirms that courage is different from pleasure. In sum:

1. Pleasure and the good are the same.
2. Courage and knowledge exist and are different.
3. Knowledge and pleasure are different.
4. Courage and pleasure are different.

We should be on the lookout for whether and how these premises reappear in the course of the argument.

When Socrates sums up these premises, he uses legal language: "Callicles of Acharnia [Acharnia is one of the demes of Athens; this is how Callicles would be referred to in court] deposes and states that pleasure and good are the same, but knowledge and courage are different from each other and from the good [i.e., pleasure]" (495d, Allen). To which Callicles responds, also in legalistic terms, "And Socrates of Alopece dissents. Or does he join us?" Socrates replies that he will not, and that Callicles himself will not, "when he sees himself correctly" (495d–e, Allen), meaning when he understands that hedonism contradicts his real convictions.

But why the legalistic language? Is Socrates responding to Callicles' accusation (which prophesies Socrates' trial) that if Socrates goes on trial, he will be helpless to defend himself? Is Socrates putting Callicles on trial? If so, Callicles does not acquit himself.

At this point, Socrates begins his first refutation of hedonism, which I summarize as follows.

> The good (*eudaimonia*) and the bad (wretchedness), cannot exist in the same person at the same time and in the same respect.
> Pleasure associated with satisfaction and pain associated with desire can exist in the same person at the same time.

Therefore, the good is not pleasure and the bad is not pain.

Let's analyze this.

Premise one: you can't be miserable and happy at the same time, wretched and happy at the same time. We must be careful here, because when Socrates speaks of happiness and wretchedness, he is talking not about feelings but about states of virtue. Now, somebody might ask, 'Can't you be courageous in battle but cowardly about disappointing your mother? So can't you be both happy (virtuous) and wretched (vicious) at the same time?'

This is why the qualifier "in the same respect" is also there: at the same time and *in the same respect*. You may be both courageous and cowardly at the same time about different objects, particularly if you are talking about courage and cowardliness as potentialities, i.e., as traits of character which don't need to be manifest at the same time. It is harder to imagine *actually* being courageous and cowardly about different objects at the same time. But you clearly cannot *actually* be both cowardly and courageous at the same time about the same objects, i.e., in the same respect.

However, pleasure and pain can exist in the same person at the same time. Here pain is associated with desire and pleasure with the satisfaction of desire. Socrates gives the example of the pain of thirst and the pleasure of drinking. Being thirsty on a hot day is feeling pain, drinking water is feeling pleasure, and the two feelings exist at the same time. I didn't say "in the same respect" because I'm not quite sure if you can make that claim. You could say that you're feeling pleasure insofar as you're satisfying yourself and feeling pain insofar as you haven't fully satisfied yourself. So, maybe the proviso of "in the same respect" doesn't apply there.

The conclusion is this: pleasure is not the good and pain is not the bad, because pleasure and pain can exist in a person at the same time while the good and the bad can't exist in a person at the same time. The underlying assumption here is that if pleasure/pain and good/bad have different ways of being, they can't be the same thing.

Callicles is unimpressed, claiming that Socrates is pulling

"clever tricks" (497a, Allen), prompting an equally testy response from Socrates. When Callicles seems to be bowing out, Gorgias interrupts and insists that Callicles answer. Callicles protests that Socrates' "little questions" are "worthless" and "narrow." But Gorgias insists. When Callicles assents, Socrates says, "You're a happy [*eudaimon*] man, Callicles; you've been initiated into the Greater Mysteries before the Lesser. I didn't think that was religiously permitted" (497b-c, Allen). Socrates is accusing Callicles of thinking he has advanced knowledge before he acquires basic knowledge, but it is not clear what body of knowledge he is referring to.

Socrates then offers a new argument, which I reconstruct as follows.

> The good and the bad do not cease together. The ceasing of the good is the bad. The ceasing of the bad is the good. They don't end at the same time. When one ends the other begins.
> Pleasure and pain cease at the same time.
> Therefore, the good is not pleasure and the bad is not pain.

As in the first argument, the underlying assumption here is that if pleasure/pain and good/bad have different ways of being, they can't be the same thing. Whereas the first argument deals with how the good/bad and pleasure/pain *exist*, this argument deals with how they *cease to exist*.

Let's consider the first premise in terms of the virtue of moderation and the vice of immoderateness. Let's focus on a single object of moderation, namely material wealth. You cannot simultaneously be both moderate and immoderate in your pursuit of material wealth. However, if you are moderate, you can become immoderate at another time. And if you are immoderate, you can become moderate at another time. Moderation ceases when immoderation begins, and vice versa.

Now let us consider the second premise, that the pleasures and pains associated with the satisfaction of desire cease at the same time. For instance, when you eat and you become full, the pleasure of eating ceases at the same time as the pain of hunger.

Socrates does not allow Callicles to respond to the second argument before moving on to the third:

> Good men are good because of the presence of goodness.
> Bad men are bad because of the presence of badness.
> Good and bad men both experience pleasure and pain.
> Good men remain good while experiencing pain.
> Bad men remain bad while experiencing pleasure.
> Therefore, pleasure cannot be the cause of goodness, and pain can't be the cause of badness.

The first two premises are pure Platonism. This man is good because he has goodness, i.e., good qualities, such as courage and honor. This man is bad because he has badness, i.e., bad qualities, like cowardice and greed. But both good and bad men experience pleasure and pain. However, if pleasure is the good, then wouldn't experiencing pleasure—a good meal, a nice massage—make a bad man good? If hedonism were true, wouldn't the best way to reform criminals be to send them to bars, restaurants, and massage parlors? And if pain is the evil, then experiencing pain—injury, illness, loss—will make a good man bad. But we see that good men remain good while experiencing pain. Indeed, standing up to pain arguably makes good men better, since the virtue of courage masters pain and fear. Moreover, bad men remain bad while experiencing pleasure. Indeed, bad men arguably become worse by experiencing pleasure, since the virtue of moderation masters pleasure. Therefore, pleasure is not the good and pain is not the bad.

At this point, Callicles throws in the towel by abandoning the claim that pleasure is the good, which entails that there are no bad pleasures. But he does not do so gracefully. Instead, he pretends that he was only joking when he defended hedonism. "Socrates, I've been listening to you for some time and agreeing, while thinking that if anybody grants you something even as a joke, you delight in it like a boy. Do you suppose that I and every other man don't believe some pleasures better and others worse?" (499b, Allen).

Callicles thinks he is offering a refinement to his hedonism, but actually he is destroying it completely. If one can recognize that some pleasures are better than other pleasures, doesn't that mean there is another standard of the good *besides* the pleasurable? If there are bad pleasures as well as good ones, then pleasure can't be the good. Conversely, if there are good pains as well as bad ones, then pain can't be the bad. This final refutation of hedonism can be articulated as follows:

> If pleasure is the good and pain is the bad, there can be no bad pleasures or good pains.
> There are bad pleasures and good pains.
> Therefore, the good is not pleasure, and the bad is not pain.

If we think about it, we can all cite examples of bad pleasures and good pains. For instance, the sugary snacks that rot one's teeth are bad pleasures, while the discomforts one endures in the dentists' chair are good pains.

But if we can distinguish between bad and good pleasures and pains, that doesn't just mean that pleasure is not the good. It also means that we *already* have a standard of what is good and bad. We *already know* what the good is. It was already operative in our thinking all along, and we didn't even know it was there. This is why Socrates said that in affirming hedonism, Callicles was not merely in disagreement with Socrates, he was in disagreement with himself.

But if all of us already know the good, then why do we disagree so violently about different conceptions of the good life? If we already know the good, then what is the purpose of moral philosophy? The answer to these questions hinges on precisely *how* we already know the good. We all have the ability to *recognize* the good and the bad. This is how, based on examples, we can *simply see* that there are good pains and bad pleasures.

One way this works is through moral sentiments like disgust and shame. Thus when Gorgias and Polus shrank back from certain ideas in shame, or Callicles shrank back in disgust from certain implications of hedonism, this is a manifestation not of social convention but of innate moral knowledge.

But this ability to recognize the good in concrete situations is more akin to practical know-how than an articulated theory. Thus matters get tricky when we start *talking about* the good, i.e., articulating in general terms what we can already see in particular circumstances. Thus as soon as we begin comparing our moral intuitions, we begin to disagree about the good.

Since we already know the good, the purpose of moral philosophy is not to impart such knowledge but rather to help us fully and accurately articulate it. Socratic moral philosophy works by articulating a view of the good (the good = pleasure), then testing these articulations in the light of our intuitive knowledge of the good (there are good pains and bad pleasures), and then trying to articulate a better account of the good.

Now let's return to the four propositions that Socrates elicited from Callicles at the beginning of this part of the argument:

1. Pleasure and the good are the same.
2. Courage and knowledge exist and are different.
3. Knowledge and pleasure are different.
4. Courage and pleasure are different.

Socrates has overthrown the first proposition. But thus far, he has said nothing about the rest, and they play no further role in the dialogue. Could this indicate that part of the original *Gorgias* has been lost?

THE REFUTATION OF LICENTIOUSNESS (499c–505d)

Once Socrates has refuted Callicles' hedonism, he turns his attention to refuting his defense of self-indulgence and licentiousness (*akolasia*) and upholding its opposite, moderation (*sophrosyne*). But in offering this refutation, Socrates draws together and sums up the argument of the whole *Gorgias* thus far and gives an overview of his moral philosophy. Thus it is an especially rich and important part of the dialogue.

Callicles has admitted that some pleasures are good and others bad. Socrates begins there and leads Callicles to assent to the following premises. Beneficial pleasures are good. Harmful pleasures are bad. Pleasures are beneficial if they do some good. Pleasures are bad if they do some evil. Pleasures that produce bodily health are good. Pleasures that destroy bodily health are evil. Some pains are beneficial. Other pains are harmful. Only beneficial pleasures and pains are to be chosen and made use of. Everything is to be done for the sake of the good, i.e., the good is the end of all our actions. The good is not pursued for the sake of other things. Thus we do pleasant things for the sake of the good, not the good for the sake of the pleasant.

Not every man can discern good and evil pleasures. Art (*techne*) is required. The bar is lower, however, for pursuing pleasure as such, regardless of good or evil consequences. All this takes is a knack (*empeiria*) for producing pleasure. As Socrates established with Polus, one knack for gratification is confectionery, meaning the ability to make tasty food, regardless of its effect on health. The corresponding *techne* that aims at bodily well-being is medicine.

At this point Socrates enjoins Callicles to be serious, evoking the name of Zeus, the god of friendship. Referring back to Callicles' claim that his defense of hedonism was joking not earnest, Socrates urges Callicles neither to say anything unserious nor to take Socrates for doing so either, because, "Our argument now concerns what even a man of little intelligence must treat with utmost seriousness, namely, the way one ought to live" (500c, Zeyl). Namely: Callicles' choice of the public life of pursuing power, for which tyranny is the archetype, vs. Socrates' choice of the private life of pursuing wisdom.

Then Socrates expands on the distinction between *techne* and knack. The *techne* of medicine considers the nature (*physis*) of the person it serves and the cause (*aitia*) of what it does. It is also able to render an account (*logos*) of both. A knack, by contrast, has no understanding of nature and causal mechanisms. It also makes no distinctions, although Socrates doesn't make clear what kind of distinctions he is talking about. What kind of distinctions do *technai* make? Instead, a knack is based simply on experiences of what works and what doesn't.

Then Socrates moves from the body to the soul. Just as there are knacks to gratify the body regardless of its health, so there are knacks to gratify the soul, regardless of its health. Just as there are arts that help perfect the body, there are arts that help perfect the soul. Callicles assents to this, but not out of conviction. He claims he is saying yes only to humor Socrates and Gorgias.

Then Socrates establishes that just as you can pander to individuals, you can also pander to groups. He gives examples from the performing arts: flute and lyre-playing, dithyrambs and choruses, and even Athens' much-vaunted tragic dramas. All these look to gratify the audience rather than to edify them. (Note: Socrates does not mention comedy here. Is this because the *Gorgias* itself is a comedy?)

Socrates then asks what you get when you subtract "melody, rhythm, and meter from any kind of poetry" so that "only speech [*logos*] is left"? Then you have public speaking. Thus Socrates says "poetry is a kind of demagoguery" and a kind of "rhetoric" addressed to all: men and women, slave and free (502c, Allen). But there is a kind of rhetoric addressed only to free men, i.e., men in political assemblies. This sort of rhetoric has been the topic of the *Gorgias* from the start.

Then Socrates asks Callicles a twofold question. First, if any of the men who speak in front of the Athenian and other such assemblies think in terms of edifying and improving their audience rather than simply gratifying them. Second, if any of the men who speak to such assemblies do not "sacrifice the common [*koinon*] to their own private [*idion*]" (502e, Allen). Socrates doesn't actually say "common good" (*koinon agathon*) or "private good" (*idion agathon*), but that is what his contrast implies. Later in the *Gorgias*, Socrates actually brings *koinon* and *agathon* together. The *Gorgias* is probably the earliest surviving statement of the standard of legitimacy central to classical political philosophy: the good regime and the good statesman pursue the common good over individual and factional interests.

Callicles' response is surprisingly thoughtful: "There are some who say what they say out of concern for their citizens, whereas others are of the sort you describe" (503a, Allen). For Callicles, then, it is at least possible for statesmen to actually care about the citizens, which encompasses both improving rather than pandering to individual citizens and serving the common good over private interests. But when Socrates asks for names,

Callicles cannot offer any contemporary examples. However, Callicles mentions earlier statesman, all of them dead: Themistocles, Miltiades, Cimon, and Pericles.

Socrates disagrees. He does not think these were good men. He thinks they were just panderers on a colossal scale, corrupting the Athenians by gratifying desires that made them worse rather than better.

Then Socrates explains how the genuine statesman would work. In every case, the good man (*agathon*) who is intent on the best (*beltiston*) when he speaks, does not speak at random. Instead, his speeches are guided by a vision of an order, pattern, or goal. Note that Socrates is now talking about all speeches (*logoi*), not just political speeches. Just as a craftsman has a model in mind that determines the materials he assembles and the acts he performs to realize the model in matter, just as the physician or trainer keeps in mind the model of a healthy body and regulates his every word and deed accordingly, so too does the good speaker keep the model of the healthy soul in view at all time. This model determines his every word and deed: everything he says or does not say, everything he does or does not do, and—in the case of the true statesman—everything he gives to or takes from his people.

Socrates claims that the good is structure (*taxis*) and order (*kosmos*) and the bad is disorder (*ataxia, akosmia*). Socrates suggests that health and strength are the proper order of the body, and Callicles agrees (503c). But Callicles is hesitant to name the proper order of the soul, probably because he senses that whatever it is, it will not be licentiousness. Thus Socrates himself provides the answer: the good structure and order of the soul is law and lawfulness, whereby souls become law-abiding (law here is *nomos*) and orderly, and these states are righteousness (*dikaiosyne*) and moderation (*sophrosyne*) (503d).

Every good statesman looks to this model when making decisions about governing the city. But to engender righteousness, statesmen must also remove injustice (*adikia*). To promote moderation, licentiousness (*akolasia*) must be discouraged. To promote virtue (*arete*), vice (*kakia*) must be discouraged (503d–e).

Callicles agrees with this, but when Socrates confronts him

with the fact that this is inconsistent with his own advocacy of licentiousness, Callicles becomes angry and sullen, saying that he doesn't know what Socrates is talking about and telling him to ask his questions of someone else. Socrates mocks this, because Callicles is rejecting the very thing that the argument concerns: correction for one's errors and vices. Callicles is humiliated and begins to sulk, claiming that he doesn't care what Socrates has to say and was only answering to humor Gorgias. When Socrates presses the matter, Callicles accuses him of being "pushy" or "overbearing" (*biaios*), and when you accuse somebody of being pushy, that's a signal that you are preparing to push back (505d). Then Callicles suggests that Socrates carry on the argument by himself.

SOCRATES' DIALOGUE WITH HIMSELF (505e–508c)

This is a rather comic turn, but Socrates is game, and Gorgias encourages him because he wants to hear the end of the argument.

Socrates says, "So as Epicharmus has it, whereas 'previously two men spoke,' I am now to suffice as one." Epicharmus (c. 550–c. 460 BC) was one of the founders of Greek comedy. In the *Theaetetus*, Socrates refers to Epicharmus as "the prince of comedy," just as Homer is "the prince of tragedy."[4] Only a few fragments of his work survive, and the context and connotations of this quote are no longer known. The best we can say about this allusion is that it underscores the farcical quality of Socrates having a dialogue with himself and it reinforces the overall point that if the *Gorgias* is a drama, it is a comic one.

But although Socrates is going to continue alone, he tells the onlookers to speak up if they hear him saying anything questionable, for Socrates thinks that the aim of their discussion—namely, the good life for man, which is the most important topic of all—will better come to light in the back and forth of dialogue, and this is "of common good to all" (506a). Here is another reference to the common good (*koinonia gar agathon*).

Socrates will lay out the argument in the way that seems best

---

[4] Plato, *Theaetetus*, 152e.

to him. But he is aware that his thoughts are hardly the final word on the matter. Thus if he says something questionable, he welcomes the audience's corrections. Socrates is not being dogmatic. Even though he's going to be the sole one talking at this point, he's not giving a speech. He's still conversing, albeit with himself. But he is inviting everyone into a dialogue with him. Also, it becomes clear that Socrates is still primarily addressing Callicles.

Gorgias encourages Socrates to continue and says that the rest of the audience appears to agree. Socrates says, "Why, I'd happily go on discussing with Callicles here, Gorgias, up until I've paid him a speech of Amphion in return for his of Zethus" (506b). This alludes to Callicles' earlier reference to Euripides' *Antiope*, in which Zethus argues for the active and public life as opposed to the private life of his artistic brother Amphion. Callicles identified himself with Zethus and Socrates with Amphion, and here Socrates seems to accept that identification. It also underscores they are still debating the choice between the public life and the private one, although in this case the public life is about politics, and the private life is about philosophy. Then Socrates addresses Callicles directly, saying that he welcomes Callicles' corrections if he should say something mistaken, since it is a great benefit to have one's false beliefs replaced with true ones. Callicles sourly tells Socrates to finish by himself (506c).

This is the substance of what Socrates establishes in his dialogue with himself. The pleasant and the good are not the same. We do the pleasant for the sake of the good, not the good for the sake of the pleasant. We are pleased by pleasure, and we are made good by the presence of the good. This much we have already heard. What comes next is new.

All things — souls, bodies, artifacts, and every living thing — insofar as they are good are made good by the presence of some virtue or excellence (*arete*). The virtue of each thing is most beautifully produced, not at random, but through proper structure (*taxis*), correctness (*orthotes*), and *techne*. The virtue (*arete*) of each thing consists in its regular and orderly (*kosmios*) structure (*taxis*). The good (*agathon*) of every kind of thing is its proper order (*kosmos*). An orderly soul is better than a disorderly one. A soul is orderly through possessing order. An orderly soul is moderate. Thus the moderate soul is good (506c–507a).

Socrates says he can find no objections to these claims and asks Callicles if he can. Callicles does not agree but simply bids him to continue.

If a moderate soul is good (*agathon*), then the soul affected by the opposite of moderation is evil (*kakon*); it is both imprudent (*aphron*) and licentious (*akolastos*). The moderate man does what is fitting concerning both gods and men. To do otherwise would be immoderate. By doing what is fitting concerning men, the moderate man is just (*dikai*), and by doing what is fitting concerning the gods, he is pious (*hosia*). He who does just and pious things is necessarily just and pious. Furthermore, he is necessarily courageous, for a moderate man would not pursue or shun what he should not. Rather, he would pursue and shun what he ought, whether things or people, pleasures or pains, and to be steadfast in doing his duty (507b–c). Thus:

> It is necessary, Callicles, that the moderate man, because he is also as we've explained just [*dikaion*] and courageous [*andreion*] and pious [*hosion*], should be a completely [*teleos*] good man [*agathon*]. The good man does what he does well [*eu*] and nobly [*kalos*]. By doing and faring well he is blessed [*makarion*] and happy [*eudaimon*]. The bad man does and fares ill and is wretched [*athlion*]. This man who is opposite to the moderate man is the licentious man [*akolastos*] whom you praised. Now, I hold these things so and say that they are true. But if true, then he who wishes to be happy must, it seems, pursue and practice moderation, and each of us must flee licentiousness [*akolasia*] as fast as our feet will carry us, and so far as possible see to it that we need no chastisement. (507c–d, Allen)

At this point, Socrates returns to the account of punishment he gave in his discussion with Polus. Just punishment restores the health of the soul, thus promoting happiness. Hence if an individual, his family, or his city need such punishment, they should be the first to suggest it. Every individual and every city must always keep the model of the happy and blessed man in sight, in order to provide all men who would live well with the necessary moderation and justice—including restraining and punishing excessive desires, lest their pursuit lead to ruin. For the man of unrestrained desires becomes antisocial, leading the "life of a robber," deprived of the community and friendship of both gods and men.

Then Socrates returns to what Heidegger called the Fourfold:

> Wise men [*sophoi*, which are something above the philosopher, who merely pursues wisdom] tell us, Callicles, that heaven [*ouranos*] and earth [*ge*] and gods [*theoi*] and men [*anthropoi*] are held together by communion [*koinonia*] and friendship [*philia*], by orderliness, moderation, and righteousness, and that is the reason why, my friend, they call the whole of this world by the name of order [*kosmos*], not of disorder [*akosmia*] or licentiousness [*akolasia*]. But you, I think, have not attended to this, for all your wisdom, but have forgotten the great power of proportional equality [*isotes*] amongst both gods and men: you recommend excess [*pleonexia*] because you neglect proportion. (507e–508b, Allen)

Recall that earlier in the *Gorgias* proportionate equality means:

Jack's merit : Jill's merit :: Jack's reward : Jill's reward.

Thus if Jill is twice as good as Jack, she will receive twice his reward. This inequality is not, however, unjust or unfair, because it is proportionate to inequalities of worth. If, however, Jack and Jill were of equal worth, it would be unjust to give them unequal rewards. Moreover, if Jill is twice as good as Jack but received ten times Jack's reward, that would also be unjust, because it is not proportionate to their differences of merit.

Now Socrates is claiming that proportionate equality exists within the Fourfold:

Heaven : earth :: gods : mortals.

What is the connection between the two senses of proportionate equality? The term that seems to link them is community. Proportional equality between Jack and Jill is a principle of distributive justice. Justice is the right order of communities. Here Socrates first speaks of community among men, claiming that the immoderate man is anti-social, like a criminal, incapable of community and friendship with his fellow men (507e). If that were all to his new discussion of justice, it would go no further than the first human-centered analysis of proportionate equality. But here Socrates also speaks of community and friendship with gods.

Does this change anything in Socrates' critique of immoderation, licentiousness, and excess? In the first analysis, if Jill were inclined to infinite acquisition, she would be constrained because she is only entitled to finite acquisition, namely finite acquisition proportionate to her finite merits. Even if she is twice as worthy as Jack, she is worthy of only twice as much, not a thousand times as much, much less infinitely more. Jill's *pleonexia* is thus constrained, as it were from below, by proportional equality.

Now let's bring the gods into the picture:

Jill's merit : Apollo's merit :: Jill's reward : Apollo's reward.

Since the Greek gods are finite in their goodness, such an analogy is possible. But note that we don't need to assign any numbers here to eliminate *pleonexia* on Jill's part. Infinite rewards would be proportional only to infinite worth. And an infinitely worthy human is simply inconceivable if there is a whole additional realm of beings that are superior to man. But note that Jill can't pursue *pleonexia* by wishing to become a god either, for the gods are finite as well, which implies they cannot justly demand infinite respect, sacrifices, etc. from us.

In the *Gorgias*, the Fourfold is introduced to constrain infinite human acquisitiveness. It plays a similar role in Heidegger. For Heidegger, the Fourfold is introduced as a foil to the *Gestell*, the modern conception of being as raw material for human projects. The *Gestell* depicts the world around us as boundlessly transparent to human curiosity and boundlessly available for human appropriation, manipulation, and consumption. One could characterize the *Gestell*'s boundless world and the boundless strivings it incubates as "Faustian" in the sense used by Oswald Spengler.[5] One could characterize Callicles' desire for infinite power and acquisition as Faustian as well. By placing man in the Fourfold, however, both Plato and Heidegger bring infinite striving to an end by containing the realm of human action within finite bounds.

Socrates brings this part of his argument to a close by challenging Callicles to refute the dual claim that righteousness and moderation are the causes of happiness and vice is the cause of wretchedness, and if it cannot be refuted, to face the consequences. The first consequence is Socrates' claim that the proper use of forensic rhetoric is to accuse oneself or one's family and friends of vice and to demand the appropriate punishments, a claim that Callicles scoffed at as unserious. The second consequence is that it is better to suffer wrong than to do it, which Callicles said that Polus agreed to only out of shame. The third consequence is that the true rhetorician must know the truth about justice, which Polus said that Gorgias agreed to only out of shame.

Socrates, in short, believes that all of his previous positions hinge on the claim that righteousness and moderation are the causes of happiness, vice the cause of wretchedness. Having established this, he now wishes to return to these arguments and finalize his victories.

---

[5] Oswald Spengler, *The Decline of the West*, Volume I: *Form and Actuality*, trans. Charles Francis Atkinson (New York: Alfred A. Knopf, 1926), pp. 183–216.

THE TRUE STATESMAN

SECURING OURSELVES AGAINST INJUSTICE (508c–513c)
Recall that one of Callicles' main arguments for prizing the *techne* of rhetoric is that it is a source of power for securing oneself against injustice. Socrates now returns to this argument and dispenses with it:

> Let us examine what you reproach me for. Is it well said or not that I am unable to help myself or any of my friends or kin, or to save them from the greatest dangers, but that I am subject, like people without civil rights, to the will of any man, whether he wishes to punch me on the chin . . . or confiscate my goods, or exile me from my city, or ultimately slay me? (508c–d, Allen)

Callicles believes that suffering injustice, up to and including an unjust death, is the worst possible thing. Socrates thinks these are bad things, but he thinks there is something worse than suffering injustice, namely committing it, and, more broadly, having a corrupt soul.

After stating this thesis, Socrates makes an important point about philosophical method.

> This appeared true in our former discussion, as I say, and it is secured and bound fast, if it is not too rude to say so, with *logoi* of adamant and iron. So, at any rate, it would seem, and unless you, or someone younger and more daring than you, shall unbind and loosen those *logoi*, it is impossible to speak well and yet say other than what I am saying now. The same *logos* is ever mine, namely, that while I do not know how things stand in these matters, I have never met anyone able to speak otherwise without being ridiculous, as now. So again, I take these to be so. (508e–509b, Allen)

When Socrates claims that it is better to suffer injustice than to do it, he does not claim to know it, in a strong sense of that word, namely knowledge that is beyond the possibility of revision. Instead, he claims that he has not yet heard a good argument against his position, but he remains open to considering one.

Then Socrates suggests a general principle, namely that the greatest *boetheia*—meaning help, aid, rescue, or deliverance—secures us from the greatest of evils (509c). Callicles agrees with this, but he and Socrates disagree about what the greatest evil is. For Socrates, the greatest evil is ultimately the corruption of one's soul, which leads to doing injustice, whereas for Callicles, the greatest evil is death, which is the worst result of suffering injustice.

Socrates then asks how we can secure ourselves against both suffering and doing injustice. In both cases, he asks whether we can do so by a wish (*boulesis*) or by a power (*dynamis*) (509d). In other words, is it enough simply to *make up our minds* not to do or suffer injustice, or do we need to *strengthen our will by acquiring additional powers*, such as the *techne* of rhetoric, which Callicles has lauded for its saving power?

It is obvious that simply wishing not to suffer injustice is not sufficient to secure us, since nobody wants to suffer injustice, but we suffer it anyway. Thus Callicles readily assents to the claim that we must acquire some sort of power not to suffer injustice.

As for not doing injustice, Socrates has already argued that all men wish to do what is good, which would include not doing injustice. But this is not enough to avoid injustice, which is rampant. Socrates also argued that if all men wish to do good, they only do bad things out of ignorance. Thus if we wish to do justice, we need more than just good intentions. We also need a certain "power or art" that reinforces our good intentions. Namely, we need *knowledge* of what justice in fact is (509e–510a).

Callicles is not particularly interested in doing the right thing, so the agreement he offers is merely perfunctory, to keep the argument moving forward.

Then Socrates suggests what power one needs not to be a victim of injustice: "One must either rule in the city oneself or even rule as tyrant or else be a comrade of the existing regime" (510a, Allen). This is music to Callicles' ears. He heartily agrees.

But then Socrates offers a critique. Like attracts like. So, if you're going to become friends with a tyrant, you must be like him. You can't be better, because he'll resent you. You can't be inferior, because he'll look down on you and treat you badly. You have to be pretty much like the tyrant. You must share his values. But you must submit to the tyrant's will. Then you will enjoy some of his power and protection. Thus no one will be able to do injustice to you with impunity—nobody other than the tyrant, of course. One will even be able to do injustice oneself, with impunity.

But there's a price. To be like the tyrant, you must share his values and activities. But tyrants, by their very nature, are corrupt, so you must become corrupt as well. If the tyrant commits injustice, then you must commit injustice as well. As Socrates sums it up: "So then, the greatest evil will befall him when he is degenerate and maimed in his soul through imitation of the master and through power" (511a, Allen). But is it worth it? In effect, Socrates is asking, 'What does it profit you to gain the whole world if you lose your soul?' Socrates says it is not worth saving one's life if one has to lose one's soul.

Callicles, however, has a ready response to this: "Don't you know that this imitator of yours [the man who becomes like the tyrant] will kill the fellow who refuses to imitate that man [the tyrant], if he wishes, and confiscate his property?" (511a, Allen). For Callicles, the worst two things in the world are loss of life and loss of property.

Callicles, in short, has a "bourgeois" value system, because he places property and self-preservation above personal honor and integrity. Socrates, however, thinks that his personal honor and integrity—the health of his soul—are more important than a long life or property. Thus he is unwilling to extend his life by corrupting his soul. Thus Socrates has an aristocratic value system that prefers death to dishonor and corruption.

Nobody wants to be murdered, but Socrates thinks that there is some solace in the fact that in Callicles' scenario, "it will be a base man killing a noble and good man" (511b, Allen). Callicles' response is that it is especially infuriating for bad men to kill good men (511b). This is an important point because it shows that Callicles understands on some level that goodness is not identical with strength, for if that were true, good men literally could not be killed by bad men, for the killer would be good by virtue of killing and the victim would be bad by fault of being the victim.

Socrates brushes this aside, though, because he wishes to focus on Callicles' underlying premise, which he formulates as "a man ought to contrive to live as long as possible and be concerned for those arts which always save us from danger" (511b-c). Callicles agrees with this statement: "Yes, by Zeus, and I'm counseling you correctly!" (511c, Allen).

Socrates' argument is that self-preservation is not the highest good. If self-preservation is the highest good, then wouldn't the arts that save lives — like piloting ships — have the highest status? The Greeks did not think so, and Socrates has an explanation: the life-saving arts don't have the highest status, because the highest value is not life itself but rather the good life. Thus it makes sense that arts that save life itself, without regard to the quality of life, do not enjoy the highest status.

Recall Socrates' hardest saying from the *Apology*: "The unexamined life is not worth living."[1] This means that *almost every* life is not worth living, because all of us start out unreflective, and only a few of us end up engaging in self-examination, i.e., philosophy.

Socrates enlists Callicles' own aristocratic prejudices against him. Callicles looks down on the people like ships' pilots. He would never let his daughter marry one of them. Yet why should he feel that way if he thinks that "virtue is simply this, saving oneself and one's own property," regardless of the quality of one's soul? By contrast, Socrates asserts that the "noble and the good" (*to gennaion kai to agathon*) — the aims of the true aristocrat — are not saving and being saved (512c-d, Allen).

Men should not be concerned with how long they live but

---

[1] Plato, *Apology*, 38a5–6. See my commentary on the *Apology* in *The Trial of Socrates*.

rather with how well they live. We should not love life as such, but the good life. We lower ourselves by trifling about making our lives longer, given that we have very little control over such factors. This was certainly true in Socrates' time, but even in modern times, science and technology may have raised average life expectancies, but the small clearing of human knowledge and control is still surrounded by a vast dragon-haunted forest of mystery and chance. Thus, although we should all take care of our health and avoid stupid risks, at a certain point we must acknowledge the fact that we cannot ultimately control death. Thus we should "turn over what concerns these things [the length of life] to the god and believe the women's[2] saying that no man may escape his destiny." Having done that, we should focus on "in what way he who is going to live for a time lives best" (512e, Allen).

Socrates insists that the best life for a man is not to become like the city in which he lives. This presages Aristotle's discussion in book three of the *Politics* of the relationship between the good man and the good citizen.[3] What makes a good man is determined by nature and is not relative to time and place. What makes a good citizen is relative to the laws of his particular time and place. The good man and the good citizen would coincide only in a city whose laws are based purely on nature.

But there are no such cities.

Thus in the Athens of Socrates' day, being a good man and being a good citizen are at odds. Since political ambition requires being like the regime, one can only buy power at the cost of one's soul. He urges Callicles to "Consider then whether this is to your advantage and mine . . . so we will not suffer what they say happens to the witches of Thessaly, who draw down the moon and cause an eclipse" (513a). According to Dodds, the Greeks believed that "a witch must pay for her powers either by a mutilation (often blindness) or by the sacrifice of a member of

---

[2] Allen suggests that this is a reference to the Eleusinian Mysteries (*The Dialogues of Plato*, vol. 1, p. 302 n9), but it could also be equivalent to the idea of an "old wives' tale" (cf. Dodds, p. 350).

[3] Aristotle, *Politics*, book III, ch. 4, 1276b16–1277b33.

her family."[4] Thus, as Socrates continues, "the choice of such power in the city would then be at the cost of what we hold most dear" (513a, Allen). In other words, political power must be paid for by the mutilation of the soul.

Socrates also cautions Callicles against sophists selling him a *techne* that will allow him to gain power merely by *acting* like the public, while remaining himself in private. Political ambition requires genuine friendship with the public, which means you must *be* like them, not merely *act* like them (513a–c). When people listen to a speech, they don't just respond to the words, they also respond to the character of the speaker. Thus if you desire to be a rhetorician and a statesman, you must share the character of the city you wish to rule.

Callicles replies, "I don't know why, but you seem to me to make sense, Socrates." This is genuine progress. But, Callicles adds, "Still, I feel the way most people do: I don't quite believe you" (513c, Allen).

GOOD STATESMEN & BAD (513c–521a)

Socrates claims that Callicles resists his arguments due to "love of the *demos*," the people of Athens, a reference to Callicles' political ambitions. Socrates tries to redirect this ambition, by convincing Callicles that the highest form of life is not the public pursuit of power at the expense of his soul but the private pursuit of wisdom, which is equivalent to the care of his soul.

To overcome Callicles' resistance, Socrates returns to his earlier arguments with Polus. There are two ways of treating people. One aims to please them. This is flattery. The other aims for the best: to edify or build them up. This is friendship. Socrates asks Callicles if the proper goal of the statesman is to build up the city and the citizens by making the citizens as good as possible. Socrates does not state the alternative, which is to build up the power of the statesman by giving the people whatever pleases them, regardless of whether it is good for them. Socrates now takes it as established that nothing good can come from placing power and money in the hands of bad men. Callicles

---

[4] Dodds, p. 351.

agrees with this to humor Socrates.

Socrates then states that if he and Callicles were to propose to build something important for the city—like walls, arsenals, or temples—their first duty would be to know themselves, specifically if they actually had the *techne* of building. But having the *techne* is not enough. One must be able to *prove* to the city that one has it by pointing to external signs. Socrates names two: the masters from whom they learned the *techne* and their portfolio of private buildings. Callicles agrees with all this (514a-b).

Similarly, if they were to propose advising the city on medical matters, they would need to prove their qualifications based on their education and experience treating patients (514d-e).

As a general rule, if we want to do something big for the public, we should be able to demonstrate that we have already done similar things on a smaller scale in private. Callicles agrees on this point as well.

Then Socrates applies this argument to Callicles himself, who is "just entering upon a public career" (515a, Allen). If Callicles wishes to become a statesman, isn't it reasonable to ask if he has made any individual citizens better in his capacity as a private citizen? Callicles is unable to cite a single example, so he deflects by accusing Socrates of being quarrelsome. Socrates claims that his question is not quarrelsome but pertinent and essential. Nobody will take Callicles seriously as an improver of the city unless he has some proof that he can improve people in his private dealings (515b-c).

Callicles becomes sullen and silent, so Socrates moves on to the topic of Pericles, Cimon, Miltiades, and Themistocles. Earlier, Callicles claimed that these former statesmen were superior to the current batch. Socrates responds that if this were true, they would have made the people better. Callicles maintains that they did. To this Socrates asks: So when Pericles began his career, were the Athenians worse than when his career ended? This causes Callicles to pause, because the answer is clearly "no." At the end of Pericles' career, Athens was at war, and the people had turned on him (515d-516e).

Of course this is hardly a fair question, because Pericles could have been a fine statesman over a city so corrupt that it could not be improved. In which case, a better question might be: Did Pericles leave Athens better off than if he had never attained power? Couldn't a statesman in a corrupt city be hailed as great simply for slowing its decline?

When asked for evidence that Pericles had made the Athenians worse, Socrates says that he hears that Pericles made the Athenians "idle and cowardly, chatterers and money grubbers" (515e, Allen) because he introduced pay for serving in public assemblies. Callicles dismisses this as the sort of thing that a Spartan-sympathizer might say. (He refers to the "men with cauliflower ears" because the Spartanizers were fond of martial arts training [515a].) Of course that doesn't make it untrue. Socrates does not dispute this. He simply moves on to another argument.

Socrates then likens statesmen to animal trainers. A dog trainer would not be considered good if he received gentle puppies and turned them into vicious curs. The same is true for the trainer of any other kind of animal. By the same token, statesmen should not be considered good if they corrupt the people they rule. Yet, Socrates argues, this is precisely what the great statesman of old did to the Athenians. Their vaunted careers ended in failure. Pericles was convicted of theft and nearly killed. Cimon was ostracized. Themistocles was exiled. Miltiades narrowly escaped execution. Thus, according to Socrates, they were bad statesmen (516a–e).

Callicles accepts this. But he maintains that Pericles and company were at least *better* than the current batch of politicians (517a–b). Socrates agrees that Pericles, etc. were better at giving the people whatever they wanted. But a true statesman does not give the people whatever they *want*, regardless of whether or not it is good for them. Instead, he does what is *best* for them, which often requires saying "no." Thus, by being better at gratifying the corrupt appetites of the citizens, Pericles and the rest were actually worse for the city than the current politicians, who might preserve some shreds of public virtue simply by being less competent at pandering to public vices.

Then Socrates cashes in on the set of analogies he established in his discussion with Polus. Mistaking Pericles for a statesman is equivalent to mistaking a chef for a trainer. A trainer seeks to improve the health of his client, whereas a chef merely titillates his palate, ruining his health in the process. Likewise, if Pericles were a true statesman, he would have made the Athenians better, not merely helped them satisfy their unhealthy desires:

> You sing the praises of those [Pericles, etc.] who threw parties for these people, and who feasted them lavishly with what they had an appetite for. And they say that they have made the city great. But they didn't notice that the city is swollen and festering thanks to these former leaders. For with no regard for righteousness and moderation, they filled the city with harbors and dockyards, walls and tribute payments, and trash like that. (519e–520a, Allen)

Socrates also issues a warning. Just as people who have ruined their health will eventually get sick, so will Athens. Moreover, men who ruin their health have a tendency not to blame the chefs who fattened them up but rather whoever is around advising them when they get sick. The same is true of a city in crisis:

> So, when that fit of sickness comes on, they'll blame their advisors of the moment and sing the praises of Themistocles and Cimon and Pericles, the ones who were to blame for their ills. Perhaps, if you're not careful, they'll lay their hands on you, and on my friend Alcibiades, when they lose not only what they gain but what they had originally as well, even though you aren't responsible for their ills but are perhaps accessories to them. (520a–b, Allen)

This "prophecy" of Alcibiades' downfall, like the prophecies of Socrates' trial and execution, have an apologetic purpose. Socrates was characterized as a corrupter of the youth in part because of his relationship with Alcibiades. In the *Greater Alcibiades*, however, Plato depicts Socrates as trying to turn Alcibiades away from politics toward philosophy and expressing the fear that the Athenians will corrupt him. In the *Gorgias*, Socrates also tries to turn Callicles from politics toward philosophy. He predicts that politics could lead Alcibiades and Callicles to bad ends, for when the crisis comes, the Athenians will blame current politicians like Alcibiades and Callicles—who are at best accessories to the crime—not the real culprits, namely past politicians, not to mention the Athenian people themselves.

But can you really establish that Pericles, Themistocles, Miltiades, and Cimon fell specifically due to the corruptions that they sowed? Maybe they fell due to corruptions that were well-established before their time. Moreover, any particular event is the result of many different wills striving against each other. So how much responsibility can one really assign to even the most powerful of statesmen?

Socrates seems to sense that this is an issue. Thus he insists that, "No leader of a city could ever be destroyed unjustly by the city of which he is a leader" (519c, Allen). Why? Socrates does not state his reasons. But he seems to be assuming that a *true* leader *necessarily* makes the people better, and if they are genuinely better, then *of necessity* they will not treat their leaders unjustly. Thus he claims that politicians who complain they are being treated unjustly by the people are liars. But again, what if even the best statesman cannot remove long-established corruptions? Would he not, then, be blameless when the people turn against him?

Socrates is also dismissive of sophists who claim to teach justice and then complain that their students are treating them unjustly by not paying their fees. He insists that there is nothing shameful about a doctor or physical trainer asking for payment up front, but if someone who claims to teach justice demands payment up front, he is obviously not confident of his wares. Socrates is probably needling Gorgias here, who might well have charged his students up front.

Socrates's argument here seems to presuppose that nothing impedes teaching or doing justice, so if a statesman or a sophist teaches it, it will be learned. He also seems to be presupposing that once justice is learned, nothing impedes people from acting on it. These are highly idealized and questionable assumptions about both politics and human psychology, akin to the idea of a frictionless plane.

Socrates can't establish the strong causal necessities that he needs. The best he can do is get Callicles to admit that it is "illogical" for statesmen and sophists to claim that they have made people good then complain that they have behaved badly. To which one might say: it may be illogical, but it happens all the time. At this point, Socrates might say, 'Yes, but no *true* statesman, no *true* sophist, would face such problems.' But this would insulate his theory against refutation only by making it unable to explain what is actually happening.

Socrates belabors this point from 519b to 520e—more than an entire Stephanus page. But beyond being weak, the whole argument is unnecessary. Socrates need not argue that Pericles *et al.* were bad statesmen because the people turned against them. After all, presumably, there could be bad statesmen that the people never turn against.

Socrates could have argued his point simply by noting that Pericles and the rest were more interested in pleasing the Athenians than making them better people, which should be less difficult to establish, since statesmen face the choice of pandering or edifying every single day.

SOCRATES AS TRUE STATESMAN (521a–522e)

Let's return now to the analogy of the self-indulgent man whose health finally breaks down. Socrates says that he is less likely to blame himself or the panderers who fattened him up long before than the people who are currently "advising" him. These advisors can fall into two categories: flatterers who tell him what he wants to hear, thus making him worse, and friends who tell him what he needs to hear in order to get better. In this case, such friends would be doctors and physical trainers.

When we move to the political realm, the current advisors who are likely to be blamed when Athens' corruption finally comes to a head would also fall into two categories: flatterers and friends. But Socrates only names flatterers like Alcibiades and Callicles, who are mere accessories to Athens' crisis, not the primary culprits. He does not mention friends of the city. These would be true statesmen who looked out for Athens' genuine interests. Such friends of the city, if they were too vocal, might also become scapegoats, in this case wholly innocent ones. Plato would have us believe that this was the fate of Socrates.

Socrates asks Callicles to tell him how he should serve the Athenians: as a friend trying to make them as good as possible (since Athens is sick, Socrates uses the analogy of a doctor not a trainer) or as a flatterer who seeks only to please them. Callicles recommends the latter, because if Socrates doesn't pander to the public, he'll get in trouble.

Socrates cuts him off, saying that he has heard it all before. But if he is killed, he will die with his honor intact, rather than sacrificing it to (perhaps) extend his life. Moreover, if his property is taken by unjust men, they will not profit by it, because to profit they must have the wisdom to use it rightly, and unjust men are *ipso facto* unwise.

Callicles says that Socrates is deluded if he thinks that he can avoid being dragged into court by staying out of the way of wicked men. Socrates says that he is no fool. He knows that he is vulnerable, but he also knows that only wicked men would attack an entirely innocent man like himself. But if it happens, Socrates fully expects to be put to death.

At this point, Socrates comes right out and says that he is a true statesman, indeed the only true statesman in Athens:

> I believe that I'm one of the few Athenians—so as not to say I'm the only one, but the only one among our contemporaries—to take up the true political art [*alethes politike techne*] and practice the true politics. This is because the speeches I make on each occasion do not aim at gratification but at what's best instead of what's most pleasant. And because I'm not willing to do those clever things you recommend, I won't know what to say in court. (521d–e, Allen)

Then Socrates appeals to the wonderful set of analogies he established with Polus. Socrates claims that if he is brought to trial in Athens, he will be like a doctor being accused by a confectioner in front of a jury of children. His accuser would claim that he is a bad man because he makes them do unpleasant things like diet, fast, and swallow bitter pills. The confectioner, however, feeds them tasty treats. What could a doctor say in his defense, especially before a jury of appetitive and immature children? The doctor would have to admit that he makes the children suffer. But when he explains that, in the long run, it is for their own good, imagine the tumult in the courtroom! It simply would not fly with the majority of jurors.

The same thing would happen if a true legislator were accused of wrongdoing by a sophist or an orator. Like children, the majority of adults are appetitive, vain, and short-sighted. Therefore, those who pander to such vices will always have the majority on their side. Thus the true legislator will always face a disadvantage when he has to compete for public favor with panderers.

Callicles then asks whether a man who is incapable of taking care of himself in such a situation is admirable (522e).

Socrates says yes, such a man is admirable as long as he has done nothing unjust in word or deed to gods or men. In other words, such a man is still admirable when he fails to triumph in court because he has taken care of something far more important, namely the most important thing of all: the cultivation of virtue in his own soul. Socrates would be ashamed if he had not done all he could to cultivate virtue. He would be ashamed to be put to death for failing to care for his soul. But he would not be ashamed to die because of his inability to pander to others at the expense of his own integrity. For no rational and courageous man is afraid of death. Instead, he is afraid of unrighteousness, which in the aristocratic scale of values is a fate worse than death.

SOCRATES THE DOG

A RATIONAL MYTH (523a)

Apropos of the topic of death, Socrates says that the worst thing is to arrive in Hades with one's soul full of injustices. He then proposes to illustrate this point with a speech (*logos*). In the context of the *Gorgias*, a speech is contrasted with the back and forth of dialogue. But the Greek *logos* does not just mean "speech." It also has the connotation of "rational account" as opposed to something irrational. Thus Socrates says that Callicles will regard his *logos* as a myth (*mythos*). But Socrates insists that it as an actual *logos* and offers it as true.

Socrates' rational myth is about the judgment of the dead in the afterlife. Socrates often swears an oath "by the dog." In the *Gorgias*, at the beginning of the conversation with Callicles, he makes clear who the dog is. He says, "by the dog, the god of the Egyptians." Socrates is swearing an oath to a foreign god. This is the sort of behavior that got him accused of impiety and executed.

Who is the dog, the god of the Egyptians? His name was Anubis. He was depicted as a black jackal or as a man with a jackal's head. The jackal was associated with the desert where the Egyptians buried their dead. In Egyptian mythology, Anubis ushered the dead before the throne of Osiris, the god of the dead, where they were judged fit to enter the afterlife. Their hearts were weighed against the feather of *ma'at* (righteousness). Those whose hearts were heavy with wickedness were devoured by a monster. Those whose hearts were light entered the afterlife.

The Greeks later identified Anubis with Hermes, the *psychopomp*, or the "guide of souls" to the realm of the dead. They even created a syncretic deity, Hermanubis, a dog-headed rather than jackal-headed god. Socrates identified himself as a *psychagog*, a "leader of souls," which is a related concept.[1] Now Socrates is

---

[1] In the *Phaedrus*, Socrates asks if rhetoric is a *"techne psychagogia tis dia logon"* — an "art of leading souls through words" in both public

taking on the role of Hermanubis and leading Callicles into the underworld to face judgment.

Socrates' dog is a foreign god who is connected with the soul and its conduct. Socrates evokes another foreign god connected with the soul, namely his *daimonion*. In the *Theages*, Socrates identifies the *daimonion* with his knowledge of "erotic things." Socrates also identifies the human soul with *eros* and the *daimonic* realm. Thus I have argued that the *daimonion* is Socrates' personification of his knowledge of human psychology. Based on this knowledge, Socrates can divine likely courses of action (character being destiny) and act prudently.[2] Could "the dog" be the *daimonion*'s littermate? Could it be another personification of Socrates' knowledge of the soul and his ability to guide it toward the good?

THE OLD REGIME OF KRONOS (523a–b)

Socrates' story is basically this. The previous age was ruled by Kronos. Human beings had foreknowledge of their time of death. When they were approaching death, they would go to a mortal judge who would assign them their place in the afterlife. Those who led good lives would be sent to the Isles of the Blessed, which was basically heaven. Those who lived evil lives would be sent to Hades/Tartarus, the equivalent of both the Christian ideas of Hell and Purgatory, where they would be punished.

But the system didn't work. The life one leads is inscribed on one's soul. Because people were judged before they died, their souls were still in their bodies. But the internal and the external don't always match up. There are people with beautiful faces and sterling reputations whose souls are corrupt and rancid. And there are decent men who have ugly faces and bad reputations, like Socrates. Moreover, because men knew when the end was near, they could live lax or wicked lives, right up to the end,

---

and private (Plato, *Phaedrus*, 261a7–8). This is a good description of Platonic dialogue, which also operates in public (as in the *Gorgias*) and private (as in the *Phaedrus*).

[2] See my commentary on the *Theages* in *The Trial of Socrates*.

then put on their best possible appearance of virtue before approaching the judges. Finally, the dying were judged by living beings, who could not see through the body, its reputation, and its behavior to the soul underneath. Thus inevitably some good people were sent to Hell, and some bad people ended up in Heaven.

THE REVOLUTION OF ZEUS (523b–513c)

When Zeus overthrew Kronos, he divided the world between himself and his two brothers: Pluto took the underworld, Poseidon took the seas, and Zeus ruled over the rest. Then Zeus rectified the judgment of the dead. Zeus decreed that men no longer have foreknowledge of their death, so they can't live laxly then prepare for judgment at the last minute. They must be prepared for death and judgment *at any time*, so they must be virtuous *all the time*.

Zeus also decreed that men be judged after death, when their souls were stripped of their bodies, so their virtues and vices were plainly visible to all. On the assumption that "like knows like," the judges must also be dead, so that naked souls judge naked souls, all external appearances and pretenses stripped.

Zeus then appointed three of his dead sons as judges of the afterlife. Aeacus judged the dead of Europe. Rhadamanthus judged the dead of Asia. Minos presided over both and had final say in case of disputes.

Under the new system, the high and mighty in this world fared very poorly in the next world if their souls were corrupt. Even the Great King of Persia entered the afterlife stripped of his pomp and reputation, with his soul naked and his sins visible to all.

This is what happens when Rhadamanthus, the judge of Asia, encounters the soul of "the Great King or some other king or potentate":

> [He] sees nothing healthy in his soul, but finds it whip-marked and full of scars from the perjuries and injustice imprinted on his soul by his every action—everything misshapen from falsehood and boasting, and nothing

straight—the result of an upbringing devoid of truth. He sees a soul filled with asymmetry and ugliness as a result of its license, luxury, insolence, and lack of control over its actions [all things praised by Callicles]; and when he sees it, he sends it away in disgrace, straight to prison. When it gets there, it will have to endure the things that are appropriate to it. (525a-b, Griffith)

Here prison means Hades, also called Tartarus. Hades is divided into two different levels. One corresponds to the Christian idea of Hell, the other to the idea of Purgatory. Both are places of punishment. Purgatory is where those who can be redeemed by punishment are sent to expiate their crimes, after which they might graduate on to Heaven. Hell is where irredeemable souls are sent to be tortured and punished for all eternity as an example for others.

Of the unredeemable, Socrates says:

Archelaus [King of Macedon] will be one, if what Polus says is true, along with anyone else who is a tyrant of that kind. In fact, I think the majority of these examples will come from tyrants and kings and potentates and those who have engaged in political life. They are the ones who have the opportunity to commit the greatest and the most unholy crimes. Homer is evidence of this, representing those who are being punished in Hades for the whole of time as kings and potentates—Tantalus, Sisyphus, Tityus. (525d-e, Griffith)

Socrates then explains why the high and mighty are more likely to be incurably corrupt than common men who lead private lives. Just as ugliness protects the virtue of women, poverty and obscurity protect the virtue of men, even the men who act wickedly. Great men sin greatly, because they have the means and opportunity to do so.

Small men sin pettily, because they lack the means and opportunity to do worse. Therefore, they are more likely to be redeemable. Socrates continues:

> No one has represented Thersites, or any other private individual who was wicked, as being in an incurable, held fast in the grip of severe punishments. He didn't have the opportunity, I suppose, which is why he was more fortunate than those who did. (525e, Griffith)

Socrates speaks here of good and bad "fortune," but he inverts the common understanding. Most men, including Callicles, think that the Great King is the most fortunate man of all, whereas a man who is humble (the opposite of the *kalon*) and unknown (the opposite of *kleos*) — in short, the opposite of Callicles, whose name basically means noble + famous — is unfortunate. For Socrates, however, the Great King is unfortunate, whereas Thersites is fortunate, for great men have more opportunities to ruin their souls than humble men.

But Socrates' analysis here leaves out something very important: wisdom. Both the great and the humble in Socrates' account take the cards they are dealt by fortune and play them badly. And, as Socrates argues in the *Euthydemus*, foolish men are better off with fewer advantages, so they have fewer opportunities to behave badly.[3] But the reverse is also true: wise men are better off with more advantages, because they can do great things with their resources. The big question is: How can wise men acquire the resources to do great things?

Socrates continues:

> No, Callicles, it is among the powerful that the really wicked people are to be found, though even among them there is nothing to stop good men coming into being, and they are entitled to great admiration when they do. After all Callicles, it is hard for someone who is born with great opportunities for acting unjustly to live his life justly. He is entitled to great credit. But people like this rarely do come into being. Here and elsewhere there have been, and no doubt will be, gentlemen with this virtue of dealing justly with whatever is entrusted to them. [Here Socrates brings

---

[3] Plato, *Euthydemus*, 280d, 281b-e, 288e-298a.

wisdom into play, in the form of the virtue (*arete*) of justice (*dike*).] One in particular, Aristides the son of Lysimachus, has become very famous all over Greece. But, with all due respect, the majority of those who exercise power turned out bad. (525e–526b, Griffith)

Aristides (530–468 BCE), nicknamed "the just" (*dikaios*), was a freeborn Athenian of moderate fortune who became a general and political leader during the Persian Wars. In short, he was born in the right stratum of society to attain power and influence without a long, corrupting climb up the greasy pole of democratic politics. Yet when he attained power, he had the wisdom to use it rightly. Aristides was truly noble and won just fame, again components of Callicles' name.

Aristides, however, was ostracized in 483 BCE. Earlier in his conversation with Callicles, Socrates claims that the ostracism of Themistocles and Miltiades were signs of their failure as statesmen.[4] This does not, however, alter Socrates' point. Aside from the fact that Aristides was soon pardoned and resumed his leading role in Athens, Socrates might have believed that Aristides was ostracized *despite* his wisdom (which cannot wholly overcome bad fortune), whereas Themistocles and Miltiades might have been ostracized due to their lack of wisdom. But, contra Socrates's earlier claims, simply being ostracized is not sufficient evidence of a failed political career.

After discussing the justice meted out to men like the Great King, Socrates then turns to the fate of men like himself:

Sometimes there is a soul which has lived a holy life, in company with truth, a soul belonging to some private individual, or somebody of that sort, or most likely, as I maintain, Callicles, the soul of a philosopher who has minded his own business in life and not poked his nose into the affairs of others. When [Rhadamanthus] catches sight of one of these [these would be philosophers from Ionia and other places in Asia], he is filled with wonder,

---

[4] Scofield and Griffith, p. 112, n126.

and sends him off to the Isles of the Blessed. Aeacus does the same [with men from Europe, such as Socrates] . . . (526c–d, Griffith)

So ends Socrates' speech, which he finds convincing.

THE MORAL OF THE STORY (526d–527a)
Then Socrates turns to the question of the practical implications of this belief:

> Well, for my part, Callicles, I am convinced by these accounts, and my concern is how I can present my soul to the judge in as healthy a state as possible. So I shall say goodbye to the honors most people are interested in, and in the practice of truth try both to live and, when I die, to die as truly the best person I have it in my power to be. And so far as lies in my power I invite the whole of the rest of mankind and you in particular, returning your invitation [namely, Callicles' invitation to pursue power in the public realm], to this life and this struggle, which I maintain is more important than all our struggles here. (526d–e, Griffith)

Here Socrates is returning to the theme of the choice of lives: the public life of pursuing power or the private life of pursuing wisdom, which means the care of one's own soul. The public pursuit of power offers certain rewards, including the ability to perform well if dragged into court. But Socrates also points out that this life has spiritual costs. To gain power over the public, one must become like it, which means that one's soul will become corrupt. As long as one keeps one's corruption hidden, one will suffer no punishment.

But in the afterlife, one faces a different court. One's soul stands naked, stripped of its body and worldly rank, one's vices visible to the judge. Socrates is confident that he will acquit himself well before such a court. Then, with evident relish, he turns the table on Callicles by forcing him to consider how he might fare in the same position:

My criticism of you is that you will not be able to protect yourself when you meet the judgment and verdict I've just been describing. You will go before that judge the son of Aegina [the nymph who bore Aeacus to Zeus], when he seizes hold of you and brings you before him, and you will go dizzy and stand there gawking, you in that place no less than I in this. Who knows, you may be given a punch in the mouth and be well and truly trampled on. (525e–527a, Griffith)

THE TRUTH OF THE TALE (527a–e)

It would be easy for Callicles to dismiss Socrates' speech as a mere myth, so Socrates immediately addresses this question:

Of course, you may regard all this as a story, an old wives' tale, and treat it with contempt. And there's nothing so very surprising about being treated with contempt, if we had somewhere else to turn in our search for better and truer answers. But as it is, you can see that you three— you, Polus, and Gorgias—who are the wisest of the Greeks alive today, and not able to demonstrate that we should lead some other life than the one which is so clearly in our best interest in the world beyond also. Among so many arguments, while the others are proved wrong, this argument alone stands its ground: that we should more beware of acting unjustly than of being treated unjustly, and that more than anything, what a man should practice both in private and in public life, is not seeming to be good, but being good. And if someone turns out badly in some respect, he should be punished. All flattery, whether directed at oneself or others, at few or many, is to be avoided. That is how rhetoric should be employed—always aiming at the just—as should any other activity. (527a–c, Griffith)

Earlier in the *Gorgias*, Socrates claims that he does not *know* that it is better to suffer injustice than to do it. This is a very strong sense of knowledge as final and unrevisable. But Socrates is willing to claim that he knows it in a weaker sense, namely that he has good arguments. Still, Socrates remains open to hearing counter-arguments. Until he hears a better argument, however, he will live his life according to the principle that it is better to suffer injustice than to do it.

Socrates has a similar attitude toward myths about the afterlife. He does not claim that they are absolute and unrevisable truths. How could he? He has not been there. But he thinks that his myths have a lot to recommend them, namely their psychagogical usefulness. So until he hears a better story, he will accept his myths as rational and live accordingly.

In my lecture, "The Myths of Plato,"[5] I discuss at some length Socrates' practice of taking up traditional Greek myths and reworking them. In the *Gorgias*, *Republic*, and *Phaedo*, for example, Socrates gives different accounts of the fate of the soul after death.

There are two questions here. First, what licenses Socrates to transform Greek and other myths and to be somewhat cavalier about making them all consistent? Second, what makes these myths rational and true? They certainly aren't rational in the sense of logical consistency. They certainly aren't true in the sense that they have been verified by experience, since Socrates was speaking on this side of the grave.

I think the same answer suffices for both questions, because the goal of these myths is the care of the soul. The Greek word *psychagogy* means "leading the soul." In Socrates' case, it means leading it to virtue. Socrates tells these stories about the afterlife to make the soul better. What makes them "rational" and "true" is being *effective* means to the end of teaching virtue. Myths don't have to be logically consistent or factually correct to have positive effects.

Thus Socrates creates the template followed by later writers like Pascal, Rousseau, Kant, and William James, all of whom offer arguments for belief in the afterlife and the moral order of the universe based on pragmatic considerations: ultimately the care of the soul.

---

[5] Greg Johnson, "The Myths of Plato," *From Plato to Postmodernism*.

Socrates ends his speech and the dialogue as a whole by inviting Callicles to follow his way of life: "Listen to me, then, and follow to that destination where, when you arrive, you will be happy both while you live and after you die, as the *logos* clearly indicates" (527c, Griffith). If forced to choose between doing injustice or suffering it, Socrates bids Callicles to suffer it, since it cannot harm the most important thing: namely his soul.

Only once they have practiced virtue can they consider turning their hands to politics. Socrates makes clear that their political involvement will consist solely in counsel. He also emphasizes that neither of them is in a position to give political advice now, and if they were to try, they would look ridiculous.

Let us now return to the question of how wise men might acquire the power and resources to do great things, the greatest of which is to establish a just regime. In the *Republic*, Socrates suggests two basic paths: philosophers must become kings, or kings must become philosophers. More broadly: wise men must pursue power, or powerful men must pursue wisdom.

In the terms of the *Gorgias*, the first path is an illusion, particularly in a democratic society like Athens, for there is no way to become great without pandering to the mob, and there is no way to pander to the mob without becoming like them, which corrupts one's soul and is thus self-defeating. Thus the only realistic path is for powerful men to pursue wisdom.

Socrates says it is difficult for the great and powerful to become wise and just. In the case of Aristides, it is not clear how it happened. Maybe he was just a freak of nature, a stroke of good fortune.

But here Socrates suggests a more reliable way for the great and powerful to become wise: listening to the counsel of the wise. Of course, Socrates isn't just talking about it, he's been *doing* it throughout the *Gorgias*. Moreover, he is not just addressing Callicles but also a large group of other upper-crust Athenians who gathered to hear Gorgias speak.

According to the argument Socrates has followed and defended, the best way of life is "to live and die practicing righteousness and the rest of virtue." Thus he invites Callicles and everybody else to follow it. Socrates concludes with brutal frankness: as for the public life in pursuit of power, "it is worthless, Callicles."

It is easy to get caught up in the drama of the *Gorgias*, assume that this conversation actually happened, and wonder what Callicles might have said in response. But maybe the fact that Callicles left no mark on history except his appearance in the *Gorgias* indicates his answer: he chose to lead a private life.

Of course, we know that Callicles is laboring under the false assumption that philosophy is confined entirely to the private realm. It is worth pondering why Socrates thought it better to leave Callicles in his mind-forged manacles.

* * *

Once you finish the *Greater Alcibiades* and the *Gorgias*, you might be tempted to read other Platonic dialogues on the same level, for instance the *Protagoras* and the *Meno*. By all means read them. But take note: once you have grappled with the *Gorgias*, you are ready to scale the heights of Plato, namely the *Republic*.

As soon as you open the *Republic*, the themes, characters, and even the outline will remind you of the *Gorgias*. You've heard this tune before. Both the *Gorgias* and *Republic* begin with a conversation with an elderly gentleman in whom subversive ideas coexist with old-fashioned virtues. Then Socrates squares off against a sophist who defends tyranny. After that, Socrates devotes the remainder of the dialogue to taming a would-be tyrant,[6] ending with a dazzling myth about the afterlife.

In the *Republic*, you will find the same moral and political themes of the *Gorgias* defended in terms of a subtler tripartite conception of the soul, culminating in a dizzying metaphysical ascent compared to which all subsequent philosophy is an anticlimax, then ending with an eschatological myth exceeded only by Dante. Moving from the *Gorgias* to the *Republic* is like studying one of Michaelangelo's charcoal sketches—and then being ushered into the Sistine Chapel. I envy you this experience, for it is unforgettable, and it can only happen once.

---

[6] Strauss, *On Plato's Protagoras*, p. 8.

A Note on Plato's *Lesser Alcibiades*

I am saving a full-fledged commentary on the *Lesser Alcibiades* for another book. Here, I simply wish to argue that Plato constructed the *Lesser Alcibiades* as a link between the *Greater Alcibiades* and the *Gorgias*. This gives credence to the Neoplatonic curriculum which began with the *Greater Alcibiades*, followed by the *Gorgias*.[1]

Since the *Greater Alcibiades* is the first conversation between Socrates and Alcibiades (103a–b), the *Lesser Alcibiades* must be set at a later date. However, when we try to pinpoint the dramatic date, an interesting parallel emerges with the *Gorgias*.

The earliest dramatic date of the *Lesser Alcibiades* is 432 BCE, shortly after the *Greater Alcibiades*. Since Pericles is mentioned as being alive (144a), the dramatic date can't be after his death in 429 BCE. The *Gorgias* mentions that Pericles has just died, so its earliest dramatic date must be 429 BCE (503c).

As in the *Gorgias* (470d), the *Lesser Alcibiades* mentions Archelaus the king of Macedon (141d). Both passages also make the same allusion to Homer.[2] Archelaus came to power in 413 BCE, so both the *Gorgias* and the *Lesser Alcibiades* must be set after then. But the *Lesser Alcibiades* mentions specifically that Archelaus has just been assassinated, which took place sometime in 399 BCE.

Alcibiades himself had been assassinated in 404 BCE. So this conversation is taking place after Alcibiades' death. Socrates

---

[1] Harold Tarrant points out many connections between the *Lesser Alcibiades* and the *Gorgias* in his essay "Ancient Readers of the *Gorgias*," in *Plato's Gorgias: A Critical Guide*, ed. J. Clerk Shaw (Cambridge: Cambridge University Press, 2024), although Tarrant believes that the *Lesser Alcibiades* is not the work of Plato but rather a "studious imitation" of the *Gorgias* by "an author presumably operating within the Academy" (p. 36).

[2] Homer, *Iliad*, 2.303.

was executed in 399 BCE, and if he died before Archelaus, then the *Lesser Alcibiades* is set after Socrates' death as well. (We don't know when Archelaus died, but surely this was known at the time. Socrates died in May or June of 399 BCE just after the return of a sacred ship from Delos, so it is slightly more likely that Socrates died first.)

If both Socrates and Alcibiades are dead, the setting would be the afterlife, where Socrates and Alcibiades are somehow unmoored in time. Could the *Gorgias* also be set in the afterlife? Perhaps, although none of the dates mentioned in the dialogue are after the deaths of Socrates and Alcibiades. If these dialogues are set in the afterlife, we must note that it does not resemble the afterlife in the myth of the *Gorgias*, or any other Platonic myth.

Just as the dramatic date of the *Gorgias* spans from 429 to 405 BCE, the dramatic date of the *Greater Alcibiades* spans from 432 to 399 BCE. The dates of the *Gorgias* fall within the years of the Peloponnesian War (431–404 BCE). The dates of the *Lesser Alcibiades* encompass the whole Peloponnesian War.

If one wished to depreciate Plato's artistry and save oneself some hard interpretive labor, one might dismiss the anachronisms of the *Gorgias* as purely a matter of chance. But the closely parallel anachronisms of the *Lesser Alcibiades* are clearly not a matter of chance. They are deliberate, meaningful, and thus part of Plato's message. We should assume that the same is true in the *Gorgias*. I share my thoughts on time and the *Gorgias* in chapter 10, above. I am saving my thoughts on time in the *Lesser Alcibiades* for a fuller treatment.

The main theme unifying the *Greater* and *Lesser Alcibiades* with the *Gorgias* is tyranny. In the *Lesser Alcibiades*, Socrates asks Alcibiades:

> Suppose the god you are on your way to pray to appeared and asked, before you had prayed for anything, if it would suffice for you to become tyrant of the city of Athens. If you were to believe that this was something of no account and nothing big, he would add tyranny over all the Greeks, and if he were to see that this still seemed

too little to you, unless all of Europe were added, he would promise this too, and not only this, but he would promise that, as you want, all men would perceive at once that Alcibiades, son of Cleinias, was tyrant. I think that you yourself would go off very pleased, thinking that you had hit upon the greatest of goods. (141a–b)[3]

This passage is so close to Socrates' "pick up" speech in the *Greater Alcibiades* (esp. 105a–c) that my first reaction was that the *Lesser Alcibiades* is not a work by Plato but simply a pastiche of the *Greater Alcibiades* and other genuine Platonic texts. I no longer think this, because if Alcibiades is a new student, it is natural that Socrates will have to repeat himself. Moreover, the repetitions include subtle differences, which are highly meaningful.

For instance, if we compare the passage above with the similar passage in the *Greater Alcibiades*, there is an important change. In the first, the "god" who speaks to Alcibiades is actually Socrates' *daimonion*. Here, Socrates meets a downcast and brooding Alcibiades on his way to sacrifice to *another* god. This unnamed god is the speaker here.

In the *Greater Alcibiades*, Socrates first told Alcibiades that only he could help the lad achieve his tyrannical aims, but by the end of their conversation, Socrates has convinced him of the need to pursue self-knowledge or moderation (*sophrosyne*), which is inherently anti-tyrannical. But it makes sense that once Socrates awakens Alcibiades' interest in ideas that he will seek out other teachers, especially teachers who might help him realize rather than abandon his dreams of tyranny.

The *Greater Alcibiades* ends with Socrates prophesying a battle between himself and his rivals, the people of Athens, for the love of Alcibiades (135e). The *Lesser Alcibiades* ends with a similar reference to rivals, specifically rival lovers (151c), but this is a different set of rivals.

In the *Lesser Alcibiades*, Alcibiades is seeking the favor of a god other than Socrates' *daimonion* (which is simply a sock-

---

[3] Trans. David M. Johnson, *Socrates and Alcibiades*.

puppet of Socrates). But Socrates would not describe a god as Alcibiades' "lovers," i.e., teachers and mentors. Those would be men. But which men?

In Plato's *Protagoras*, which is set around the same time as the *Lesser Alcibiades*, we see Alcibiades in the company of some of Socrates' rivals: the great sophists Protagoras, Hippias, and Prodicus, as well as Critias, later of the Thirty Tyrants.

Thus I read the *Lesser Alcibiades* not as a clumsy pastiche but as an artful continuation of the *Greater Alcibiades*.

Another continuity between all three dialogues are references to public debates about topics like city walls, arsenals, warships, harbors, etc. (*Greater Alcibiades*, 134b; *Lesser Alcibiades*, 144e–145a; *Gorgias*, 455b, 514a, 520a).

In the *Lesser Alcibiades* (146b), Socrates quotes Euripides' play *Antiope*, where Zethus says to his brother Amphion that men have a bias toward the things they are good at. In the *Gorgias*, Callicles quotes the same passage at greater length to Socrates (485e–486a).

Another connection between the *Lesser Alcibiades* and the *Gorgias* are Socrates' references to foreign gods, specifically Egyptian ones. In the *Gorgias*, Socrates swears an oath "by the dog" (461b) and more specifically "by the dog, the god of the Egyptians" (482b). This is a reference to Anubis, the jackal-headed god who guided the dead to the throne of Osiris for judgment. In the *Lesser Alcibiades*, the Egyptian god is Ammon (148c–150b). But Socrates does not introduce Ammon to Athens. Instead, the Spartans send a delegation to Ammon's oracle to ask him a question.

In sum, the *Lesser Alcibiades* is chronologically and thematically very close to the *Greater Alcibiades*, which it points back to. Moreover, the *Lesser Alcibiades* is also closely connected to the *Gorgias* not just in the central theme of tyranny, but also because it uses the same historic figures (Pericles and Archelaus) to establish a similarly anachronistic setting, as well as the same quotes from Homer and Euripides, the same topics of political debate, and even the same pantheon of foreign gods, the Egyptian.

BIBLIOGRAPHY

I found the following works useful, although not all of them ended up being cited.

GENERAL

Aristotle. *Aristotle's Art of Rhetoric*. Trans. Robert C. Bartlett. Chicago: University of Chicago, 2019.
Boesche, Roger. *Theories of Tyranny from Plato to Arendt*. University Park: Penn State Press, 1996.
Corey, David D. *The Sophists in Plato's Dialogues*. Albany: SUNY Press, 2016.
de Romilly, Jacqueline. *The Great Sophists in Periclean Athens*. Trans. Janet Lloyd. Oxford: Oxford University Press, 1992.
Dillon, John. "Tampering with the *Timaeus*: Ideological Emendations in Plato, with Special Reference to the *Timaeus*." *The American Journal of Philology*, vol. 110, no. 1 (Spring 1989): 50–72.
Friedländer, Paul. *Plato*. 3 vols. Trans Hans Meyerhof. New York: Bollingen, 1958, 1964, & 1969.
Gagarin, Michael and Paul Woodruff, eds. *Early Greek Political Thought from Homer to the Sophists*. Cambridge: Cambridge University Press, 1985.
Grote, George. *Plato and Other Companions of Sokrates*. 3 vols. Cambridge: Cambridge University Press, 2009.
Howland, Jacob. *Glaucon's Fate: History, Myth, and Character in Plato's Republic*. Philadelphia: Paul Dry Books, 2018.
Johnson, Greg. "Freedom of Speech." *Toward a New Nationalism*. 2nd ed. San Francisco: Counter-Currents, 2023.
———. "The Myths of Plato." *From Plato to Postmodernism*. San Francisco: Counter-Currents, 2019.
———. "Notes on Philosophical Dialectic." *From Plato to Postmodernism*. San Francisco: Counter-Currents, 2019.
———. "The Relevance of Philosophy to Political Change." *New Right vs. Old Right*. San Francisco: Counter-Currents, 2013.
———. *The Trial of Socrates*. San Francisco: Counter-Currents, 2023.
Moore, Christopher. *The Virtue of Agency: Sôphrosunê and Self-Constitution in Classical Greece*. Oxford: Oxford University Press, 2023.

Munn, Mark. *The School of History: Athens in the Age of Socrates*. Berkeley: University of California Press, 2000.

Nails, Debra. *The People of Plato: A Prosopography of Plato and Other Socratics*. Indianapolis: Hackett, 2002.

Plato. *Complete Works*. Ed. John M. Cooper. Indianapolis: Hackett, 1997.

———. *Laws*. Trans. C.D.C. Reeve. Indianapolis: Hackett, 2022.

———. *Plato's Letters: The Political Challenges of the Philosophic Life*. Ed. and trans. Ariel Helfer. Ithaca: Cornell University Press, 2023.

———. *The Republic*. Ed. G.R.F. Ferrari, trans. Tom Giffith. Cambridge: Cambridge University Press, 2000.

———. *The Republic of Plato*. Trans. Allan Bloom. New York: Basic Books, 1968.

Romm, James. *Plato and the Tyrant: The Fall of Greece's Greatest Dynasty and the Making of a Philosophic Masterpiece*. New York: Norton, 2025.

Schleiermacher, Friedrich. *Introductions to the Dialogues of Plato*. Trans. William Dobson. London: John William Parker, 1836.

Sprague, Rosamond Kent, ed. *The Older Sophists*. Indianapolis: Hackett, 2001.

Strauss, Leo. *The City and Man*. Chicago: University of Chicago Press, 1978.

Taylor, A.E. *Plato: The Man and His Work*. London: Methuen, 1926.

Thucydides. *The Peloponnesian War*. Ed. P.J. Rhodes. Trans. Martin Hammond. Oxford: Oxford University Press, 2009.

Waterfield, Robin. *Plato of Athens: A Life in Philosophy*. New York: Oxford University Press, 2023.

Welliver, Warman. *Character, Plot, and Thought in Plato's Timaeus-Critias*. Leiden: E.J. Brill, 1977.

Wilburn, Joshua. "The Problem of Alcibiades: Plato on Moral Education and the Many." *Oxford Studies in Ancient Philosophy*, vol. XLIX. Ed. Brad Inwood. Oxford: Oxford University Press, 2015.

Xenophon. *The Landmark Xenophon's Hellenika*. Ed. Robert B. Strassler. New York: Pantheon, 2009.

Xenophon. *Memorabilia*. Trans. Amy L. Bonnette. Ithaca: Cornell University Press, 1994.

Xenophon. *Symposium*. Trans. O.J. Todd. Xenophon, vol. IV. Loeb Classical Library. Cambridge: Harvard University Press, 1923.

Zuckert, Catherine. *Plato's Philosophers: The Coherence of the Dialogues*. Chicago: University of Chicago Press, 2009.

THE *GREATER ALCIBIADES*

Aeschines of Sphettus. *Alcibiades*. Trans. David M. Johnson. *Socrates and Alcibiades: Four Texts*. Newburyport, Mass.: Focus Philosophical Library, 2003.

Ahbel-Rappe, Sara. *Socratic Ignorance and Platonic Knowledge in the Dialogues of Plato*. Albany: SUNY Press, 2018.

Alfarabi. *The Philosophy of Plato and Aristotle*. Trans. Muhsin Mahdi. Ithaca: Cornell University Press, 2001.

Altman, William H.F. *Ascent to the Beautiful: Plato the Teacher and the Pre-Republic Dialogues from* Protagoras *to* Symposium. Lanham, Maryland: Lexington Books, 2020.

Annas, Julia. "Self-Knowledge in the Early Plato." *Platonic Investigations*. Ed. Dominic J. O'Meara. Washington, D.C.: The Catholic University of America Press, 1985.

Bartsch, Shadi. *The Mirror of the Self: Sexuality, Self-Knowledge, and the Gaze in the Early Roman Empire*. Chicago: University of Chicago Press, 2014.

Belfiore, Elizabeth S. *Socrates' Daimonic Art: Love for Wisdom in Four Platonic Dialogues*. Cambridge: Cambridge University Press, 2012.

Carlini, Antonio. "Studi sul testo della quarta tetralogia platonica." *Studi italiani de filologia classica*, vol. 34 (1963): 169–89.

Corrigan, Kevin. *Love, Friendship, and the Good: Plato, Aristotle, and the Later Tradition*. Eugene, Oregon: Cascade Books, 2018.

de Romilly, Jacqueline. *The Life of Alcibiades: Dangerous Ambition and the Betrayal of Athens*. Trans. Elizabeth Trapnell Rawlings. Ithaca: Cornell University Press, 2019.

Dillon, John. "A Platonist *Ars Amatoria*." *The Classical Quarterly*, vol. 44 (1994): pp. 387–92.

Faulkner, Robert. *The Case for Greatness: Honorable Ambition and Its Critics*. New Haven: Yale University Press, 2007.

Forde, Steven. "On the *Alcibiades I*." *The Roots of Political Philosophy: Ten Forgotten Socratic Dialogues*. Ed. Thomas L. Pangle. Ithaca: Cornell University Press, 1987.

Gill, Christopher. "Self-Knowledge in Plato's *Alcibiades*." *Reading Ancient Texts*, vol. 1., *Presocratics and Plato*. Ed. Suzanne Stern-Gillet and Kevin Corrigan. Leiden: E.J. Brill, 2007.

Gordon, Jill. "Eros and Philosophical Seduction in *Alcibiades I*." *Ancient Philosophy*, vol. 23 (2003): 11–30.

Helfer, Ariel. *Socrates and Alcibiades: Plato's Drama of Political Ambition and Philosophy*. Philadelphia: University of Pennsylvania Press, 2017.

Iamblichi Chalcidensis. *In Platonis Dialogos Commentariorum Fragmenta*. Ed. and trans. John M. Dillon. Lydney, UK: The Prometheus Trust, 2009.

Jirsa, Jakub. "Authenticity of the *Alcibiades* I: Some Reflections." *Listy filologické*, vol. 132 (2009): 225–44.

Johnson, David M. "A Commentary on Plato's *Alcibiades*." Ph.D. Dissertation. University of North Carolina at Chapel Hill, 1996.

_____. "God as the True Self: Plato's *Alcibiades I*." *Ancient Philosophy* 19 (1999): 1–19.

Moore, Christopher. *Socrates and Self-Knowledge*. Cambridge: Cambridge University Press, 2015.

Olympiodorus. *Commentary on the First Alcibiades of Plato*. Trans. L.G. Westerink. 2nd ed. Amsterdam: Hakkert, 1982.

_____. *Life of Plato and On Plato First Alcibiades 1–9*. Trans. Michael Griffin. London: Bloomsbury, 2015.

_____. *On Plato First Alcibiades 10–28*. Trans. Michael Griffin. London: Bloomsbury, 2016.

Pigliucci, Massimo. *The Quest for Character: What the Story of Socrates and Alcibiades Teaches Us about Our Search for Good Leaders*. New York: Basic Books, 2022.

Plato. *Alcibiades*. Ed. Nicholas Denyer. Cambridge: Cambridge University Press, 2001.

_____. *Alcibiades I*. Trans. D.S. Hutchinson. Plato. *Complete Works*. Ed. John M. Cooper. Indianapolis: Hackett, 1997.

_____. *Alcibiades I*. Trans. David M. Johnson. Plato and Aeschines of Sphettus. *Socrates and Alcibiades: Four Texts*. Newburyport, Mass.: Focus Philosophical Library, 2003.

_____. *Alcibiades I*. Trans. W.R.M. Lamb. Loeb Classical Library, Plato, vol. XII. Cambridge, Mass.: Harvard University Press, 1927.

_____. *Alcibiades I*. Trans. Carnes Lord. *The Roots of Political Philosophy. The Roots of Political Philosophy: Ten Forgotten Socratic Dialogues*. Ed. Thomas L. Pangle. Ithaca: Cornell University Press, 1987.

Plutarch. *Alcibiades. Greek Lives*. Trans. Robin Waterfield. Oxford: Oxford University Press, 1998.

Proclus. *Alcibiades I*. Trans. William O'Neill. The Hague: Martinus Nijhoff, 1971.

Ramsay, Reuben. "Plato's Oblique Response to Issues of Socrates' Influence on Alcibiades: An Examination of the *Protagoras* and *Gorgias*." *Alcibiades and the Socratic Lover-Educator*. Ed. Marguerite Johnson and Harold Tarrant. London: Bloomsbury, 2012.

Renaud, François and Harold Tarrant. *The Platonic* Alcibiades I: *The*

Dialogue and its Ancient Reception. Cambridge: Cambridge University Press, 2015.
Scott, Gary Alan. *Plato's Socrates as Educator.* Albany: SUNY Press, 2000.
Tarrant, Harold. "Olympiodorus and Proclus on the Climax of the *Alcibiades.*" *International Journal of the Platonic Tradition*, vol. I (2007), pp. 3-29.
Wohl, Victoria. "The Eye of the Beloved: *Opsis* and *Eros* in Socratic Pedagogy." *Alcibiades and the Socratic Lover-Educator.* Ed. Marguerite Johnson and Harold Tarrant. London: Bloomsbury, 2012.

THE *GORGIAS*

Arieti, James A. "Plato's Philosophical *Antiope*: The *Gorgias.*" *Plato's Dialogues: New Studies and Interpretations.* Ed. Gerald A. Press. Lanham, Maryland: Rowman and Littlefield, 1993.
Gómez-Lobo, Alfonso. *The Foundations of Socratic Ethics.* Indianapolis: Hackett, 1994.
Guthrie, W.K.C. *History of Greek Philosophy*, vol. IV, *Plato: The Man and His Dialogues. Earlier Period.* Cambridge: Cambridge University Press, 1975.
Kahn, Charles H. "Drama and Dialectic in Plato's *Gorgias.*" *Oxford Studies in Ancient Philosophy* 1(1983): 75-121.
_____. *Plato and the Socratic Dialogue: The Philosophical Use of a Literary Form.* Cambridge: Cambridge University Press, 1996.
McKim, Richard. "Shame and Truth in Plato's *Gorgias.*" *Platonic Writings, Platonic Readings.* Ed. Charles L. Griswold, Jr. New York: Routledge, 1988.
Olympiodorus. *Commentary on Plato's Gorgias.* Trans. Robin Jackson, Kimon Lycos, and Harold Tarrant. Leiden: E.J. Brill, 1998.
Plato. *Gorgias. The Dialogues of Plato*, vol. 1. Trans. R.E. Allen. New Haven: Yale University Press, 1984.
_____. *Gorgias: A Revised Text with Introduction and Commentary.* Ed. E.R. Dodds. Oxford: Clarendon Press, 1959.
_____. *Gorgias.* Trans. Terence Irwin. Oxford: Clarendon Press, 1987.
_____. *Gorgias.* Trans. W.R.M. Lamb. Loeb Classical Library, Plato, vol. III. Cambridge, Mass.: Harvard University Press, 1925.
_____. *Gorgias.* Trans. James H. Nichols, Jr. Ithaca: Cornell University Press, 1998.
_____. *Gorgias.* Trans. Robin Waterfield. Oxford: Oxford University Press, 1994.

_____. *Gorgias*. Trans. Donald J. Zeyl. Plato. *Complete Works*. Ed. John M. Cooper. Indianapolis: Hackett, 1997.

_____. *Gorgias, Menexenus, Protagoras*. Ed. Malcolm Schofield. Trans. Tom Griffith. Cambridge: Cambridge University Press, 2010.

Strauss, Leo. "*Gorgias* Note," 1973. Ed. Nathan Tarcov and Svetozar Minkov. Leo Strauss Center, Audio and Transcripts.

_____. *On Plato's Protagoras*. Ed. Robert C. Bartlett. Chicago: University of Chicago Press, 2022.

_____. Plato's *Gorgias* (1957). Transcript. Ed. Devin Stauffer. Leo Strauss Center, Audio and Transcripts.

_____. Plato's *Gorgias* (1963). Transcript. Ed. Devin Stauffer. Leo Strauss Center, Audio and Transcripts.

THE LESSER ALCIBIADES

Plato. *Alcibiades II*. Trans. W.R.M. Lamb. Loeb Classical Library, Plato, vol. XII. Cambridge, Mass.: Harvard University Press, 1927.

_____. *Alcibiades II*. Trans. David M. Johnson. Plato and Aeschines of Sphettus. *Socrates and Alcibiades: Four Texts*. Newburyport, Mass.: Focus Philosophical Library, 2003.

_____. *Second Alcibiades*. Trans. Anthony Kenny. Plato. *Complete Works*. Ed. John M. Cooper. Indianapolis: Hackett, 1997.

Sharpe, Matthew. "Revaluing *Megalopsychia*: Reflections on the *Alcibiades II*." *Alcibiades and the Socratic Lover-Educator*. Ed. Marguerite Johnson and Harold Tarrant. London: Bloomsbury, 2012.

Tarrant, Harold. "Ancient Readers of the *Gorgias*." *Plato's Gorgias: A Critical Guide*. Ed. J. Clerk Shaw. Cambridge: Cambridge University Press, 2024.

Tarrant, Harold. *The Second Alcibiades: A Platonist Dialogue on Prayer and on Ignorance*. Las Vegas: Parmenides Publishing, 2023.

INDEX

Numbers in bold refer to a whole chapter or section devoted to a particular topic.

A
actions, 51, 71, 98, 107, 123, 157, 206, 231
Adam, 45, 59
Aeacus, 230, 234–35
Aegina, 235
Aeschines of Spettus, 49; *Socrates and Alcibiades: Four Texts*, 50n4
Aeschylus, 2
afterlife, **228–38**, 240
Agesilaus II, 46
Agis II, 20, 46, 47
agreement, 36, 52–57, 134, 157, 187, 187, 216; see also: concord; friendship; oneness of mind
Alcibiades, 1–3, 7–10, **15–29**, **30–43**, **44–51**, **52–57**, **58–65**, **66–75**, **76–84**, 103, 105, 108, 130, 152, 165–66, 223, 225, 239–42; his tyrannical ambitions, 3, 8–9, 22, 29, 83
Alexander the Great, 27, 55
Allen, R.E., vi
Amestris of Persia, 47–50
Ammon, 248
Amphion, 178, 210, 248
analogies, 3, 44, 48, 66, 130, 150, 153, 156, 162, 188, **189–90**, 196, 197, 213, 222, **225–26**; Pythagorean, 196; Socratic, 189–90; *techne*, 190
Anaxagoras, 42–43, 132

Andron, 11n18, 182
Antiope, 178
Antiope (Euripides), 85, 177, 178, 186, 210, 242
Antiphon, 93
Anubis, 120, 167, 228, 242
Apollo, 71, 87, 92, 213
appetites, 47, 193–94, 222–23
Archelaus, king of Macedon, 85, 141, 142, 147, 149, 231, 239–40, 242
archetype, 206
Archidamus II, 47
Archytas of Tarentum, 5
Aristides, 233, 237
aristocratic ethos, 14; prejudices, 217; values, 217, 227
Aristophanes, 11, 85, 87, 96, 117, 157, 172n2, 175–77, 179; *Birds*, 87; *Clouds*, 11, 87, 96n14, 117, 157, 172n2, 175–77, 179; *Wasps*, 85, 87
Aristotle, v, 25, 52, 62, 66, 85, 88n6, 107, 109, 140, 149; works: *De Anima*, 66n1; *Metaphysics*, 22n8, 88n6; *Nicomachean Ethics*, 28, 52n1, 106n2, 140n4; *Politics*, 227n3; *Rhetoric*, 109–10
arithmetic, 150, 190
art (*techne*), 13, 32, 50, 52, 58, 64, 78, 91–93, 96, 100, 102–104, 113, 117, 119, 206, 216;

a power (*dunamis*) to do things, 115; architectonic, 52, 54; each needs its own rhetoric, 161–62; Gorgias' art, 97, 101, 103–104, 106; has a practical dimension, 125; justice is the most important of the arts, 147; master art, 13, 115, 120, 122, 133, 150, 154; morally neutral, 13, 115, 117, 123, 133; of courage, 151; of divination, 83, 100; of "good advice" (*euboulia*), 52; of justice, 150; of medicine, 147, 150; of money-making, 147; of persuasion, 13, **111**; of rhetoric, 91, 97, 106, 109, 114, 116, 122, 125, 133; of seduction, 68; of ship-building, 112; of Socratic questioning, 101, 103; of the gentleman, 52, 107; of the judge, 147; of the sophists, 105; of verbal magic, 93; philosophy is not an art, 125, 177; political art (*politike techne*), 52–54, 76–77, 115, 165; ruling art, 116, 154; true art can give a rational account (*logos*) of itself, 125–26; two kinds of, 107; versus quackery, 122, 125, 133; wisdom is not an art, 153; see also: analogies, *techne*; craft; knack; master art; quackery; ruling art; sophistry; *techne*; technology

Artaxerxes I, 45, 47, 48

Asia, 27, 70, 230, 233
Aspasia, 47
Athenian Stranger, 5
Athens, 1, 2, 8–11, 15–16, 19–20, 22, 26, 35, 36, 41–42, 44, 46, 48, 73, 83, 85, 87–90, 108, 113, 130, 142, 156, 160, 162, 165, 182, 200, 207, 219–21, 223, 225–26, 233, 237, 240–42

B

bad (*kakon*), **144–45**, 211
Bacciarelli, Marcello, vi
base (*poneros*), 40, 64, 92, 110, 112, 185, 217; see also: wretched
belief (*pistis*), 91, 97, **111–13**, 118–19, 123, 132, 145, 167, 210, 234, 236; see also: knowledge
beneficial (*ophelimon*), 37, 57, 97, 129, 205, 210
bestial people (Aristotle), 140, 149
beautiful (*kalon*), beauty, 16, 26, 44, 64, 67, 102, 129, 144, 146, 175, 229; see also: fine
blessed (*makarios*), 211, 229; see also fortunate
body (*soma*), 37, 39–40, 58, 60–61, 64–65, 66, 75, 96, 102n22, **125–32**, 139–140, 147, 162, 168, 189, 198, 206, 208, 230
Boesche, Roger, 4
bourgeois *ethos*, 14, 217

C

Calippus, 1

Callicles, 7, 10–14, 26, 30, 89–90, 146–47, 156–60, **163–73, 174–82, 183–91, 192–214, 215–27, 228–38**; a sophist, 89; asks Socrates what rhetoric is, 125, 129, 132–36, 138, 141–44; biography, 88–89; capable of shame, 124, 171, 181, 198, 204; defends the idea that freedom is doing as one pleases, 13; has a philosophical soul, 10; his idea of philosophy, 11, 173–76, 238; lack of shame, 89, 173; love of power & of the people, 165, 173, 220; not gentlemanly, 89; 89–90; refuted by Socrates, 144–45; role in *Gorgias*: defender of tyranny, 10; tries to shame Socrates, 198–99

care of the soul, 126, 129, 132, 162, 236; guided by knowledge of the good, 132; see also: politics; soul

Carlini, Antonio, 80

Chaerephon, 11, **87–88**, 90, 99–105, 117–118, 163; a copy of Socrates, 105

chaos, 132; contrast: order

character (psychological), 2, 3, 6–8, 14, 18, 23, 27, 70, 92, 108, 127, 141, 174, 201, 220, 229; as destiny, 3, 229

Charmides, 1–2, 8, 20, 88

choice, 11, 26n18, 168, 178, 206, 210, 220, 225, 234; choiceworthy, 11, 39

Cicero, 179; *Tusculan Disputa-*

tions, 179n2

Cimon, 207, 221–24

city states, 2, 19, 88; see also: Athens; Leontini; Syracuse

Cleinias, father of Alcibiades, 15, 16, 22, 27, 77, 165, 241; brother of Alcibiades, 43; beloved of Critobulus, 67

comedy, 96, 207, 209

common good, 2, 4, 6, 55, 150, **207–209**

community, 130, 189, **212–13**

concord (*homonoia*), 53–55; see also: agreement; friendship; oneness of mind

consequences, 3, 40–41, 110, 176, 199, 206, 214

convention (*nomos*), 129, 169, 193, 208

correctness (*orthotes*), 210

cosmos, see: order

courage (*andreia*), 24, 39, 46–47, 139, 150–51, 168, 191–93, 199–201, 203, 205; & knowledge, 199–200, 205; & pleasure, 200, 205; see also: virtue

cowardice (*deilia*), 39–40, 98, 139, 146, 203

craft(s), 52–53, 55, 112; craftsman, 208; see also: art; *techne*

crime & punishment, 9, 130, 141–62, 223, 231; deterrence, 129, 148, retribution, 129, 148

Critias, 1–2, **6–7**, 20, 26n18, 50n5, 88, 115, 190n2, 242

Crito, 67

Critobulus, 67

Cupid, see: Eros
Cyrus, 27

D
daimonion, 22–23, 27–29, 50–51, 57, **70–71**, **72–73**, 74, 78–79, 82, 84, 100n20, 229, 241
Damascius, 59–60
Damon, 42, 43
Dante Alighieri, 238
Darius I, 49, 50, 170
death, 14, 18, 26n18, 37–40, 82, 85, 90, 139, 148–49, 157, 159, 171, 176, 195, 215–17, 219, 226–27, 228–30, 236, 239–40; death penalty, 149, 176; unjust, 215
Deinomache, 15, 48, 27
Delphic injunction ("Know thyself"), 58, 63, 66; see also: self-knowledge
Delphic oracle, 71, 87, 100
demagoguery, 65, 207
democracy, 3–4, 12–13, 20, 112, 194
Demos, 11n18, 165–66
demos, Athenian, 22, 64, 118, 165–66, 220
Denyer, Nicholas, v, 48, 74, 80; *Alcibiades*, v, 41n2, 48n2, 58n1, 74n9, 80n7
desire, 3–4, 12, 14, 26, 28, 63–64, 78, 82, 94, 132, 168, 172, 186, **192–97**, 200–202, 214; infinite, 3, 10, 26, 63, 64, 77, 194, 195; limited, 196; see also: soul; reason
desire-driven men, 3; societies, 4; see also: tyrants

dialectic, 31n2, **62–63**, 104, 107
dialogue (*dialogos*), as means of self-knowledge, 60; Platonic, 18, 27n19, 62n9, 153, 229n1, 238; Socratic, 49n3, 82n13, 83n15, 87
Dillon, John, iv n1, 75
Dion, 1–2
Dionysius I, 1–2, 6, 24
Dionysius II, 1–2, 6, 24
Diotima, 47
dishonor, 3, 218
disorder (*akosmia*), 3, 208, 210, 212; contrast: order
Disraeli, Benjamin, 86
divination, see: *daimonion*; oracles
division of labor, **53–54**, 56
Dodds, E.R., v, 93, 182, 219
dog (the), 120, 166, 167, 228, 242; see also: Anubis
doing well (*eu prattein*), 40; see also: noble action
drug addiction, 13

E
education, 7, 44, 46–47, 126–27, 142, 148, 174, 181, 221; liberal, 174, 177; moral, 21, 153; philosophical, 29, 125; sophistical, 30
Egyptian myths, 167, 228, 242
elite (Athenian), 11
Empedocles, 88
endurance, 47
Epicharmus, 209
equality (*isotes*), 171–72, 184–85, 194, 212–13; proportionate, 212–13; two concepts of, 188–91

Eros (Greek god), 22, 82
eros, 22, 51, 82, 84, 229; see also: love
Euripides, 85, 174, 177, 178, 186, 196, 242; works: *Antiope*, 85, 177n2, 178, 186, 242; *Phrixus*, 196n3, *Polyidos*, 196n3
Europe, 27, 70, 230, 234, 240
Eurysaces, 45
Eusebius of Caesarea, 73
expertise, 32, 109, 114; technical, 31–32, 109; moral, 158; versus common knowledge, 52–57; versus oneness of mind, 53–55; see also: knowledge, expert

F
family life, 46, 53–54
Faustianism, 214
Ferrari, G.R.F., 5
fine (*kalon*), 50, 82, 89, 102, 123–24, 144, 146, 157, 169, 172, 174, 184, 193, 198, 221; see also: beautiful
fitting, 148, 175, 211; see also: beautiful
flattery (*kolakeia*), 6, 122, 126, 128, 132–33, 136–37, 165–66, 220, 225; vs. friendship, 122, 166, 220; vs. rhetoric, 165, 235; see also: quackery
flight to the logoi, 60
Forms (Platonic), **59–63**, 79; see also: ideal objects; Ideas
Fourfold (the), 189, 212–14

fortune, 49, 186, 232; see also: blessed
frankness (*parrhesia*), 106, 180–81, 195, 237
freedom (*eleutheria*), 13, **77–78**, 89, 108, 122, 124, **135–38**, 141, 164, 194; Athenian, 124; personal, 108; true, 78, 141; see also: liberty
friendship (*philia*), 53–57, 62n9, 72, 126, 128, 136, 166, 168, 186, 206, 212–13, 220; god of (Zeus), 72, 186, 206; produces oneness of mind, (*homonoia*), 54–55; see also: agreement; concord; oneness of mind

G
geometry, 24, 150
Gestell (the), 214
Gill, Christopher, 58n1, 69n8
Glaucon, 1, 7, 238
God, **73–75**; see also: god, the; gods
god, the, see: *daimonion*
gods, **71–72**, 227; oath "by the gods," 57, 72; of Athens, 9n17, 16, 73, 78, 94, 132, 180, 240–41; Egyptian, 167, 228, 242; foreign to Athens, 16, 242; in the Fourfold, 189; 211–13; Persian, 46; see also: Ammon; Anubis; Apollo; *daimonion*; the dog; Eros; friendship; God; Hermes; Kronos; Muses; oaths; Osiris; Poseidon; Pluto; Zeus
goodness, 115, 183–84, 213,

218; & pleasure, 192–93
goodwill (*eunoia*), 180–81
Gorgias of Leontini, 12, 30, 85, **90–100**, **100–105**, **106–24**, 130, 134, 161, 167, 237, 238; life: arrival in Athens, 85; on timing in rhetoric, 86; other innovations, 91–92; student of Empedocles, 88; anti-metaphysics, 88; very much a gentleman, 88; may have settled in Athens, 88; friend of Chaerephon, 88; ambassador to Athens, 88; surviving books & speeches, 90; *Defense of Palamedes*, 90, 130; *Encomium of Helen*, 90, 93–96, 130; *On Non-Being*, 90–91; in the dialogue: Gorgias' art, 97, 101, 103–104, 106; his art of verbal magic, 93; display speeches of, 98–99, 130, 161; unable to explain rhetoric, 104, 106ff; better than anyone else at short answers, 106; thinks very highly of himself, 106; his two surviving speeches, 110, 130; rhetoricians vs. experts, 113–14; his brother Herodicus, 114; willing to answer questions on anything, 114; definition of rhetoric, 114; trains men for "contests of virtue," 116; regards rhetoric as the ruling art, 116, 120, 133; the daimonic power of rhetoric, 116–17; rhetoric is morally neutral, 117; Socrates catches him in a contradiction, 117–20, 121, 169, 181; tries to back out of the dialogue, 118; sense of shame, 118–19, 120–21, 123, 169, 180–81, 198–99, 204, 214; rhetoric secures freedom, 122
gratification, 3, 161; gratifying the people, 207–208, 222; gratifying the body or the soul, 206
greed, 203; see also: *pleonexia*
Griffith, Tom, v
guardian spirit, see *daimonion*
gymnastics, of the body or soul, 131

H

Halcyon, 87
Hamlet, 97
happiness (*eudaimonia*), 13, 15, 21, 49, **77–78**, 140, 142–43, 194, 196, 199, 201, 211, 214; & well-being, 13, 40, 49, 78
harm, **139–40**, 145, 147, 158–59, 237
harmony, 166–68; of the soul, 167–68, 189; see also: virtue
health, 33, 81, 102n22, 108, 119, **126–28**, 131–33, 135–36, 147, 149, 151, 155–56, 161–62, 167, 189, 205–206, 208, 211, 217, 219, 222–23; bad, 78, 126; good, 126; of the soul, 211; spiritual, 129, 131, 147, 156, 161–62,

167
hedonism, 14, **199–205**
Heidegger, Martin, 107n3, 189, 212–14; the Fourfold, 189, 212–14; the *Gestell*, 214; works: *Being & Time*, 107n3, 189n1; *Poetry, Language, Thought*, 189n1
Helen of Troy, 90, 93, 110, 130
Heracleitus, 55
Hercules, 45
Hermes, 19, 228
Herodicus, 102, 114
Herodotus, 91
Hipparchus, 2
Hippias, the sophist, 30, 242; the tyrant, 2
Hobbes, Thomas, 194n1, 195n2
Homer, 56, 90, 106, 176, 209, 231, 239, 242
honor, 3, 8, 14, 39, 47, 119, 142, 157, 173, 203, 217, 226, 234
hubris, 27, 29
Hutchinson, D.S., vi n11, 80

I
Iamblichus, iv, 7n14, 15, 16n2
Ideas, 55, 59, 75, 84; see also: Forms
ignorance, 19, 31, 34, 42, 57, 79, 137, 146, 182; moral, 142; Socratic, iv, 10, 34, 62n9, 142, 182, 216
induction, 96
injustice (*adikia*), 14, 34, 37, 110–11, 120, 156–57, 159, 161, 171, 188, 208, **215–17**; doing injustice, 138, 141, 144–45, 171, 216, 237; doing injustice is more shameful than suffering it, 144–46, 171, 184–85; doing vs. suffering, 138–40; suffering injustice, 138, 140, 144–45, 218;
intellect (*nous*), 23, 55, 68, 80
Ionia, 233
irony (*eironeia*), 25, 186
Isles of the Blessed, 234
Isocrates, 93

J
James, William, 236
Johnson, David M., vi n11, 24, 59n11, 68n7, 80, 82n11, 241n3
Johnson, Greg, works: *From Plato to Postmodernism*, 7n13, 31n2, 62n10, 236n5; *New Right Versus Old Right*, 21n6; *The Trial of Socrates*, 9n17, 12n19, 22, 79n3, 87n2, 96n14, 100n20, 117n9, 132n2, 155n2, 157n3, 172n2, 218n1, 229n2; *Toward a New Nationalism*, 81n9
Jowett, Benjamin, vi n11, 101n20, 103
Julius Caesar, 27
justice (*dike, dikaiosyne*), 10, 33–36, 44, 46, 52–53, 55–56, 75, 77–78, 84, 110–12, 117, 119–21, 123–24, 126, 130–31, 138, 141–42, 144, 147–52, 158–59; & expediency, **37–43**, 48; as a *techne*, 158; as health of the city, 161; as health of the soul, 155,

157, 162; as helping one's friends & harming one's enemies, 159–50; as removal of "spiritual sickness," 129; criminal justice, 149–50, 156, 160, 162; definition of, 159–160; fine & just, 172, 193; highest value of politics, 34; just things, 38, 41, 146; justice & injustice, 34, 110–11; knowledge of, 36, 112, 158; rehabilitative justice, 148; see also: virtue

K

Kant, Immanuel, 236
king(s), 2, 5–6, 10, 45–48; distinguished from tyrants, 2–3; Persian, 45–46; Spartan, 45; see also: philosopher-kings; see also names of particular kings
Kipling, Rudyard, 56
knack (*empeiria*), 104, **122, 125–26**, 133, **150–53**, 161, 206; morally neutral, 151; see also art; *techne*
knowledge (*episteme*), 32, 42, 61, 122, 142, 199, 202, 216, 219, 235; advanced versus basic, 202; & courage, 199–200, 205; & disagreement, 36; & pleasure, 199–200, 205; based on experience, 30; common, 52–57; expert, 56, 153, 158, 161; from ourselves or from another, 30; implicit, 63; induction, 96; innate, 31, 35–36, 75, 124, 181; intuitive, 205; moral, 120, 142, 150, 153, 158, 204–205; not belief or opinion, 95, **111–13**, 119; of erotic things (*ta erotika*), 22–23, 51, 229; of justice, 36, 112, 158; of the good, 13, 76, 15, 115, 124, 132, 179, 181, 205; of the human soul or nature, 23, 62–63, 65, 70, 72–73, 79, 83, 100, 127; of the just & the unjust things, 35–36, 120, 158; of ultimate causes 60, 74, 84; philosophy is the highest form, 120; Socrates' knowledge of human nature, 70, 72, 82, 229; specialized, 54–55; tacit knowledge, 158; technical, 33; virtue as a kind of knowledge, 120, 154; wisdom as a higher-order knowledge, 64; see also: belief; courage; craft; expertise; ignorance; moderation; self-knowledge; virtue; wisdom
Kronos, 229–30

L

Laches, 19
Lamb, W.R.M., vi n11, 24, 59
Lampito of Sparta, 47–48, 50
leisure, 55
Leonitini, 85, 88
Leotychides of Sparta, 46
liberalism (modern), 12, 14
libertarianism, 137
liberty, 4, 80, 84, 137, 194;

negative, 13, 137; positive, 13; true, 84; see also: freedom
licentiousness (*akolasia*), **205–209**, 211–13; contrast: moderation
logic, 15, 107
logos, see: rational account
Lord, Carnes, v, 27n19, 59n2,
love (*eros*), 53, 64–65, 82, 85, 94, 166; of children, 148; of life, 218; of power, 173; of the people, 165, 220, 241; of truth, 111, 165; of truth versus love of victory, 117–19; of wisdom, 173; see also: *eros*
Lysimachus, 233

M
madness (*mania*), 68
Magian lore, 46
magnanimity (*megalopsychia*), **23–25**, 47; contrast: pride; see also: virtue
Meno, 116, 121
might & right, 163–73
Miltiades, 207, 221–22, 233
Minos, 233
misery, 13, 140, 143
moderation (*sophrosyne*), 10, 12, 75, 77–78, 84, 98, 127, 179, 202–203, 205, 208, 211–12, 214, 223; & self-knowledge, 63–65, 76; & self-rule, 192–95; & statesmanship, 76–77; contrast: licentiousness; see also: virtue
monarchy, 2–3; see also: king(s); one-man rule; tyranny
moral sentiments, 204; see also: shame
morality, 89–90, 122; of slaves & masters, 172
Muses, 33, 71
music, 32–34, 43, 52, 71, 107, 178, 217
myth (*mythos*), 44, 63, 161, 167, 180, 228, 235, 238, 240; goal of myths is care of the soul, 236; see also: *logos*; rational account
myth of the metals, see: noble lie

N
nature (*physis*), 169, 194, 206
Nausicydes, 11n18, 182
Neoplatonic canon, iv, iv n6, 239
Neoplatonists, iv, v, 7, 16n2, **59–62**
Nicias, 19
Nietzsche, Friedrich, 172, 194
Noble action, 40, 145; see also: doing well
noble lie, 97, 180

O
oaths, 16, 34, 35, **71–72**, 120, 167, 186, 228; "by the gods," 57, 72
oligarchy, 3, 10, 20, 193–94
Olympiodorus, 7n14, 59, 67, 87, 97, 98, 102n22, 118; *On Plato First Alcibiades*, 59n5, 60n6, 67n2, 80n5, 87n3, 99n18, 102n22

one-man rule, 2–5; see also: monarchy; tyranny; tyrant(s)
oneness of mind (*homonoia*), 53–55; see also: agreement; concord; friendship
oracle(s), 79; of Ammon, 242; Socrates' personal oracle, 79; see also: Delphic oracle
order (*kosmos*), 3, 12, 132, 189, 208, 210–13; moral, 173, 236; contrast: disorder; see also: structure
Osiris, 228, 242

P

pain, 68, 94, 96, 129, 144, 145, 157, 197, **200–204**
Palamedes, 90, 130
pandering, **122–40**, 161, 168, 207, 222, 225, 237
Pangle, Thomas L., v n9, 27n19
Pascal, Blaise, 236
paternalism, 122, 137
peace, 19, 32–33
Peace of Nicias, 19
Peisistratus, 2
Peloponnesian War, 18–20, 86, 98, 110n5, 116, 240
Perdiccas, 141
Pericles, 16–17, 28, 34, 42–43, 44, 47–48, 50, 71, 82n13, 85, 113, 207, 221–25, 239, 242; guardian of Alcibiades, 17
Perseus, 45
Persia, 10, 44–45, 29, 230
Persian Wars, 233
Philip II, 55
philosopher(s), 5–6, 8, 9, 10, 12, 21, 60, 87, 91, 100, 112, 153–54, 180, 233, 237; Callicles' idea of, 11, 173–76, 238; moral, 195n2; not rhetoricians, 142; not sophists, 134; of nature, 42, 87, 169; Socratic, 115; the soul of a philosopher is golden, 180; see also: philosopher-king(s)
philosopher-king, 3, 5, 12; philosopher-statesman, 5, 9, 11
philosophy, 11, 21, 238; a knack, not a *techne*, 153; as private care for the soul, 162; Callicles' idea of philosophy, 11, 173–76, 238; cannot be taught, 125; connected with self-knowledge, 101; differs from sophistry, 28; highest form of knowledge, 120; medicine for the soul, 189; moral, 205; natural, 96; & practical reason, 179; the rightful ruler of all human affairs, 97
phren, 24
piety, 9n17, 59, 78, 92, 158; impiety, 2, 9n17, 21, 34, 228
Plato, 1, 11, 16–17, 21–22, 24, 46, 47, 59, 63, 74–75, 82–83, 85, 86, 88n6, 90, 92–93, 97, 98, 102–103, 105, 110, 119, 125, 133–34, 150, 153, 155n2, 166–67, 170, 178–79, 192, 214, 223, 225, 236, 239, 241; doctrines: noble lie,

97; the parts of the soul, 3, 132–33, 192, 196, 208; wonder is the beginning of philosophy, 114; works: *Apology of Socrates*, 110; *Charmides*, 8, 87, 150; *Critias*, 7n12; *Crito*, 90; *Gorgias*, iii–vi, 7–14, 16n2, 17, 26, 30, 32, 37, 41, 63–64, 78, **85–238,** 239–240, 242; *Greater Alcibiades*, iii–vi, 2, 6–10, 12, 14–15, **16–84,** 85, 98, 101, 103, 136, 160, 166, 223, 238, 239–40, 242; *Laws*, 5, 189; *Lesser Alcibiades*, iv, 6, 7n12, **239–242;** *Letters*, 6; *Meno*, 43, 63, 116, 119, 150, 238; *Menexenus*, 47; *Protagoras*, v, 6, 13n21, 30, 43, 119–120n10, 169n1, 238, 242; *Republic*, 1, 3–5, 7–9, 11, 24, 37, 41, 46, 56, 63n12, 117, 132, 159, 180, 192, 194, 236–38; *Seventh Letter*, 1n1, 5; *Symposium*, 4n3, 7n14, 17n1, 22n9, 23–24, 67–68, 81n10, 82, 152; *Theages*, 22–23, 29, 43, 88n6, 100n20, 152, 229; *Timaeus*, iv n6, 7, 16n2, 61, 75n10

pleasure, 14, 87, 94, 126, 132, 144, 147–48, 170; & goodness, 192–213; & pain, 201–203; see also: appetites, courage, craft, desire, fine, rhetoric, virtue

pleonexia, 14, 189, **112–13**

Plotinus, v

Pluto, 230

poetry (*poiesis*), as demagoguery or rhetoric, 207; defined by Gorgias as a kind of speech with meter, 94

politicians, 144, 165, 174, **222–24**

politics, 7n13, 10, 12–14, 22, 27, 31, 36, 37, 41, 44, 54, 65, 173, 178, 183, 210, 223–24 226, 233, 237; as care of the soul, 129; highest value is justice, 34, 111; the true master art, 133; versus sophistry, 189; see also: craft; democracy; philosophy; power politics

Polus, 7, 10–13, 30, **88–89, 122–40; 141–62,** 167, 189, 220, 226, 231, 238; a copy of Gorgias, 105; a student of Gorgias, 10, 88, 89; defeated by his sense of shame, 89, 123–24, 145, 163–64, 169–72, 180–81, 198–99, 204, 214; defends freedom as doing what one pleases, 13; displays rhetoric but can't explain it, 103–104; embraces an amoral & technocratic idea of rhetoric, 116, 123; less gentlemanly than Callicles, 89, 122, 134, 169–71; less of a philosopher than Callicles, 173–74; on crime & punishment, 141–44, 211; on doing and suffering injustice, 138–40; praises tyranny, 7, 11; refuted by Socrates, 144–47,

155–60; two kinds of freedom, 135–37
Poseidon, 230
Potidaea, Battle of, 17–18, 37, 88
power (*dynamis*), 1, 3–5, 10, 12–15, 20, 26–28, 32, 44, 48–49, 57, 64, 66–67, 70, 77, 81, 100–101, 105–109, 117, 122, 129, **135–38**, 141, 164, 168, 170–73, 183–85, 195, 206, 212, 214, **215–21**, 233–37, 237, 237; & freedom, 137; daimonic, 72–73, 114–15, 117; military, 129; of drugs, 96; of incantations, 94; of rhetoric, 105, 114, 117; of speech, 95–97; political, 5, 13, 109, 122; real or true, 135–37; versus wisdom, 174–77; see also: power politics; wealth & power
power politics, 86, 89, 98, 122
pride (*megalophrona*), 23–26, 44, 46; contrast: magnanimity; see also: virtue
Proclus, 7n14, 15, 23, 59; *Greater Alcibiades*, 15n1, 23n12
Prodicus, 242
Protagoras of Abdera, 13n21, 30, 43, 242
protreptic (genre), 7, 84
prudence (*phronein, phronesis*), vi, 5, 51–52, 69–73, 82, 121, 193
public speaking, 207
pusillanimity, 25
Pyrilampes, 85, 165, 166

Pythagoreans, 5, 88, 196
Pythocleides, 42, 43

Q
quackery, **122–25**, 133; see also: flattery
queens, 47–49, 52; Persian, 47–49

R
rational account (*logos*), 125, 228; see also myth; *techne*
rational men, 3
reason (part of the soul), 3, 7, 12, 32, 167–68, 192, 200; see also: desire; rational men; *thumos*; soul; spiritedness
recollection, 63
Renaud, François, v, 41n2, 69, 59, 80n5
Rhadamanthus, 230, 233
rhetoric (*rhetorike*), 28, 86, 88, 90–93, 104–105, 123, 143; & flattery, 165, 235; & tyranny, 124; as a source of power, 97; as the art of manipulating opinions & appearances, 91; as the art of persuasion, 111; as the art of taking & keeping comprehensive political power, 122; bridges the gap between the few who know & the many who do not, 105; *daimonic* power of, 114; each art needs rhetoric to communicate with laymen, 161–62; kinds of rhetoric: deliberative, 110, 112, 160, 161; ep-

ideictic, 109–110, 112, 160–61; forensic, 110, 112, 155, 159, 160–61, 214; king of the arts, 97; legislation & justice are not forms of rhetoric, 161; limits of, 167; morally neutral, 92, 117, 123, 133, 169; needed for self-defense, 177, 215–16; not an art but quackery, 125–33; paradoxical uses, 156–59; philosophical rhetoric, 134; poetry as rhetoric addressed to all men, 207; restoring spiritual health, 156; secures the greatest good, 108–109, 122; sham rhetoric in law, 155, 162; Socrates as sophist (Aristophanes), 176; subordinate to knowledge of the good, 179; true & false rhetoric, 102n22; versus expert knowledge, 113–14; versus *logos*, 106–108; versus philosophy, 115–16, 120, 122

righteousness (*dikaiosyne*), 208, 214, 223, 228; see also justice (*dike*); virtue

Rousseau, Jean-Jacques, 137, 236

S

Salamis, Battle of, 47

satisfaction, 170, 194–95, 200–202; self-satisfaction, 8

Scythians, 170

Second Sailing, 60

seduction, art of, 68

self-control (*enkrateia*), 192, 196; contrast: weakness of the will (*akrasia*)

self-cultivation, 48–51, 58, 64, 84

self-defense, 159, 177

self-improvement, 45

self-knowledge, 10, 31, 23, 52, 57, **58–64**, 72, 76–77, 86, 101, 192, 141; & moderation, 63–65, 76, 241; & philosophy, 101; as anti-tyrannical, 10; as knowledge of the individual soul, 62; by means of dialogue (*dialogos*), 60; prerequisite to know other things, 31; see also: Delphic injunction

shame, 33, 44, 47, 89, 122, 147, 193, 204; is natural, 124, 173; Socrates uses shame to defeat his opponents, 33, 44, 47, 89, 118–19, 121, 123–24, 169, 172–73, 181, 198–99, 204, 214; see also: moral sentiments

shameful (*aischron*), 33, 38, 50, 88–89, 118, 123, 142, **144–46**, 163, 169, 171, 174, 178, 181, 184–85, 193, 196

Socrates, as enemy of tyranny, 1; believed that the soul is perfected by virtue & marred by vice, 37; did not teach virtue, 152; his art of divination, 83, 100; his art of questioning, 101, 103; his art of seduction (*erotike techne*), 68; his *dai*-

monion, 23, 27–29, 50–51, 57, 78, 84, 229, 241; his golden soul, 180; his greatest rivals were the sophists, 28, 117, 122; his knowledge of human nature, 70, 72, 82, 229; insists on short answers, 106, 167, 179; master of rhetoric in his own way, 177, 179; proposed use of a Noble Lie to justify social inequality, 180; redirected philosophy from theoretical questions to moral questions, 179; regarded tyranny as a disease of the soul & society at large, 6; saved Alcibiades at Potidaea, 37; Socratic Paradox, 143, 216; sought to turn tyrants toward the good, 6; steels himself against shame, 198–99; swears by the dog, 228, 242; teacher of Alcibiades, Charmides, & Critias, 1; teaches rhetoric or sophistry (Aristophanes), 176, 179; thinks shame is natural, 124, 173; thought to instill tyrannical ambitions, 9, 134; uses shame to defeat his opponents, 33, 44, 47, 89, 118–19, 121, 123–24, 169, 172–73, 181, 198–99, 204, 214; see also: ignorance, Socratic

sophistry, 13, 14, 28, 31, 89, 116, 118, 128, 129–31, 150, 161, 176, 189; Aristophanes thinks it is nourished by natural philosophy, 132; as pandering, 161; as "fake legislation," 129–31, 161, 189; as the master art, 13, 150; corrupts the city, 161; differs from philosophy by its goals, 28, 116, 134; as route to political power, 13; value-neutral, 13, 116

sophists, 10, 13–14, 26, 28, 30, 85–86, 89, 95–96, 105, 106, 114–17, 121–22, 129, 179, 220, 224; & the primacy of the ever-changing moment, 86; & the variability of conventions & opinions, 86; as moral subjectivists, 13–14, 89, 116, 121, 150, 170, 194; differ from philosophers by their goals, 134; nourished by natural philosophy, 96, 169; Socrates' greatest rivals, 28, 117, 122; taught pursuing freedom for oneself through power over others, 164; teachers of political science, 115; teachers of rhetoric, 114; teachers of tyranny, 105

Sophocles, 2, 43

soul (*psyche*), 3, 6, 12, 14, 24, **37–40**, **59–65**, **66–70**, 85, 92, 94, 122, 131, 178, 180–89, 206, 228; an orderly soul is better, 210; & moderation, 210–11; & well-being, 127; as the mirror of the body,

66–69; as the true self, **58–63**, 84; Callicles' soul, 90, 219; care of the soul, 126–27, **129–32**, 162, 220, 227, 236; Christian interpolations, 73–75; civic, 60; contemplative, 60; corruption of the soul, 215–17; *daimonic* nature, 72–73, 229; embodied, 60; harmed by bad deeds, 139, 141; harmony of the soul, 167–68, 189; human, 3, 23, 51, 74, 229; immune to bad fortune, 140, 141; individual, 61–62; judgement after death, 229–34; justice restores health to the soul, 155, 211; leading the soul (*psychagogy*), 236; myth of the soul's preexistence in the *Meno*, 63; parts of the soul, 3, 132–33, 192, 196, 208; perfected by virtue & marred by vice, 37; philosophical, 190; political power mutilates the soul, 219–20; power of speech over the soul, 96; rational, 59; rehabilitative punishment as medicine for the soul, 122, 146–49, 156, 160; since the soul is more important than property & the body, justice is the most important of the arts, 147; testing the golden soul, 179–80; the best part of the soul, where reason resides, akin to a god, 72; the evil of the soul is the greatest evil, 146–47; the soul as the mirror of another soul, 69–73; ultimately rules itself & the body, 132; versus the body, 126, 132, 138–39, 141, 168; see also: desire; reason; spiritedness

Sparta, 10, 15, 19–20, 44–50, 52, 222; Spartan virtues, 47

Spengler, Oswald, 214; *The Decline of the West*, vol. I: *Form and Actuality*, 214n5

spiritedness (*thumos*), 3, 24, 46, 132, 179; see also: desire; reason; soul

spiritual health, **129–31**, 147, 156, **161–62**; see also: virtue

statesmanship, 76–77; guided by knowledge of the good, 13

Stobaeus, Joannes, 73

Strauss, Leo, vi–v, 246n6

structure (*taxis*), 55, 208, 210; see also order (*kosmos*)

stupidity, 42, 182, 193

success, 5, 14

suspension of disbelief, 97

Syracuse (Greek colony), 1, 2, 5–6, 19, 24, 88; see also: Calippus; Dion; Dionysius I; Dionysius II

T

Tarrant, Harold, v, 41n2, 69, 59, 80n5, 239n1

Taylor, A.E., 83n14–15

techne, 13, 32, 50, 64, 68, 76, 92,

96, 100, 106, 115, 120–21, 125–26, 150–56, 158, 169, 190, 206, 210, 215–16, 220–21; morally neutral, 13, 64, 115, 120, 151–52, 154, 169; of building, 221; of medicine, 206; of morality (impossible), 153, 155, 158; of rhetoric, 215–16; true techne as knack (*empeiria*) plus rational account (*logos*), 125; see also analogies, *techne*; art; knack; technocracy; technology

technocracy, 13, 115, 116, 155; morally neutral, 13; dangerous, 155; see also: *techne*; technology

technology, 13, 219; morally neutral, 13; see also *techne*; technocracy

temperance (*sophrosyne*), 47, 150, 151; intemperance, 147

Thales, 5

Theages, 29

Themistocles, 49, 85n1, 113, 207, 221–24, 233

Thersites, 232

Thirty Tyrants, 1, **87–89**, 130, 242

Thrasymachus, 7, 238

Thucydides, 18n4, 19, 93, 110; *The Peloponnesian War*, 18n4, 19n5, 110n5

thumos, see: spiritedness

Timaea, 20, 56

Timaeus (statesman), 5n8

timeliness (*kairos*), 86, 91–92

Tisander, 11n18, 181–82

tragedy, 4, 97, 178, 207, 209

tyranny, 1–3, 6–8, 10–12, 21, 26, 65, 77, 80, 84, 105, 108, 122, 124, 141, 166, 194, 206, 238, 240–42; & pleonexia, 77; & the worship of numbers & size, 77; as disease of the soul & society at large, 6; main theme unifying the *Greater & Lesser Alcibiades* with the *Gorgias*, 240–42; praised by Polus and Callicles, 7; sophists as teachers of, 105; see also: one-man rule; tyrant(s)

tyrant(s), 1–2, 4–8, 11, 15, 21, 24, 71, 77, 105, 126, 141, 143, 149, 184, 217, 231, 240–41; distinguished from kings, 2–3; fear the courageous and proud citizen, 24; see also: one-man rule; Thirty Tyrants; tyranny

U

unity, 53–55

Unmoved Mover, 8

untimeliness, 86

useful (*chresimon, ophelimon*), 144, 145, 147, 153, 157–59

V

vengeance, 148, 158

vice (*kakia*), 14, 37, 81, 98, 128, 133, 146–47, 150, 202, 208, 214

virtue (*arete*), 9n17, 10, 24, 37, 40, 45, 46, 64, 76, 77, 81, 82, 116, 120, 152, 153, 154, 166,

167, 195, 201, 208, 210, 236, 237; & happiness/well-being (*eudaimonia*), 13, 40, 49, 78; as knowledge, 76, 120, 154; as spiritual health, 167; four cardinal virtues, 46; Gorgias as a teacher of virtue, 116; not a *techne* but a knack, 152, 166; of the soul, 73; Spartan, 47; teachability of virtue, 152–53, 158; see also: courage; harmony; justice; magnanimity; moderation; pride; righteousness; spiritual health; wisdom

W

war (*polemos*), 19, 32–33, 86, 88, 97–98, 221; war & peace, 33; Peloponnesian War, 18–20, 86, 98, 110n5, 116, 240; Persian Wars, 233
warrior aristocracy, 3
weakness of the will (*akrasia*), 196; contrast: self-control
wealth, 10, 14, 26, 31, **45–49**, 77, 92, 135, 164, 170, 183, 202; & power, 14, 48–49, 170
well-being, 40, 49, 79, 115, **125–28**, 137, 152, 206; & happiness, 13, 40, 49, 78; & the soul, 127; requires knowledge, 120
Welliver, Warman, 7n12
wisdom, 13, 21n6, 32, 43, **48–51**, 64, 72, 77, 84, 97, 100, 115, 173, 175, 177, 179, 181, 192, 206, 212, 220, 226, 232–34, 237; medical, 190; moral, 84, **150–55**; not morally neutral, 13; practical (*phronesis*), 49, 52, 69, 72, 115, 153, 175–76, 178–179, 187; theoretical (*sophia*), 47, 49, 72, 179
wise (*sophoi*), 4, 6, 43, 49, 101, 155, 177–78, 180–81; wise men, 2, 42, 187, 189, 232, 237
wish (*boulesis*), 216; wishing, 213, 216
wonder (*thaumazein*), 22, 29, 114, 233
work, 55–6, 107, **126–28**, 149, 156
worthy, 21, 25, 45, 50, 64, 140, 157, 159, 175, 213
wretched (*athlios*), 138, **141–43**, 193–94, 198, 201, 211; see also: base

X

Xenophon, 7n13, 12n20, 26n18, 53n5, 67–68, 82n13, 87, 190n2; *Apology*, 87; *Memorabilia*, 6n11, 7n13, 12n20, 26n18, 53n5, 82n13, 87, 190n2; *Symposium*, 67–68
Xerxes I, 27, 47, 170

Z

Zethus, 177, 178, 186, 210, 242
Zeus, 34, 35, 45, 71–72, 101, 170, 186, 206, 218, 235
Zeyl, Donald, 99
Zopyrus the Thracian, 47
Zoroaster, 46

About the Author

Greg Johnson, Ph.D., is Editor-in-Chief of Counter-Currents Publishing Ltd. and the Counter-Currents.com webzine.

He is the author of twenty-four books (all published by Counter-Currents, unless otherwise noted): *Confessions of a Reluctant Hater* (2010, 2016), *Trevor Lynch's White Nationalist Guide to the Movies* (2012), *New Right vs. Old Right* (2013), *Son of Trevor Lynch's White Nationalist Guide to the Movies* (2015), *Truth, Justice, & a Nice White Country* (2015), *In Defense of Prejudice* (2017), *You Asked for It: Selected Interviews*, vol. 1 (2017), *The White Nationalist Manifesto* (2018), *Toward a New Nationalism* (2019, 2023), *Return of the Son of Trevor Lynch's CENSORED Guide to the Movies* (2019), *From Plato to Postmodernism* (2019), *It's Okay to Be White: The Best of Greg Johnson* (Ministry of Truth, 2020), *Graduate School with Heidegger* (2020), *Here's the Thing: Selected Interviews*, vol. 2 (2020), *Trevor Lynch: Part Four of the Trilogy* (2020), *White Identity Politics* (2020), *The Year America Died* (2021), *Trevor Lynch's Classics of Right-Wing Cinema* (2022), *The Trial of Socrates* (2023), *Against Imperialism* (2023), *Novel Takes: Essays on Literature* (2024), *The Best of Trevor Lynch* (2025), *Is America Doomed?* (2025), and the present volume.

He is editor of *North American New Right*, vol. 1 (2012); *North American New Right*, vol. 2 (2017); and *The Alternative Right* (2018), plus books by Julius Evola, Francis Parker Yockey, Alain de Benoist, Savitri Devi, Collin Cleary, Kerry Bolton, and Jonathan Bowden.

His writings have been translated into Arabic, Czech, Danish, Dutch, Estonian, Finnish, French, German, Greek, Hungarian, Norwegian, Polish, Portuguese, Russian, Slovak, Spanish, Swedish, and Ukrainian.